# Graphic Design Rules

REVISED EDITION

# Graphic Design Rules

## 365 Essential Design Dos and Don'ts

**Sean Adams · Peter Dawson · John Foster · Tony Seddon**

PRINCETON ARCHITECTURAL PRESS · NEW YORK

Published by
Princeton Architectural Press
A division of Chronicle Books LLC
70 W 36th Street, 11th Floor
New York, NY 10018
www.papress.com

FSC
MIX
Paper | Supporting
responsible forestry
FSC® C016973
www.fsc.org

27 26 25  6 5 4

ISBN: 978-1-61689-876-2

Editor: Linda Lee
Design: PAPress
Cover concept: Peter Dawson

Special thanks to: Paula Baver, Janet Behning, Abby Bussel,
Jan Cigliano Hartman, Susan Hershberg, Kristen Hewitt,
Stephanie Holstein, Lia Hunt, Valerie Kamen, Jennifer Lippert,
Sara McKay, Parker Menzimer, Wes Seeley, Rob Shaeffer,
Sara Stemen, Jessica Tackett, Marisa Tesoro, Paul Wagner,
and Joseph Weston of Princeton Architectural Press
—Kevin C. Lippert, publisher

Library of Congress Cataloging-in-Publication Data
available upon request.

# Contents

# The Book of Rules

Sean Adams

Being a designer requires possessing
certain dissociative identity disorder characteristics. Previously known as multiple
personality disorder, its symptoms result in
a designer possessing two personality states.
The first is obsessively focused on the
most minute details of type: serif forms or
the optical appearance of hanging quotation
marks. The second personality is open to
radical new ideas and can view any problem
with comprehensive and open-ended
solutions. Unfortunately, there is no alternative. To succeed as a designer requires being
able to acknowledge both ways of seeing
the world.

The title of this book, *Graphic Design
Rules*, identifies a life-saving suggestion that
will prevent the viewer from assuming that

the designer is merely a small child or house cat that has learned how to use the computer. But, in the right hands and with radical thinking, one might find a use for Comic Sans (although highly unlikely, as it is remarkably clumsy and overused). The thing about rules is that they often work best when broken. Without experimenting with that which is considered entirely incorrect, we might still be using medieval medical techniques, for example. Here, then, is the dilemma: when to follow the rules and when to ignore them.

Experience should be the guide when determining if one should ignore convention and choose low-quality paper stock, combine multiple serif typefaces, or use expected and bland stock photography. On one project, I chose the most inferior quality of paper possible to communicate authenticity. On another, I combined Garamond, Bodoni, Caslon, and Century Expanded because I wanted to. And I've applied terribly banal stock photos to a project to add humor. One viewer might be enchanted with these choices, while another might find them disturbing and entirely misguided. But I decided to make these choices after doing the right thing and following the rules for more than twenty years.

Design is not only about research and great concepts. Craft is a vital component that separates us from cows. Recently, a designer who travels in radical avant-garde circles told me that *craft* was the *c* word. Somehow, the idea that a designer focused on the refinement of form and excellence in execution was equated with vapid and "aesthetically attractive" work. I disagree entirely. Why would a solution that employs sloppy typography, grammatical errors, and dour colors be more intelligent? If our job as designers is to communicate a concept, shouldn't seducing the viewer be preferable to repulsing him or her?

Much of *Graphic Design Rules* is oriented to assist the designer with issues of craft through rules, suggestions, and methods. This incorporates approaches to typography, composition, color, and images. These are the ingredients, with a strong concept, that create a design solution. If I were a chef, I would strive to work with the best ingredients: produce, choice of meat, and herbs. I would not expect an excellent meal if I replaced the fresh ahi tuna with canned tuna or tomato sauce from scratch with Chef Boyardee or SpaghettiOs. The same is true with design. Working with a well-designed version of a typeface, such as Garamond, a custom color palette, and extraordinary photography will produce a superior solution rather than the free downloaded typeface, the default palette in a software program, and random stock photography.

Once one has mastered the "right" way of designing and is confident that every en dash is appropriately typeset, it is acceptable to allow that other personality to rise to the surface. He or she can then imagine remarkably unexpected and provocative solutions, challenge the status quo, and explore alternative processes in production. However, that personality hell-bent on following the rules and on creating perfection needs to step in periodically to make sure the solution communicates clearly and delights the viewer.

# Type &
# Typography

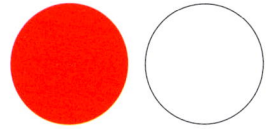

# DON'T use Comic Sans

Comic
Sans

Well, we had to put it in, didn't we? Comic Sans is arguably the most inappropriately used typeface in history since its first appearance in 1995. It was designed for Microsoft a year earlier by Vincent Connare (who incidentally is very philosophical about his notoriety among type fans) to supply user-friendly menus for people who were a bit scared of computers. When it was included as one of the font choices in Windows 95, it took off faster than a speeding bullet. Everyone with a computer and the notion they could do graphic design started using it on their homemade letterheads, party invites, curricula vitae, shop signs, well, you get the picture. Comic Sans wasn't designed to do all these things, so why did everyone like it so much? Connare thinks people like to use it because "it's not like a typeface." Ouch! What better reason can there be to *not* use Comic Sans? **TS**

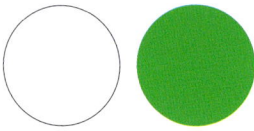

# DO use Comic Sans…ironically

Did I just say you shouldn't use Comic Sans? Well, I was only kidding. One of the great things about typefaces that are vilified due to inappropriate application or overuse is they gain a platform from which they can be used to portray irony, sarcasm, satire, and so on. If you've got a dispiriting message that you want to make light of, for instance "Turning forty-six next week and really happy about it—party on!" Comic Sans might just be your typeface of choice. The problem is that those invitees who aren't graphic designers won't get the joke. Using type ironically can be very effective and indeed great fun, but only if the irony isn't wasted. Therefore, think carefully before you decide to use Comic Sans, Child's Play, Dot Matrix, Bullets Dingbats, or any other novelty typeface that requires anyone to figure out why you chose the typeface in the first place. If the joke isn't immediately transparent, you should probably have gone for Times New Roman instead. Ha ha—do you get it? No? **TS**

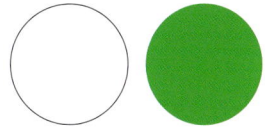

# DO accept that Times New Roman has its uses

# Boring!

Times New Roman is an incredibly useful typeface. It's well designed, with elegant letterforms, and displays excellent readability and legibility characteristics. It's also very economical with space, a property that harks back to its origins as a typcface designed for the *Times* newspaper in 1932. Its biggest problem is that it's so totally ubiquitous, it has lost its personality. Everyone with a computer can identify it, thanks once again to Microsoft, who's bundled it with Windows since 1992 and made it the default typeface for Word before switching to Calibri in 2007. It's also one of the most widely used typefaces in mass-market paperbacks, particularly in the United States. This is why we graphic designers get all haughty about using it. Are we being fair? I'm not so sure. If it's not such a great typeface, how come it's used more than any other for so many varying applications? I think it's time to accept Times New Roman for what it is and give thanks for its usefulness. But will I be using it for my next commercial design commission? No way—it's Times New Roman, for goodness' sake! **TS**

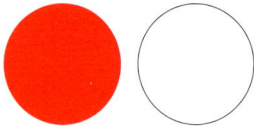

# DON'T use Zapf Dingbats

Good design is about good ingredients. A talented chef uses the best spices, vegetables, and meats. A bad chef chooses the premade cake mix rather than making a wonderful cake from scratch. Zapf Dingbats are well drawn and have an excellent pedigree, created by Hermann Zapf. But they are ubiquitous and off the shelf. They work well for handmade signs for lost dogs or birthday parties. Like most design elements, a good rule of thumb is to ask this question: would my mother design this? Unless your mother is a noted designer, she will likely design an invitation for her weekly bridge game using Zapf Dingbats. Your poster for a client, such as the Melbourne Opera or the Louvre, deserves better. Unfortunately, while they are useful and in some instances (the triangle and simple star) acceptable, Zapf Dingbats will create work that is dull, ordinary, and expected. As a designer, one of our jobs is to create delight. Invent a custom form for an arrow, asterisk, or scissors. If great design is in the details, why would choosing a banal detail be the right choice? **SA**

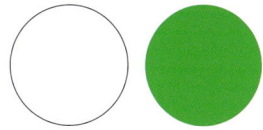

# DO worship classic typefaces

| | |
|---|---|
| **Helvetica** | **Akzidenz Grotesk** |
| **Futura** | Frutiger |
| **Garamond** | Univers |
| **Clarendon** | Sabon |
| Bodoni | Mrs Eaves |
| Avenir | Meta |
| **DIN** | **News Gothic** |

What designates a typeface as a classic? First, it doesn't mean the typeface has to be a hundred years old, as any typeface providing a marker for a prominent graphic style can be considered a classic. In 2009, I was fortunate to work with designer and writer Tamye Riggs on a book about classic fonts. She came up with a great analogy to automobiles: every year seems to produce its own classic car; the same can be said of fonts. Any typeface that makes a credible mark on typography has a right to join the classics club—Sentinel (as used in this book) is a good example of a relatively new font that has become a classic very quickly. The digital revolution has placed thousands of (often quite bad) fonts at our disposal, but for me it's the typefaces that have best made the transition from movable type to digitized font that are the true classics. These are fonts that will always remain relevant and should indeed be worshipped, although respected is probably a better word. Use them wisely and often—they'll never let you down. **TS**

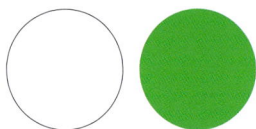

# DO learn about typographic classification

# Humanist serif Optima

# Old Style serif Caslon

It's normal to make type choices based on the feel you get from a typeface, but knowing at least a little about typographic classification (the grouping of typefaces that share similar design characteristics) can help you reach a more informed decision about using specialist type. For example, Transitional serif typefaces from the mid-eighteenth century, such as Baskerville, are evolved interpretations of Old Style serifs dating back as far as the late fifteenth century; they are more elegant and easier to read. This means Transitional serif typefaces are particularly well suited to the setting of long-form text. Some background knowledge on a typeface's origins can go a long way, especially when a specific historical period is referenced in the text. Using Futura to set your headings for that article about the Industrial Revolution isn't necessarily wrong, but Baskerville might look a little more appropriate. **TS**

Transitional serif <small>Baskerville</small>

Rational serif <small>Bodoni</small>

**Grotesque slab** <small>Clarendon</small>

Geometric slab <small>Rockwell</small>

Humanist sans <small>Gill Sans</small>

Geometric sans <small>Futura</small>

*Formal script* <small>Bickham Script</small>

*Casual script* <small>Jazz Script</small>

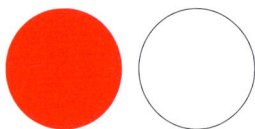

# DON'T choose the latest typeface for every new project you work on

_Graves and Sons_

**MORTICIANS**

As designers, we're all susceptible to a bit of typeface mania every now and again. You know how it is—a *MyFonts* newsletter arrives in your inbox, you scroll down, and there it is. You think, My God! That font is amazing. I must buy it and use it on the project I'm just about to start. But hold on just a second. It might be a great typeface that you can't live without, but is it truly right for the project? More to the point, will your client respond well to it? For example, if you're working on a new logo for a mortician, MetroScript might not be a good choice, no matter how much you like it. Likewise, Futura might not be ideal for the badge of the local amateur baseball team's uniform, unless, of course, they all work together at an interior design shop and are fans of 1920s European architecture. These are extreme examples, of course, but think carefully about the appropriateness of your font choices, and try not to get carried away by your own personal favorites when a tried and trusted font might serve you better. **TS**

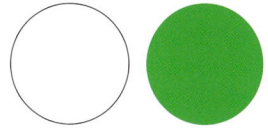

# DO learn that trendy typefaces do not always prevail

*Curlz*

Life is full of regrets and errors. Why did I say yes to that last cocktail? Perhaps the adoption of twelve children was overkill? Trendy typography is one of the most egregious of these errors. Curlz may seem wacky and fun, but it will ruin your life. As designers, we have the pressure of remaining aware of shifts in popular culture. Understanding what is trendy is part of the job. The obvious reason for choosing classic over trendy typefaces is that the trendy fonts will likely soon fall out of style. Classic fonts have survived the test of time. Consider your haircut in high school. Is that school photo the one that you use as your headshot for publications? No. Each of us, at some point, has fallen into a trendy and tragic hairstyle. Trendy type is the same. Template Gothic was groundbreaking in 1990. Four years later, all of these projects were dismissed as "so 1990." These projects now sit unseen in designers' flat files, like high school senior photos, hidden from public view. **SA**

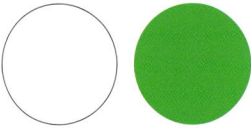

# DO accept that legibility and readability are more important than typographic styling

Our purpose as designers is to communicate effectively, but the number of options available to us can often be overwhelming. First of all, any number of typographic stylings can be applied to a headline or a body of text; designers often submit text matter featuring numerous typefaces. (We jokingly refer to this type of designer in my studio as a Ten-Typeface-Terry—apologies to Terrys everywhere!) Sadly, this approach not only makes it very hard for the reader to navigate the text and understand the content but also makes for an unpleasant reading experience. I always turn the page if it is typographically confusing—if the audience decides to do the same, then the designer has failed in providing legibility and readability. Keep it simple, choose appropriately, and respect the words. **PD**

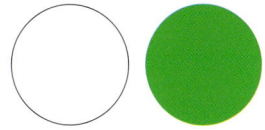

# DO throw legibility and readability out the window

Legibility and readability are not always of utmost importance. You only have to look at the hugely influential body of work created by David Carson during the 1990s, when he was art director of *Raygun* magazine—an era that pioneered what later became known as grunge typography. This style of typography was often practically illegible, relying on the visual impact of the type to convey the core meaning of the layout. Admittedly, much of the work produced during that period now looks dated, but, graphically, much of it also still looks spectacular, almost more art than graphic design. Where does art end and graphic design begin, though? There's a good question. The bottom line: If you're designing a public service leaflet for a government department or a book about Swiss furniture design, grunge typography really isn't the way to go. However, if your audience is likely to respond to typography that is a little more radical, legibility and readability may indeed be sidelined. **TS**

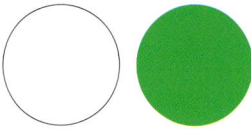

# DO learn about the anatomy of letterforms

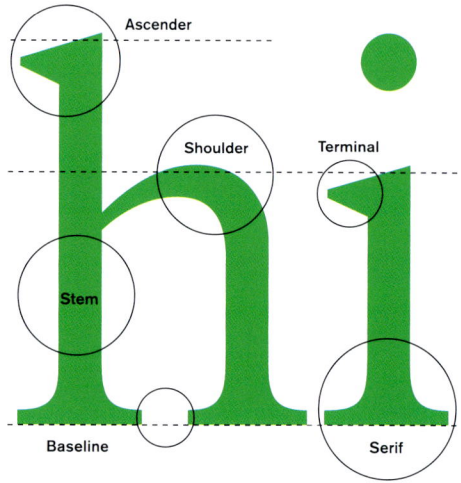

Ascender
Shoulder
Terminal
Stem
Baseline
Serif

I've always been fascinated by how many intriguing terms there are for the components that make up letterforms: ascenders, balls, chins, dots, and so on. Any designer worthy of the title should really spend time learning the names of these components that make up characters. You'll find it most useful when it comes to choosing typefaces for a design, as you'll understand how the individual letterforms are constructed and be able to compare particular typefaces with an expert eye. This is especially important when considering which typeface to use for text matter— you can use this knowledge to help evaluate the appropriateness and legibility of a typeface. If you decide to take on the challenge of designing your own typeface, it's even more important that you know about the anatomy of letterforms and how these elements have an effect on a typeface's appearance and structure. **PD**

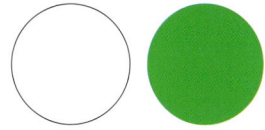

# DO make font format choices based on their intended use

9:41

Some years ago, it would have been a bad idea to use TrueType fonts for a print project because there were issues outputting the format to RIPs (raster image processor) or laser writers. Software improvements to print and PDF workflows mean that this is not a major issue today, but format choice is still important for web use, as different browsers prefer different formats. The TrueType format (TTF) and its much improved successor, OpenType, is probably the best choice overall. Web Open Font Format (WOFF) is a much better option, as it is widely supported, as are Scalable Vector Graphic (SVG) fonts, which work particularly well on phones and tablets. **TS**

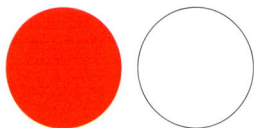

# DON'T use "free" fonts, unless you are sure they are of good quality

**100% FREE!***

*No guarantee of quality or usability

Since the emergence of digital design technology, there has been an explosion in the number of typefaces. This is thanks to the development of relatively easy-to-use typeface-creation software and the rise of websites dedicated to the sharing or selling of typefaces. Many of the typefaces are available online to download free of charge or for a nominal fee. However, on a number of occasions, my studio has found that "free" fonts don't work as they should— whether on a printout, in a PDF, or within live files. Either they have failed to display properly, or they do not work at all. This has, obviously, created great difficulties because, by that stage, the design has been established, refined, and approved—the only solution is to find a replacement typeface. If there is a deadline to meet (and there always is!), this can cause tension between you and the client. Always check the type-face's integrity, and make sure it works as it should before incorporating it into your design. **PD**

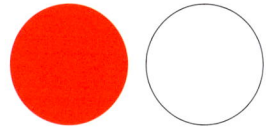

# DON'T design for print using system fonts

Verdana

Times New Roman

## Arial

Palatino

Courier

Trebuchet

Tahoma

Georgia

Lucida

System fonts are made for civilians. These are basic choices provided so everyone can exchange Word documents easily and so a child can make a sign for their bedroom door. Some system fonts, such as Times Roman and Helvetica, are beautiful typefaces. Times Roman was designed for the *Times* of London in 1932, and Helvetica was designed in 1957. They are legible, clear, and refined. Unfortunately, they are also everywhere. And anything that is everywhere can easily becomes background noise or wallpaper that we do not see. Telephone poles are a good example. Now, there are exceptions. Arial and Georgia are system fonts that are good choices for websites. They are poor choices for printed materials and for instances when you need a distinctive voice. "But Verdana is perfectly fine," you may say. And yes, it is. But so is raw concrete. I'd rather choose another surface for my house. It is important to have a broad knowledge of typefaces. Recognizing a refined cut of Univers as opposed to system Verdana is what separates a good designer from those designing telephone directory ads. **SA**

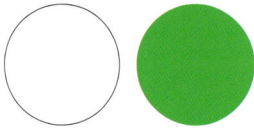

# DO mix typeface choices to create typographic texture

## Typography Today
{ The Summer Lecture Series }

· · ·

## 1800–1850
### The Fann Street Foundry
British typeface design and its lasting influence on American typographic culture.

Different typefaces don't always work together naturally, but good combinations of fonts from opposing type families can create wonderful typographic texture. For an experienced typographer, the process is largely intuitive; let's face it, everyone is going to have their own opinion about which typefaces combine well. However, it's useful to have a few ground rules to follow. First, look for historical links between typefaces and try combinations in which the features of each font underpin its role in your layout. For example, an early grotesque slab for headlines with an elegant transitional serif for the text. Second, look at the proportions of different typefaces and select font combinations with harmonious links between, say, character heights and widths. Third, try to pick up on any qualities that different typefaces might share, such as elegant stems and bowls, consistent stroke thickness, and so on. The important thing is to identify exactly what role each font has to play in the layout and take care to stick to the plan. If you don't, you'll end up with typographic soup. **TS**

# DON'T
# mix typefaces
# to create
# hierarchy

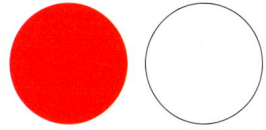

3 VACATIONS FOR THE PRICE OF 1!!

This vacation package includes:

a **4 day** and **3 night**
**CARRIBEAN CRUISE**
and scuba diving excursion
Meals and Entertainment included!!

5 days and 4 nights in Orlando plus:

**3 days** and **2 nights** in

# Puerto Rico

5 days and 4 nights in Orlando plus:

*Only $299.99 per person!*

Includes roundtrip airfare for two!!

1-888-123-4567

Postcards for raves and nightclub events are a wonderful cacophony of typography, color, and sparkly objects. "Look at me! Look over here! No, look here!" they shout. It's great fun until you need to find an address. Many designers make the error of creating hierarchy using similar techniques, the ill-advised practice of using multiple elements rather than employing sound typographic practices. This leads to solutions that are confusing, chaotic, and desperate. Desperation is not pretty at a singles bar, and it is not pretty in design. Creating clear hierarchy is an exercise in patience and restraint.

- Choose one typeface for body copy
- Choose a size
- Choose a color
- Choose a weight
- Choose a case style

Now for the headline: change one attribute, and only one. Change the weight, size, color, or case. Then stop. Do not change the typeface, add a color, make the headline larger, and use all caps. That is good for postcards for a rave, not for clear information. **SA**

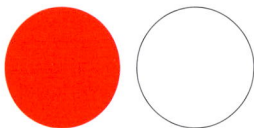

## DON'T mix serif fonts in a layout

# Mixing serif fonts
Sabon
# in a layout is always
Bodoni
# a bad design decision.
Bembo

Few people can successfully mingle stripes and plaids. Edward, the Prince of Wales, managed to mix plaids and plaids, but he had hours of free time to perfect this, and when you're very rich, everyone assumes you are correct. When one of us attempts something similar, we end up looking like a member of a barbershop quartet. This is why mixing serif fonts can be disturbing. I'm talking here about mixing serif fonts, such as Garamond with Bembo. They are both beautiful typefaces, but they are too similar. If you are designing a publication to be read only by an educated group of typophiles, the reaction might be: "Isn't that ironic?" The rest of us will only see something that looks like a mistake. This will result in the same response as seeing someone mixing plaids: "That's just sad and wrong." **SA**

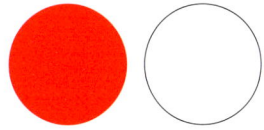

# DON'T use ultrathin typefaces for logo design

There are times when a client requests something that defies the laws of physics. They may request larger type and with additional copy inside a smaller space. Or they may ask for a logo with ultrathin letterforms. Most logos are reduced to fit on a business card or in the corner of a website. The laws of physics dictate that a thin typestyle will be thinner when reduced in scale. If a logo is made with ultrathin letterforms, at some scale these letterforms will appear to be as thin as a single atom. No printer will be able to print this, and nobody will see it. The solution is to create logos that can be scaled to a small size and remain clear. Additionally, good logos are strong and confident. No company or organization should be portrayed as being weak, ineffectual, and anemic. **SA**

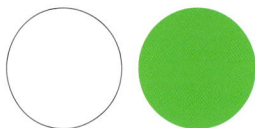

# DO always choose a typeface with an acceptable range of weights for body text

Arno Pro Regular / *Italic* / **Semibold** / ***Semibold Italic*** / **Bold** /
***Bold Italic*** / Light Display / *Light Italic Display* / Caption / SmText / Subhead /
Display / *Italic caption* / *Italic SmText* / *Italic Subhead* / *Italic Display* /
**Semibold Caption** / **Semibold SmText** / **Semibold Subhead** /
**Semibold Display** / ***Semibold Italic Caption*** / ***Semibold Italic SmText*** /
***Semibold Italic Subhead*** / *Semibold Italic Display* / **Bold Caption** /
**Bold SmText** / **Bold Subhead** / **Bold Display** / ***Bold Italic Caption*** /
***Bold Italic SmText*** / ***Bold Italic Subhead*** / *Bold Italic Display*

When you need to typeset any amount of body text, please be sure to select a typeface with at least a couple of weights in both roman and bold, and more importantly, one with true italics. It's a surprisingly common mistake for designers to choose a font based purely on its looks (not a bad thing per se, so don't shout me down here) but with little or no consideration for its versatility. Imagine the scenario: the presentation is completed, and the industrial theme looks wonderful with DIN 1451 as the text font. Then the editor calls you up and says, "I want to introduce italics in the running text. How can I do that with this font?" Disaster—there are no italic weights, and don't you dare add a slant to the roman font! Okay, you could switch to Linotype's DIN Next, which has lots of italic weights, but if you don't already own it, and the client insists they like the typeface you've used, you've got an unexpected expense against the project's budget. Serves you right! **TS**

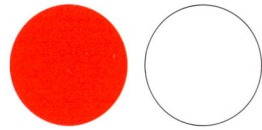

# DON'T use any more typefaces in one layout than is absolutely necessary

Now, this does seem like a bit of 𝔬𝔳𝔢𝔯𝔨𝔦𝔩𝔩. The more I think about it, chances are that we could have managed with one font. Don't you think?

**Hello? Anyone home?**

*Anyone?*

This is one rule that leaves a little ambiguity. However, a solid gauge is that as soon as you notice that a layout has a lot of fonts, it probably has too many. If we all take an honest approach, we can admit that we rarely need more than one sans serif and one serif font to complete most assignments. Sticking to typefaces that have full sets so that we have usable bold, italics, and whatnot will bring most any document to fruition. If you find that your design uses different fonts for the introductory paragraphs, drop caps, captions, folios, body copies, and pull quotes—well, then you have six typefaces in action already, along with a confused reader, and we haven't even talked about headlines. Give me back four of the fonts, and let's try this again. You'll thank me later. **JF**

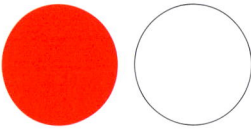

# DON'T set body copy using a script typeface

*From the highway, take the second exit for Pepper Lake which you reach by following the road for approximately three miles. Just before you reach Pepper Lake itself, take the small road to your right next to the Tourist Information building. Follow the road for approximately two miles until you come to a fork, take the left-hand fork and drive for another 400 yards until you reach the clearing where the wedding ceremony will take place. See you on Saturday!*

Have you ever tried to read a block of running text set in a formal script typeface? I repeat, have you ever tried to read a block of running text set in a formal script typeface? It's hard work, isn't it? This explains why designers in the know tend not to make that type choice. I've racked my brains trying to think of a situation in which you might want to do this, and with the possible exception of a wedding invitation, I really can't think of one. In fact, I can't think of a good reason to use a script font for the text on a wedding invitation either, if you expect any of the guests to actually read it. I'm sounding very antiscript here, which I'm not, but for important text that needs to be read easily and understood clearly, scripts aren't a good choice. Do use scripts for flamboyant headlines, highly characterful logos, or elegant branding, but not for the directions to the church, or your client may find that nobody turns up on the big day. **TS**

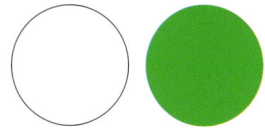

# DO manually
# kern script fonts

-170    -2    -4    -1    -4

When you do find an occasion to use a script typeface (you see—I'm not completely antiscript), it's important to pay close attention to the kerning, as, invariably, several character pairs will need manual adjustment. Script typefaces evolved from the formal handwriting styles of the seventeenth century, and many of the characters feature strokes that join them to the next letter in a word. The kerning pairs built into every typeface will take care of some, but not all, instances of inconsistencies, for example, a lowercase *e* and an *n* or a *p*

and an *r*. The adjustments are often tiny but will make all the difference in the elegant flow of your type, particularly at large point sizes, which makes clearly visible even the slightest misalignment. By the way, if you're using Adobe InDesign, don't be tempted to use the optical setting for kerning with a script font. It works very well with other typeface classifications when set at larger point sizes, but for scripts you should stick with metrics for the best results. **TS**

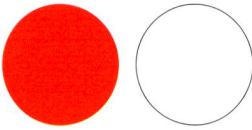

# DON'T set body copy in a novelty typeface

I turned to my trusty *Oxford English Dictionary*, which defines *novelty* as "a decorative or amusing object relying for its appeal on the newness of its design." The dictionary also uses the word *strangeness*, which for me is the more appropriate explanation for the unsuitability of novelty typefaces for setting text. To be fair, there is a place in the design world for novelty typefaces, and some clients might love the idea of an entire brochure set in Jokerman.

When used appropriately, good novelty typefaces can work, but it takes a good eye and a measured judgment on the part of the designer to get it right. I know I'm sounding like a terrible type snob here, but it's true—believe me. As for setting body copy in a novelty typeface, it breaks all the rules of legibility and readability (and taste, quite frankly), so if you want to be taken seriously as a typographer, don't go there. **TS**

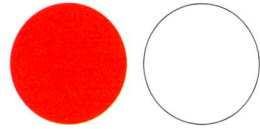

# DON'T use display fonts for body copy

For this rule, we should first establish the definition of a display typeface to understand how this differs from other fonts. In essence, *display* refers to the use of type at large sizes, such as 72pt, which may be used for titles on a magazine or headlines in a newspaper. As such, display fonts are "cut" differently because they do not have to contend with being printed small. A significant difference, for example, might be display faces with removed "ink traps" (indents in and around the corners of the letter strokes), which may be used with typefaces to compensate for overinking when printed to retain the letterform's integrity. Using a display face at smaller sizes will mean running the risk of overinking at the printing stage and thus changing the letterform's appearance. In addition, many display typefaces appear only in upper-case and have a narrower character set. **PD**

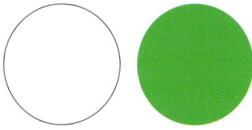

# DO use real handwriting for convincing handwritten text

Organic design that showcases the unique handwork of the designer is something magical. It is one of the very few instances in which only you can provide a specific solution for the client in question. This appeal has led to a proliferation of fake handwritten type-faces. They look like a perfect solution, or at least a quick fix, when seen in a catalog or on a website, yet in practice, they are far less convincing. The key to handwritten type is that it is one of a kind. You know what's not one of a kind? A font that anyone can have for a couple of dollars, or worse, freeware that is the hacked-together scribbles of a first-time fontographer. What's the harm, you say? Well, just look at a word with the letter *e* in it three times and see how it compares to the nuances in your own handwriting. Your *e* never quite looks the same. The font never changes. And everyone knows the difference. **JF**

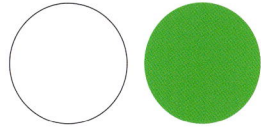

# DO use ligatures if your choice of typeface accommodates them correctly

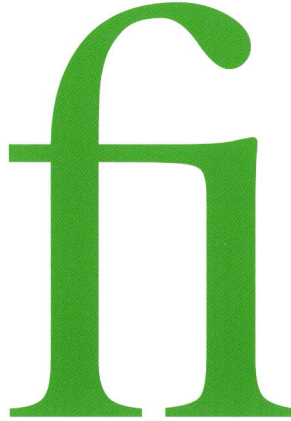

To enhance your typographic skills and to improve your work, the employment of ligatures should be a consideration when setting large volumes of text. This is not law by any means, but could be a benefit to the reader and your work. When characters share a common design feature, they could be replaced by a single character, a ligature. (For example, an *f* followed by an *i* replaced by fi.) Ligatures enhance the reading experience by improving legibility and also help to make the typesetting more attractive. Not all typefaces possess ligatures, but many serif families do. Some OpenType families may have additional, "discretionary" ligatures, which can include other character pairs, such as ct, st, and cp. When considering a typeface, check what is available within the character set, and compare this against other families to determine which gives you the most options. **PD**

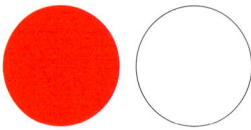

# DON'T slope a roman font to create an italic font

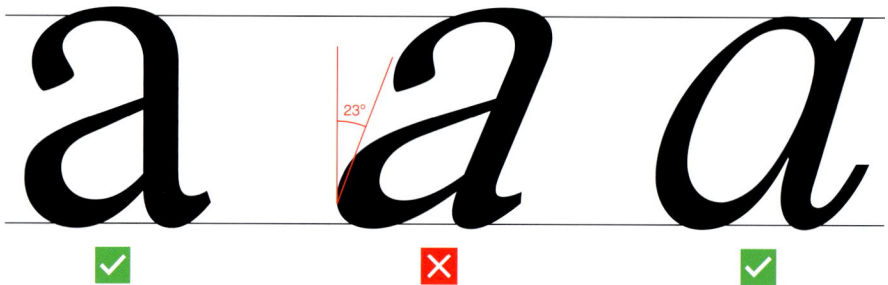

I'm always amazed when a designer takes a word and, having set it in a roman cut of a typeface, then forces it to be italic by sloping it at an angle using their design software. This, of course, is not a true italic but merely a word leaning over. A giveaway for spotting this is the fact that few lowercase italics possess a double-story a. Although true italics retain many of the core typeface's design principles, they also include changes to each letter's strokes.

When a character is forced to tilt, however, it displays none of these alterations. With italics, a more hand-drawn, cursive approach is evident, and some of the characters link together and more ligatures are incorporated into the cut. There is no need to slope; with the wealth of typefaces available, a good typeface family will contain italic styles of most, if not all, roman weights. **PD**

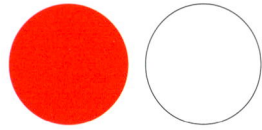

# DON'T falsely darken fonts to create bold weights

Just as you shouldn't slope a roman typeface to make it appear italic (because it isn't true to the typeface's design), lighter weights shouldn't be adjusted to make them appear bolder. Not only is this unnecessary (just pick a typeface that has a variety of weights instead), it also increases the size of the letterform by placing a border around it, which knocks it out of alignment with the rest of the text on the baseline, x-height, and cap-height rules. Distorting the design of the letterform means it loses its inherent personality—you will find that the counters (the enclosed or partially enclosed circular or curved negative space [white space] of some letters) and serifs quickly fill in and become bloated in appearance. Desktop publishing and illustration packages do allow you to apply a stroke around words, but it is a rather lazy approach and, for the reasons described above, is poor design practice. There are stylistic exceptions to the rule, such as when applying outlines to headlines or titles, but for text matter, use a bold variant and don't falsely mimic a bold font. **PD**

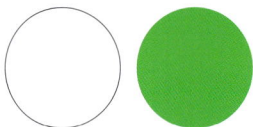

## DO reward typefaces that work well as body copy with long-term commitments

# I ♥ Trade Gothic

When you first start out as a professional, you find yourself drawn to numerous relationships, each with certain benefits (and drawbacks). Some may be mentoring alliances, offering long-term benefits, while others carry the thrill of a whirlwind romance. As we mature, we find ourselves drawn to relationships that provide stability and reliability. Someone who shows up on time and always pays their bill at the bar. Later still, we notice that some people not only are the anchors in our stormy seas but also strive to make us look better than we actually are and oftentimes succeed. It may not have the rush of the new romance, but it is far more fulfilling. If we have any sense whatsoever, we marry these people (professionally or otherwise). You do know we are talking about typefaces, right? **JF**

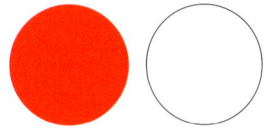

# DON'T buy into the twelve-good-typefaces theory

## 12 12

The great designer Massimo Vignelli was arguably the most prominent champion of the theory that you only need twelve good typefaces. Now, I'm a massive fan of Vignelli's work. He designed the New York subway map and the original iconic American Airlines logo, and his work for Knoll during the 1970s still informs the company's work to this day. Despite all this, I don't agree with him on this one. It's true, to an extent, that we now have so many thousands of typefaces because type design as an industry continues to produce typefaces as commercial products. It's also true that thousands of those typefaces are pretty awful and practically unusable. However, there are more than twelve good typefaces. The important point to make here is that a typeface choice is about appropriateness as well as the design of the typeface itself. We no longer have to restrict ourselves to the narrow selection that was available to typographers in the past—so why do it? By all means, build a selective catalog of typefaces you favor, but don't stop at twelve, and never stop searching for perfection. **TS**

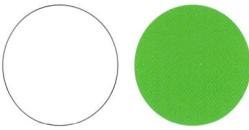

# DO increase a serif font's italics by .5pt in body copy

Read *Book Title*

24pt

Read *Book Title* ✓

24pt 24.5pt

Gustave Flaubert said, "Le bon Dieu est dans le détail." This roughly translates to "God is in the details." A part of being a good designer is having the ability to think in broad strokes and simultaneously being detail-orientated. In some instances, an italic font is created artificially by simply slanting the roman version. This is a sin. True serif italic fonts are completely unique letterforms, distinct from the roman version. They may be thinner and smaller optically than their roman companion.

The type may be uniformly set as 8pt Garamond with roman and italic words, but the italics may look smaller. You can ignore this and state that you are a purist, and all type should be left to their original size, but that would be lazy. A good option to solve this optical problem is to increase the serif italic copy by .5pt. In headline situations, the size adjustment should be explored optically. The fine details in the craft of typography help a project transcend the ordinary to become spectacular. **SA**

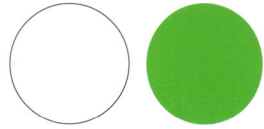

# DO optically adjust point sizes in mixed-serif and sans-serif body copy

I'm not burying my head in the sand and I understand the challenges and problems we face. As Jack Kennedy said, "We do these things not because they are easy, but because they are hard." We need to use our talents to solve our problems with smart dialogue and good old-fashioned action.

8pt

I'm not burying my head in the sand and I understand the challenges and problems we face. As Jack Kennedy said, "We do these things not because they are easy, but because they are hard." We need to use our talents to solve our problems with smart dialogue and good old-fashioned action.

8pt

7pt

Similar to the optical issues of roman and italic serif fonts, mixing sans-serif typefaces with serif typefaces requires optical adjustments. Serif fonts have changing thick and thin stroke weights in each character. Their overall proportion is meant to work well as body copy. Sans-serif fonts have fairly consistent stroke weights within each character. Their x-height is often slightly larger than a serif font. If using a mixture of sans-serif and serif fonts within the same headline, or body text, adjust the size of the sans serif to optically match the serif. This usually requires a slight reduction in the size of the sans-serif font. If ignored, the viewer will read the copy and see the optically larger sans-serif words as shouting over the other copy. It is rare that this is the author's intent unless the text is accusatory and angry. **SA**

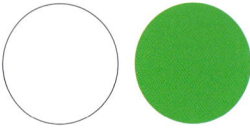

# DO use oldstyle figures with U&L typography

August 15, 2011
Aligning Figures

August 15, 2011
Oldstyle Figures

Years ago, a designer received typewritten pages from a client. A typesetter took these pages and set the copy. Good typesetters were masters of fine detail. Today, designers have taken on the task of typesetting, and the responsibility to maintain the same high standards of quality has changed hands. Oldstyle figures, also called expert figures, are these: 0123456789. Aligning figures are these: 0123456789. Oldstyle figures are similar to uppercase and lowercase letters. They have ascenders and descenders. This allows the text to look uniform. A date set within the body copy 12/23/2017 will read as uppercase and lowercase letters. Alternatively, a date set with aligning characters, 12/23/2017, will look like a line of capital letters. Oldstyle figures also exist in italic form, and as with italic text, a slight size adjustment may be necessary. Some typefaces, such as Century Expanded, do not have accompanying oldstyle figures, indicating that the designer, such as Morris Fuller Benton, designed the font without them. **SA**

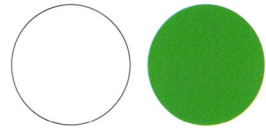

# DO use aligning figures with all caps

VIRGINIA 1607

VIRGINIA 1607

When we read, we look at individual characters, and reading becomes difficult when the characters are too similar. Imagine reading *War and Peace* typeset entirely in Helvetica. Reading is also interrupted when there is an abrupt change of shape. ALIGNING FIGURES, 0123456789, MAINTAIN THE SAME SHAPE AS CAPITAL LETTERS. They do not have ascenders or descenders and are uniform in height. Sans-serif fonts traditionally rejected classical forms and only included aligning figures, although recent typefaces such as Joanna Sans Nova, designed by

Terrance Weinzierl for Monotype, do feature oldstyle figures. A common typographic error is to use oldstyle figures alongside all capital letters as a headline. In the hopes of creating a design that is classic and traditional, a designer may be tempted to use the seemingly more formal oldstyle figures. This creates a disjointed reading experience. Reading a line of all capital letters inexplicably switches to uppercase and lowercase characters. Do not be tempted by this affectation. It may look "fancy," but it is only incorrect. **SA**

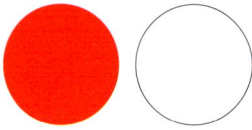

# DON'T use horizontal or vertical scaling to distort fonts

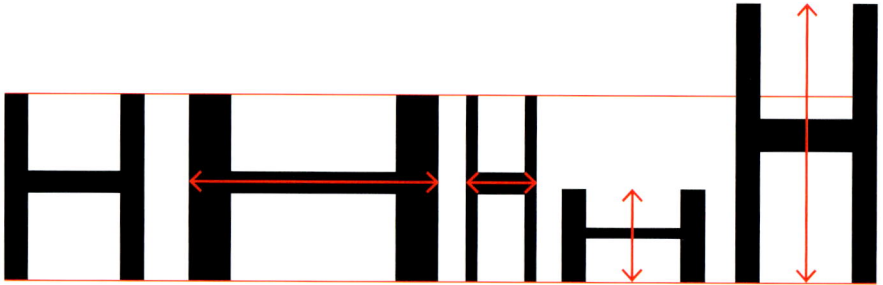

Don't be surprised if there's a gasp of horror and a shake of the head anytime someone asks if this is an acceptable treatment of type. As one of the most universally accepted "bad practices" in typography, it is still common among inexperienced graphic designers and typographers. Distorting the type in such a way plays havoc with the balance of the typeface's structure and creates unusual and awkward stroke widths in the characters. In short, it just looks awful! After the typeface designer and/or foundry have spent so much time and skill creating a beautifully weighted, consistent font family, stretching or squeezing it to "improve" it shows a serious lack of respect! If you do wish for a typeface with a wider character width or a typeface that is compressed with a large cap height, then there are plenty of extended and condensed (sometimes called compressed) type-faces available. **PD**

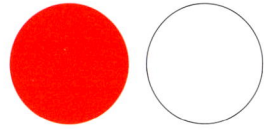

# DON'T stroke your type so that it destroys the integrity of the letterforms

## stroke

Look, everyone enjoys a little stroke now and again, but let's not get carried away. If the stroking becomes too heavy, you can barely recognize the form being smothered with such heavy attention. Innuendos aside, there are few times when stroking a typeface can be justified (production needs and trapping notwithstanding). When a little fat-tening is absolutely necessary, it is important to truly consider what you're hoping to accomplish. If you're applying more than a point of stroke, there is a good chance that you're forcing the letterforms to do things they were never designed to do. Should you look closer, you will likely find that you have created some odd jags and such as well. If you really must have your type carrying such heft, perhaps try a bolder font. After all, what's the point in using a typeface if it is no longer recognizable? **JF**

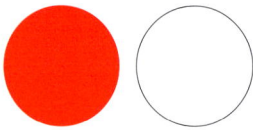

# DON'T ruin a typeface with a filter effect

# FILTER EFFECTS

The computer allows us to stretch, squeeze, slant, and warp type. There are a multitude of filters that open the door for this abuse. You may argue that this activity is acceptable because filters exist. Cars can be driven into trees, but that doesn't mean they should be. If you consider type as being made of the hardest substance in the universe, your life will be better. Type is not rubber. It is not soft clay. Claude Garamond did not spend decades cutting Garamond, only to have it inflated and distorted. If you need a specific effect for a project, find a typeface that has the desired attributes. Rather than warping a typeface to create something taller, find a well-drawn condensed font. It is the mark of a poor designer to rely on filters and special effects. A good, solid idea will not require the Ocean Glass Ripple filter for the headline. Simple, clear, and beautifully crafted elements create good solutions. Adding filters and effects to create interest is comparable to pouring ketchup over a perfectly grilled steak. **SA**

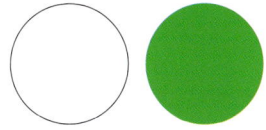

# DO learn how to customize type successfully

EyeQ Opticians

Not to be confused with a "custom type-face," which is a face designed from the ground up for a specific use or client, there are two situations in which one might refer to type as customized. One situation would be when a designer has taken an existing letterform and redrawn it slightly by extending the serifs, by adding a swash, by removing part of a bowl, and so on. It's quite common for logo-design specialists, for example, to customize a typeface in this way in order to set it apart from the original and to create a unique font for their client's identity. When this is done well and when the concept behind the editing is supportive of the rationale for the changes, highly successful results can be achieved. The other (less desirable) option might be to take an existing typeface and alter its personality by applying a filter effect, something we discourage on page 50. Especially in the latter case, always try to honor the character of a typeface when you attempt any customization in order to retain the qualities conceived by the face's original designer. **TS**

# DON'T reverse 6pt text out of a black background

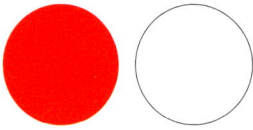

Do not try this, it will never work.

One of the goals of most clients is to create solutions that communicate. In order to communicate clearly, it is necessary to be able to read the copy. While small, delicate typography in white looks wonderful on the screen, most of us need to enlarge the view to 200 percent to read it. A computer-screen image is made of light. Light passes through the monitor onto our optical nerves. The result is a glowing and bright white on a solid black surface. Printed matter is different. Light bounces off the surface of a printed object. The white copy will never be as bright as a screen, and the black solid will never be as dense and consistent. Reversing small type sizes out of black does not work. It is easier to read black copy on a white background. In printed work, a solid black back-ground requires heavy ink coverage. Smaller type will begin to "fill in" as the coverage is denser. The only available option will be to decrease ink coverage, resulting in a thin and light black. The solution is to maintain a size and weight that will not be adversely affected. **SA**

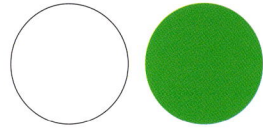

# DO specify at least one plate as 100 percent tint for colored type

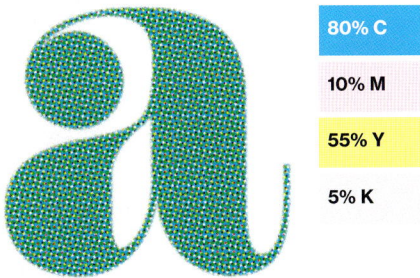

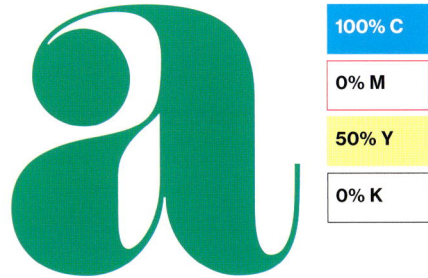

| | |
|---|---|
| 80% C | 100% C |
| 10% M | 0% M |
| 55% Y | 50% Y |
| 5% K | 0% K |

One of the negative aspects of the digital age is the lack of understanding of the physical world. When designing on the computer, everything looks perfect. The colors are solid; the lines are precise. The type created with 58 percent cyan and 12 percent magenta looks like a nice blue. The printouts that are shown to the client look fine, and we explain that the colors may be slightly different when actually printed. Then tragedy strikes. On press, the type is soft and blurry. The printer adds more ink, and the problem is exacerbated. Hopefully, the type will become sharper when the press sheets dry. But it doesn't. Why did this happen? Because when the type is created with percentages of cyan and magenta, a halftone screen is created. Halftone screens are made up of tiny dots. Hence, the letterforms are made of tiny dots and will always be soft. The solution is to always use one process color at 100 percent value. One plate will be clean line art, with no halftone dots, and your type will therefore be sharp and refined. **SA**

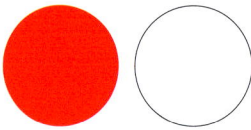

# DON'T use excessive leading in body copy

But we can perhaps remember—if only

for a time—that those who live with us are our

brothers, that they share with us the same

short moment of life, that they seek—as do we—

nothing but the chance to live out their lives

in purpose and in happiness, winning

what satisfaction and fulfillment that they can.

Let's begin with the basics. Leading is the space between lines of text. The name comes from the actual strips of lead that were used to separate text rows when metal type was set by hand. Appropriate leading allows us to read clearly. Too little leading will make copy too dense and hard to read, as if someone were mumbling. Too much leading and the copy will be too open and hard to read. There will be too much space between the lines, and it will read as if someone were speaking with long pauses in the middle of a sentence. At the end of each line, the reader will need to stop, go get a glass of water, and then start the next line. Traditionally, type exists to be read. It is not meant to occupy space as a funny compositional element that serves no other purpose. Excessive leading may be "interesting" visually, but it is unreadable. And, in the end, making typography unreadable is passive-aggressive behavior toward the reader. **SA**

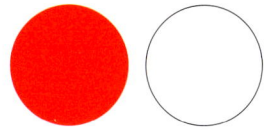

# DON'T use CAPS for long passages of body copy

WE'VE ALREADY DISCUSSED IN RULE #9 THE IMPORTANCE OF KEEPING THE TYPEFACE SIMPLE IN ORDER TO ENSURE THE LEGIBILITY OF LONG PASSAGES OF TEXT. HOWEVER, WITH EVEN JUST THE ONE TYPEFACE EMPLOYED, IT'S STILL EASY TO CREATE DIFFICULTIES FOR THE READER BY SETTING ALL THE TEXT IN CAPITAL LETTERS (OR UPPERCASE) THROUGHOUT. IT'S UNIVERSALLY RECOGNIZED (AND MUCH RESEARCH HAS BEEN DONE ON THE SUBJECT) THAT MIXED LOWERCASE AND UPPERCASE BLOCKS OF TEXT ARE EASIER TO READ THAN ALL UPPERCASE. THIS IS PRIMARILY DUE TO THE FACT THAT, DESPITE UPPERCASE TEXT APPEARING LARGER WHEN SET AT THE SAME SIZE, IT HAS NO ASCENDERS OR DESCENDERS. AS SUCH, THE LOWERCASE LETTERS HAVE MORE VARIATION IN THEIR APPEARANCE AND ARE THEREFORE EASIER TO RECOGNIZE, SPEEDING UP THE PROCESS OF READING. ANOTHER KEY POINT IS THAT USE OF UPPERCASE CAN COME ACROSS AS AGGRESSIVE AND SO GIVE THE IMPRESSION THAT THE AUTHOR IS SHOUTING AT YOU. EMPLOYING MIXED CASE FOR THE BULK OF THE TEXT CREATES A GENTLER, MORE MODERATE TONE AND HELPS GIVE THE OCCASIONAL USE OF CAPITALS

We've already discussed on page 22 the importance of keeping the typography simple in order to ensure the legibility of long passages of text. However, with even just the one typeface employed, it's still easy to create difficulties for the reader by setting all the text in capital letters (or uppercase) throughout. It's universally recognized (and much research has been done on the subject) that mixed lowercase and uppercase blocks of text are easier to read than all uppercase. This is primarily due to the fact that, although uppercase text appears larger when set at the same size, it has no ascenders or descenders. As such, the lowercase letters have more variation in their appearance and are therefore easier to recognize, speeding up the process of reading. Another key point is that use of uppercase can come across as aggressive and give the impression that the author is shouting at you. Mixing cases for the bulk of the text creates a gentler, more moderate tone and helps give the occasional use of capitals greater impact. **PD**

# DON'T have excessive amounts of reversed-out text

This is too much reversed out tex much reversed out text. This is to out text. This is too much reverse is too much reversed out text. Thi reversed out text. This is too muc text. This is too much reversed ou too much reversed out text. This i reversed out text. This is too muc text. This is too much reversed ou too much reversed out text. This i reversed out text. This is too muc text. This is too much reversed ou too much reversed out text. This i reversed out text. This is too muc text. This is too much reversed ou

There are few truths as self-evident as the fact that black text on a white background is the easiest way for the eye to digest information and communicate it back to our brain. What we do with it after that is up to the individual, but the first part is true for most everyone. Thousands of years of writing, and no shortage of academic and scientific study, have proved this. Given that most texts are presented as such, for this very reason, reversing the course can have a huge impact. You still retain contrast, yet reversed-out text grabs your attention just by being different. It's like a feathered hat. Few people are wearing them, so everyone notices. But you know what will burn your retinas? A feathered skirt, blazer, and boots combo. That only works on Big Bird. The same is true for reversed-out text. Anything more than just a little is difficult to enjoy. **JF**

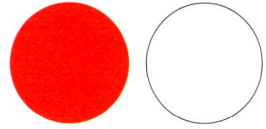

# DON'T overstyle headings

**DO NOT OVERSTYLE HEADLINES**

In the design a book, for instance, the purpose of the headings and subheadings is not only to separate and order the text but also to aid in navigation. Over the course of hundreds of pages, it is vital that the reader is able to find, with ease, the section or subsection they wish to read. It is, therefore, important that headings remain stylistically consistent throughout. It's tempting, with so many styling variables at our disposal, to start applying treatments to headers until we end up with a hodgepodge of typographic applications. Keep it simple and concentrate more on balancing the size of the headings with the size of the body text to get a clear hierarchy among the different heading levels and a visual connection between those levels. Using a secondary typeface that differs from the body text is also fine, but remember to practice restraint at all times; by doing so, your designs will be cleaner and more professional. **PD**

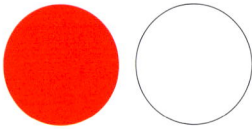

# DON'T add two spaces after a full stop

es. ⋅ ⋅ Ab

Ever since the introduction of movable type, the correct amount of space following a full stop has been a source of debate. Type set by hand utilized variously sized "spacers" depending on the chosen font, and it was down to the compositor to decide what looked right. The introduction of the typewriter in the late nineteenth century changed all this because the type was monospaced, with each letter allocated the same character width. A single space after a full stop was deemed insufficient, so the practice of double-spacing was taught widely, with hot-metal Linotype operators adopting the convention alongside regular typing-pool employees. Nowadays, modern digital fonts contain proportional kerning pairs, and a slightly wider space is always added after a full stop, so a double space is no longer required. It's ultimately up to the typographer, but the convention is: always add a single space after a full stop. **TS**

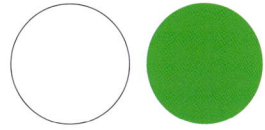

# DO apply an indent to the beginning of each new paragraph of body copy

Large amounts of body copy will typically be divided into paragraphs, which are made up of multiple sentences that ease the reading process and create pauses for the reader. When a new paragraph begins, it will start on a new line, and there are rules regarding how this new paragraph should be presented. If there is no clear line break preceding the new paragraph, then the first line of the new paragraph should be indented to signify that a new paragraph starts. You should never indent and have a line break, as the two treatments are in effect a duplication of each other. You only need to signify it once. However, there are exemptions from indenting: never the first paragraph and never after a heading or subheading. **PD**

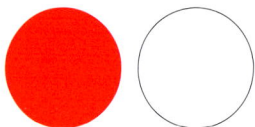

# DON'T indent a paragraph that follows a heading or paragraph break

As explained on page 59, when setting large amounts of body copy, it will be structured as paragraphs; a styling has to be applied to create paragraphs that signify pauses for the reader. It may be that you decide to include line breaks between each paragraph so that they are clearly separated. This approach would probably be used more in literature or promotional print items than in other types of publishing such as newspapers because, in the latter, space is at a premium. Be aware that this approach breaks up the flow when reading and is a bit too stop and start. If you are employing line breaks, you should never indent—the two treatments fulfill the same function. Likewise, if a heading precedes the start of a new paragraph, there is no need to indent. **PD**

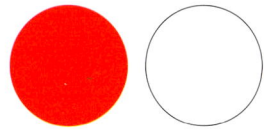

# DON'T indent a paragraph that starts at the top of a column or page (unless house style says otherwise)

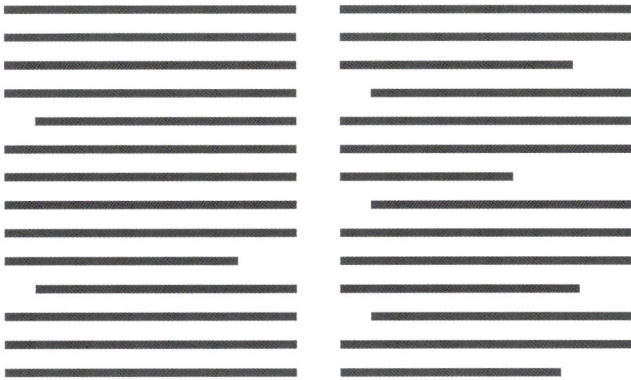

The rules governing the indentation of paragraphs are invariably linked to either a publisher's house style or style rules in corporate guidelines, so a degree of flexibility is important. That said, it is essential to be consistent when setting the text, particularly where a new paragraph begins at the top of a column or page. In the books I have designed, body text is indented when a new paragraph begins at the top of a column or page. In corporate literature, however, I find that, because the page grid will often have more columns of text per page, it's cleaner not to indent at the top of a column. Discuss with the client whether there are any house styles before you begin, as the decision may have already been made for you. **PD**

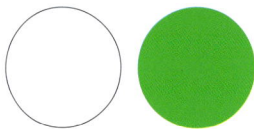

# DO set the first few words of a sentence following a drop cap in small caps

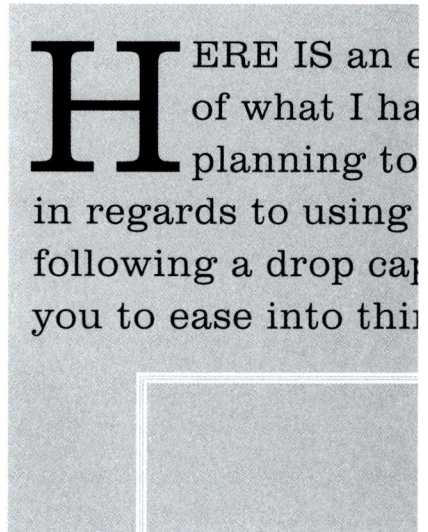

Think of this in the same way you might a foyer in a house, or better yet, a hallway or atrium before you enter a huge performance space. The heart of the space still lies ahead, where you will spend hours digesting a barrage of information, unless it is a night at the opera, when you might just catch up on some sleep—but that is another book altogether. Outside the arena, there are blaring and bold signs welcoming you in. Those are the drop caps in our typographic world. Once we are settled in our rows, the body copy is getting ready to take the stage—the meat of the evening. What is needed is a visual transition from the huge drop cap to the workmanlike body copy. Enter the sensible small cap to walk us to our seat. **JF**

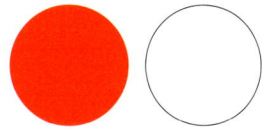

# DON'T use tabs to create indents

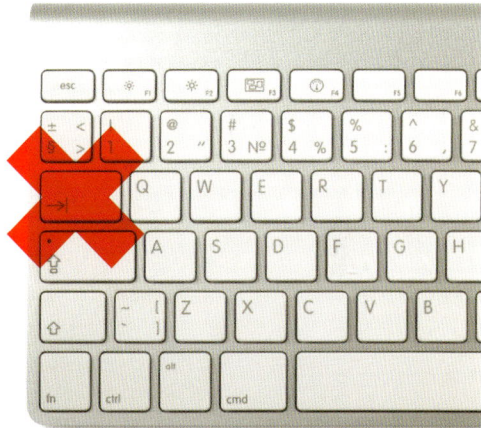

Tabs exist to position text at specific measurements within a line length. They are useful when creating tables of information. Tabs should not be used to create indents. Indents move the text inward from the left or right edge of the line length. Indents should be used, oddly, to create indents. Once the first line indent of a paragraph is set, each subsequent paragraph can follow the same measurement. If a tab is used to do this, the designer will need to insert a tab space manually. When multiple paragraphs need indents, this manual approach may lead to errors. A tab might be forgotten. The tab measurement may be set incorrectly. If there are copy revisions—and there always are copy revisions—a manually set tab may move and end up in the middle of a line. A first-line indent is the correct approach. This will not affect any copy changes, and the manual input of individual tabs is not necessary. **SA**

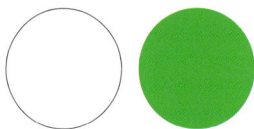

# DO hang lines of text from a tab in a bulleted list

1. When a bulleted or numbered list contains items that run to more than one line, it is common to "hang" the text from the bullet or number.

2. A paragraph may also be hung from the first line of text—often with a run-in head of bold or italic when no bullet or number is present. In either case, the hanging indent more clearly marks the item in the list.

3. When a bulleted or numbered list contains items that run to more than one line, it is common to "hang" the text from the bullet or number.

4. A paragraph may also be hung from the first line of text—often with a run-in head of bold or italic.

A solid swath of body copy is like a team: to be successful, it needs everyone to fully understand and perform their roles. When someone starts to go rogue and do their own thing, it weakens the whole operation. Each piece has a job, with specific functions, and with good reason. When you have a bulleted list, one must understand each role thoroughly; then all of the decisions that follow are easy. You have a title or main head that deserves some attention on its own. This means that it starts on the left to grab your eye immediately. You might have some intro copy. Not as important, but still needs your attention, so it starts on the left. Then you have the tabbed copy, indented to show that it is a subsection. The copy with each tab is a self-sufficient little burst and belongs together as a single notion. So why would you let it slip over to the left on the next line? It's not a header or body copy. It's a tab and proud of it. **JF**

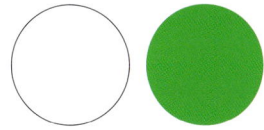

# DO learn the difference between a typeface and a font

80pt

Designers regularly refer to typefaces and fonts as the same thing, but there's an important, albeit subtle, terminological difference. A typeface is a set of characters that is independent of an individual point size but shares other characteristics such as the width of its strokes, the style of its serifs, indeed whether it is serif or a sans serif, and so on. Given this, you can say that Neue Haas Grotesk Text Bold (used for the headlines on each page in this book) is a *typeface*. A font, on the other hand, is all the characters, including numerals, punctuation, glyphs, and so on,

for a typeface at one specific point size. Therefore, 80pt Archer Bold is a *font*. It's a simple distinction but one worth knowing, especially if you have a tendency toward type geekiness. This rule is applied less rigidly now that OpenType is the established font format because a single OpenType file contains *all* point sizes of a particular weight or style, making the term more interchangeable. However, it is still useful to observe the distinction when discussing typographic specifications for a project. **TS**

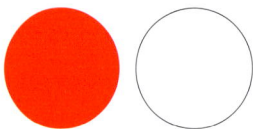

# DON'T confuse x-height with cap height

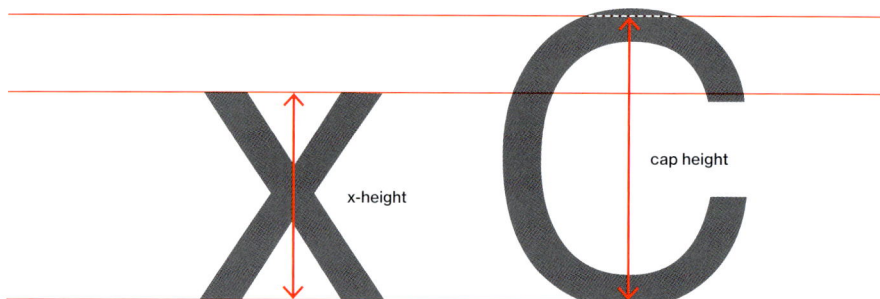

x-height

cap height

It's a very important rule to remember, and, once learned, the definitions of each will stay with you forever. To clarify, the x-height of a typeface starts from the baseline, on which all the characters sit, and reaches up to the height of the lowercase letters (not including their ascenders and descenders). To see how differing typefaces have a range of x-heights, create a line of type, duplicate it, change the font, overlay it, and examine the differences. The ascenders and descenders on letters with small x-heights will look more pronounced. Larger x-heights will make the text look heavier and more solid, so an increase in the leading may be required to compensate. The cap height simply refers to the height of the capital letters from the baseline to the top. Be aware that rounded uppercase letters sit above the cap height and below the baseline, so this measurement doesn't apply to them. Their additional size is called an overshoot. **PD**

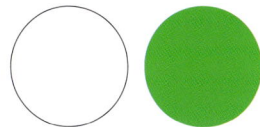

# DO consider a font's x-height when specifying leading

Everything on this line is 26pt

When I select which typeface I'm going to use for a new project, I like to start by setting blocks of 9pt body text with 12pt leading to see how my various choices look. The $^9/_{12}$ text setting isn't an arbitrary choice but rather a rough average of the values one might choose for the point size and leading of body text. One of the first things I tend to note is the variation in the x-height between my font choices, partly because the x height contributes largely to the feel of the setting but also because it

influences the leading required for comfortable line-by-line scanning. A font with a large x-height (for example, Helvetica) will likely need a little more leading (or a reduction in point size) than a smaller x-height (for example, Centaur) would require, and this needs to be taken into account when planning your layout and grid. You should also take the height and depth of the ascenders and descenders into account when specifying line feed. **TS**

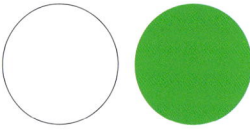

# DO learn what *leading* means and what it does

Leading is named as such based on the strips of lead that old typesetters used to separate lines of metal type. In essence, it is the distance from the baseline of one line of type laid out to another. You may also hear it referred to as line spacing in conversation.

*Leading* is a term derived from the early days of typesetting, and it is one of the most important things to understand in becoming a competent designer. You may also hear this called line feed, but that is usually from people who don't fully grasp leading. The term comes from when typesetters would use strips of lead to create specific space between lines of metal type. The way it is applied in the modern era is much more varied and powerful. Based on a premise of using 120 percent of the size of the type being displayed, the default setting for most programs works fairly well. But this is an area with which the designer can instantly create a response from the viewer interacting with the layout (feeling tense and claustrophobic as I tighten the paragraph leading or airy and loose as I increase it?) and should be fully explored and understood. **JF**

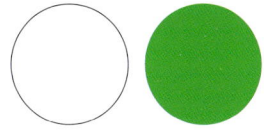

# DO keep consistent leading within a paragraph

Consistent leading within a paragraph is extremely important. Changing this can create an unplanned effect on the reader as they are made uncomfortable. One has to consider that the paragraph is intended to contain a single thought and should therefore be kept cohesive.

Now that we know how powerful leading is—and it is incredibly powerful—we have to understand why we can't abuse it. If you walk down a corridor and it gradually narrows, you will feel pretty uncomfortable by the end; certainly, you are having a different experience than when you started. A corridor that opens up widely by the end creates the reverse effect, but it is just as jarring. The same is true if you tinker with the leading in a paragraph. By nature, a paragraph is a complete thought and should retain cohesiveness. The viewer has to have the same experience at the beginning as at the end. No matter what the desired effect is, the point is to remain consistent in order to achieve it. **JF**

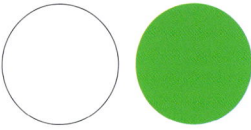

# DO understand paragraph spacing and use it wisely

In speaking about paragraph spacing, one should take into account a number of factors, such as how the information is to be received and digested. How much space is available on the page? Should the designer be creative with an option? Or is it best to go with a tried and true solution like the following half line?

In speaking about paragraph spacing, one should take into account a number of factors, such as how the information is to be received and digested. How much space is available on the page? Should the designer be creative with an option? Or is it best to go with a tried and true solution like the following half line?

Paragraphs are formed so that we can digest the information in reasonable blocks. This is a simple idea but one that some designers fail to take into account. With that perspective, the space between paragraphs takes on a heightened importance. There are a number of ways to accomplish getting our eyes to acknowledge that we have finished one paragraph and are starting another, and each one has its benefits and deterrents. The trick is in finding the best solution for your particular project—indents (or for the true wild child, outdents) are not as visually clean as a line break with a half-line space, but they do conserve space. Typographers of the past used various creative ways to make this happen, rarely with readable results, but the masters could finesse it at times (for example, symbols marking the space between paragraphs as the body copy continues to run and run and run— a magazine sidebar mainstay). If you understand the process, the answers become more evident. **JF**

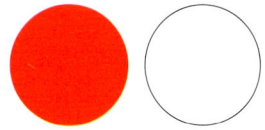

# DON'T apply excessive tracking to body copy

The terms tracking and kerning quite often get confused. As described in rule #58, kerning is the adjustment of space between individual letter pairs, whereas tracking is the adjustment of letter spacing of entire lines or paragraphs of text. Tracking is a useful feature when setting body text but it must be used sparingly so as not to cause problems with legibility. Too much negative tracking and a sentence or paragraph will appear dense compared to the rest of the text. Too much positive tracking and the text will look too airy, blurring the distinction between letters and words and making it difficult to read. The benefits of tracking are that you can apply it to entire paragraphs, to single lines, or to a single word, and this can enable you to pull back widows and orphans and tidy up awkward line breaks.

The terms *tracking* and *kerning* quite often get confused. Kerning is the adjustment of space between individual letter pairs, whereas tracking is the adjustment of letter spacing of entire lines or paragraphs of text. Tracking is a useful feature when setting body text, but it must be used sparingly so as not to cause problems with legibility. Too much negative tracking and a sentence or paragraph will appear dense compared with the rest of the text.

Too much positive tracking and the text will look too airy, blurring the distinction between letters and words and making it difficult to read. The benefits of tracking are that you can apply it to entire paragraphs, to a single line, or to a single word, and this can enable you to pull back widows and orphans and tidy up awkward line breaks. As a rule of thumb, when using a software package like Adobe InDesign, I would never go past +/−25 on the outside. **PD**

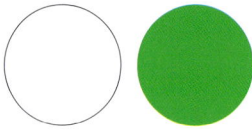

# DO always kern unsightly character combinations

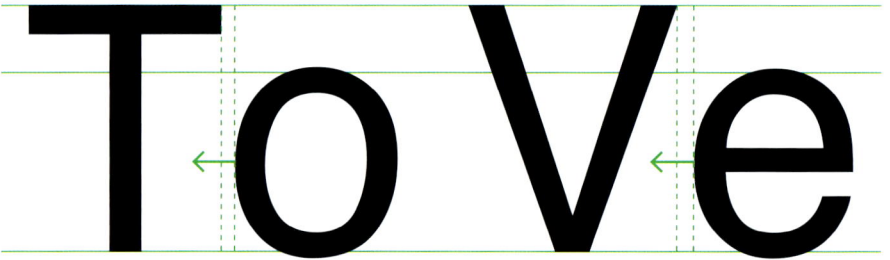

To Ve

Quite often, although the typeface you have chosen may be working well, the spacing between some of the letters may look uneven. This is a very common aspect of typography that designers deal with on a day-to-day basis; to compensate, you need to kern the letters. When setting uppercase text, the issues are more evident, as is the case with letters such as *T*, *V*, and *W*, which force the subsequent letter to sit some distance away. When creat-ing their fonts, typeface designers do consider many of the letters that sit awkwardly together (for example, *Kn*, *To*, *Ve*, *Wi*) and create kerning pairs to eliminate the spacing issues. More often than not, however, it's up to you to adjust and eliminate the unsightly spacing. To do so, simply decrease (or increase) the kerning between the characters to improve balance and create an appearance of even spacing in relation to the rest of the word. **PD**

# DO always kern headlines manually

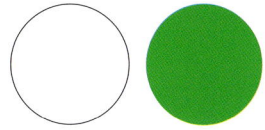

kern ✅

**kern**

The familiar adage "The bigger they are, the harder they fall" can be applied to type too. Design software and kerning pairs work in tandem to control the character spacing of all type, and at point sizes below 14pt it's hardly ever necessary to apply any manual kerning. That's fortunate—imagine the amount of work that would be needed to sort all that out. However, as point sizes increase for crossheads and headlines, the character spacing becomes more visible, and some attention is often required. Problem pairs can involve, but aren't limited to, any characters that don't have vertical stems at the side, so *A*, *K*, *T*, *V*, *W*, and *Y* are common culprits. In reality, any number of character pairs in both uppercase and lowercase may need some manual kerning—depending on the typeface. When you're searching for potential kerning problems, try squinting at the setting—it helps in making the awkward white spaces between characters more prominent. **TS**

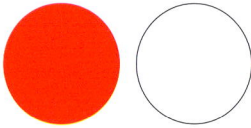

# DON'T use negative letter spacing

# NEGATIVE

If you've ever tried to squeeze too many people onto a sofa at a party, then you know what we're talking about with negative letter spacing. This doesn't mean that you can't nuzzle together to get the job done on occasion; some tracking work to pull up an orphan up here and there might be required.

What we are talking about is the tightening together of letterforms to the point that they are uncomfortable or right on top of one another. They weren't designed to work that way, much in the same manner that too many people crammed on a couch or sitting on our lap is suffocating. **JF**

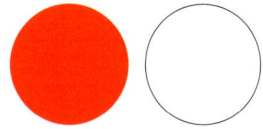

# DON'T exceed eighty characters per line

For the sake of readability, the designer should ensure that the measure (or line length) isn't too long. Very long lines can mean that the reader may lose their place midsentence or when shifting their eyes to the start of the following line—a frustrating experience if you have a whole book ahead of you! A way of getting around this is to check the character count in an individual line. A generally accepted standard is around 45–75 characters per line. In a pinch, you can go up to 80, but this depends on the typeface chosen. On the flip side, a very short measure means that the reader's eyes will be continually zipping back and forth, ensuring a disagreeable reading experience. Working within or close to the limits will help to improve your design. **PD**

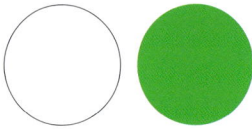

# DO set the second line of a paragraph longer than the first

That is why we like to have the second line of a paragraph set longer than the first.

Once we start walking, we definitely appreciate some forward progress. Any step that has to be retraced, even if it's a half-step pause, is wasted motion. When we read, that same quality takes over, and once we get going, it's hard to stop us on our stroll toward comprehension. That is why we like to have the second line of a paragraph set longer than the first. The indented white space, if it is shorter, gives us pause. Creating this is a combination of selective line breaks and tracking as needed. Ragging our copy is an art form in its own right. It is important to note that this should not take precedence over other hard rules of typography (don't end the second line with a dangling "a" or "it" or track out +60 just to make it happen), but it should be attempted wherever possible. **JF**

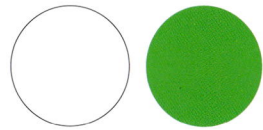

# DO set the penultimate line of a paragraph longer than the last

Paragraphs are there so that we can digest information easily. Thus, we have come up with numerous tools to let the reader know exactly when a paragraph is ending and another one is starting.

In order for these to work, one of the most important aspects is that the last line of set type be shorter than the line before it, creating a bit of white space to alert the eye to a change.

As we have already discussed, the paragraph is a construct of writers; it doesn't actually occur naturally like a sentence (which is a full thought as if uttered in conversation). Paragraphs are there so that we can digest information easily. Thus, we have come up with numerous tools to let the reader know exactly when a paragraph is ending and another one is starting. In order for these to work, one of the most important aspects is that the last line of set type be shorter than the line before it, creating a bit of white space to alert the eye to a change. A simple meal is structured in much the same way: appetizer (slightly shorter first line), entrée (slightly longer second line, going into the body of the paragraph), and the dessert (shorter final line). If the dessert is larger than the entrée, you have no idea what kind of meal you have just eaten or if it is over. **JF**

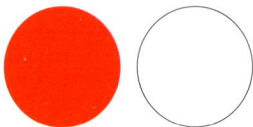

## DON'T allow a line to break on the words *it* or *is*

When working with a justified paragraph, it ✕ is harder to accomplish,

This is one of those rules that really showcases those who are the true masters of paragraph ragging. You won't find it in any manual or stated as a hard-and-fast rule in a textbook, but if you work with savvy folks who have been in the trenches of publication design, this is often one of the first tips that they pass on. When working with a justified paragraph, it is harder to accomplish, but when you have one flushed left or right, you should be willing to rework a paragraph seven different ways to make it happen. Why do we care so much? Because finishing a line as such leaves a massive hanging thought and causes an awkward pause in our comprehension. The easiest practice is simply to read the text aloud. Once you do that, you will never let a line end in it or is again. We would never talk that way; why should we force ourselves to read that way? **JF**

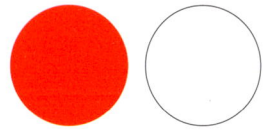

# DON'T hyphenate words of less than seven characters

One should not hyphenate wor- ❌
ds of less than
seven charac- ✅
ters

Many designers are happy to hyphenate shorter words, but for me the minimum acceptable number of characters a word should contain before it can be hyphenated is seven. This in turn means a minimum of four characters before a hyphen and no fewer than three characters following a hyphenated line break. These parameters can be set in a paragraph style sheet at the beginning of a project to ensure the consistency of all body copy (see page 82). Why seven? It's partly a visual thing, as I don't believe two characters followed by a hyphen look that great, but it's also an editorial consideration, as I don't think a word of five characters or less reads cleanly when it's hyphenated. Experienced readers store words as shapes to speed up the reading process, and seeing the first few characters of a word helps us to fill in the rest before scanning the start of the next line. If you have only one or two characters to work with, this process won't happen. **TS**

# DON'T mix centered and flush-left or flush-right text

**The Great Basin
A Tragedy in Four Parts**

Good

**The Great Basin
A Tragedy in Four Parts**

Not good!

For hundreds of years, typographic layouts used a largely symmetrical, centered approach. Headlines, subheads, and body text were centered or justified. Symmetrical typography was a product of available technology and the printing press. In the 1920s, Jan Tschichold championed asymmetrical typography. His frustration with the complex and illegible Victorian and Gothic German forms led him to a system of sans-serif fonts, more negative space, and asymmetric typography. He considered asymmetry to be more legible, vibrant, and powerful. This does not make centered typography wrong. It is entirely appropriate in certain contexts. Mixing centered and flush-left or flush-right text, however, is wrong. It is similar to mixing a simple white T-shirt with red velvet pantaloons. It's not pretty, and it looks foolish. As in most things in life, maintaining consistency creates clarity. A consistent centered layout tells the viewer how and where to look for information. The same is true for an asymmetric layout. Mixing the two creates confusion and chaos. **SA**

**80**     TYPE & TYPOGRAPHY

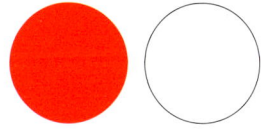

# DON'T use justified text over a short measure

**Too few characters, and the word spacing will b e c o m e enormous to create a justified axis.**

If a designer has several years of experience refining the word spacing and kerning of justified paragraphs, then justifying a short line is okay. For those with less than a decade of experience, this is a bad idea. Justified type requires a minimum number of characters. Too few characters, and the word spacing will become enormous. Large word spacing will create "rivers" of negative space within a paragraph and make reading more difficult. The underlying logic of good typography should be invisible while facilitating reading and understanding. Creating a justified line length that feels effortless is the correct solution to good typography. Typography stops being invisible when we are faced with discrepancies, such as unexpectedly large word spaces. When justifying text, a good rule of thumb with line-length measures is to use no more than eighty characters and no fewer than twenty-six characters. But the best approach is to set the text with a line measure that has an optically consistent amount of word and letter spacing. **SA**

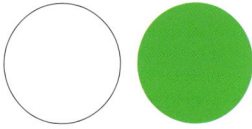

# DO check justification settings for justified text

| | Minimum | Desired | Maximum |
|---|---|---|---|
| Word Spacing: | 85% | 100% | 125% |
| Letter Spacing: | 0% | 0% | 0% |
| Glyph Scaling: | 100% | 100% | 100% |

Justification

OK

Cancel

☑ Preview

Auto Leading: 150%

Single Word Justification: Align Left ⌄

Composer: Adobe Single-line Composer ⌄

The desktop publishing programs InDesign and QuarkXPress both provide the means to apply manual settings for justification. The settings are only applicable to justified text, as ragged text uses the optimum letter and word spacing built into a font. If you opt for justified alignment and the word spacing at your chosen font size looks too gappy or too tight, the justification settings will help fix things. A value of 100 percent for word spacing or 0 percent for letter spacing is equal to "no manual adjustment" in real terms. If you want to close up space, enter a value less than 100 percent for word spacing or -0 percent for letter spacing; opening up space requires a value greater than 100 percent for words or +0 percent for letters; and so on. Play around with a paragraph of dummy copy to see how different values reflow the text—it's the best way to learn how the functionality works. My tip would be to concentrate on the minimum and maximum word spacing, leaving the desired setting at the optimum 100 percent, and always leave the letter spacing set to 0 percent. **TS**

# DO avoid creating "rivers" in justified text

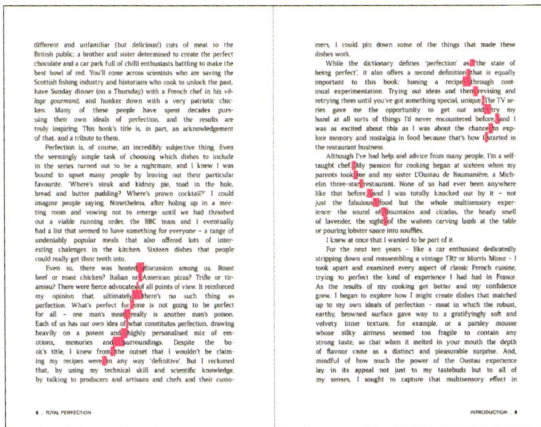

When a text is justified, a distracting visual oddity can often occur: Spaces between words arrange themselves on top of one another, forming a curving white line running vertically through the paragraph. This is referred to as a "river." This can appear in flush-left, flush-right, and centered type, but because of the way justified type increases the word spacing by forcing the line of type to the full measure, the chance of creating rivers increases. Rectifying the problem is straight forward. The first step is to introduce hyphenation into the setting—this can be done manually if you wish to reduce the number of hyphens that appear, or it can be set up automatically in your desktop publishing software. Alternatively, you can track some of the affected lines in or out to compensate, and problem solved! **PD**

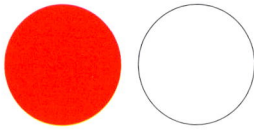

# DON'T allow widows to appear in text

*Widows*, one of typography's more unusual terms, occur so often that even some of the most beautifully crafted works, on closer examination, have been marred by their presence. Different than orphans, they are single words or lines of text that have been separated from the rest of the paragraph and are either sitting alone at the top of the following column or pushed over to the opposite page. There, they sit all on their own, away from the rest of their text, creating

an unsightly visual anomaly at the top of the column or page. To rectify and rescue the widow, review the column or page from where it has been forced over and track back these lines, which are more open if justified or are shorter if flush left, to eliminate the widow. The end result will be that the bottom of the column or page finishes cleanly with the end of a paragraph, and the next page starts with a new one. **PD**

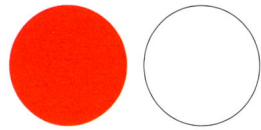

# DON'T allow orphans to appear in text

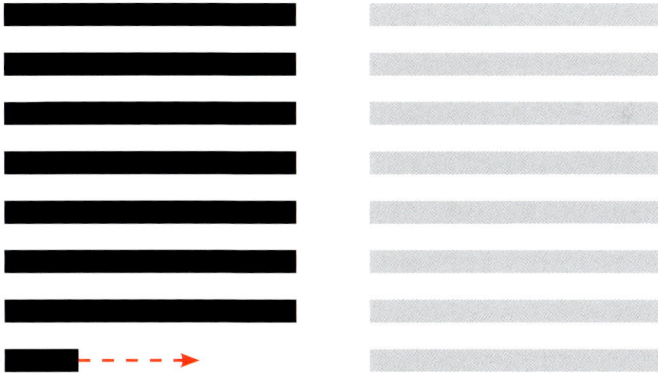

An orphan (which, in my view, is commonly and mistakenly referred to as a *widow*—see page 84 for a definition) can be described as a single word sitting on its own at the end of a paragraph, or it can be the first line of a paragraph on its own at the bottom of a column or page. Visually, it is not very nice to look at, and it hinders the flow of reading. In order to rectify this, either put in some soft returns in the text preceding it, pushing words over to the next line and adding to the single word, or, if there is space, track back certain lines to pull back words and pull the orphan back up to the previous line. The same goes for the single line at the bottom of the column or page, although I would take the view that it is better to push it over than take it back so that the paragraphs have clean breaks between columns or pages. Better still, if you are working directly with an editor, ask them if the text can be edited in order to fix the problem. **PD**

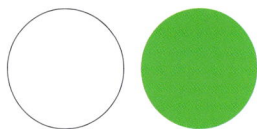

## DO check that text is not formatted with "justify all lines" selected

# creating a pleasing re-sult with justified text is often difficult to a c h i e v e .

There are three ways to set justified text, each of which treats the final line of a paragraph differently. The usual method is designated "justify with last line aligned left." This means any text on the final line of a paragraph will effectively not be justified at all—it will be ragged left. The character and word spacing probably won't match that of the lines that appear before it, but that is the nature of justified setting and the reason that creating a pleasing result with justified text is often difficult to achieve. The second option is "justify with last line centered," which is never really going to work with running copy. The third option is "justify all lines," where the final line of a paragraph is set to the full measure regardless of how many words or characters it contains. If a line of copy almost fills a measure, falling short by only an em or so, this option will work perfectly well. Under any other circumstances, it is best to avoid the option altogether. Never choose it as a default setting when building style sheets. **TS**

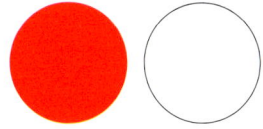

# DON'T hyphenate text that is ragged right*

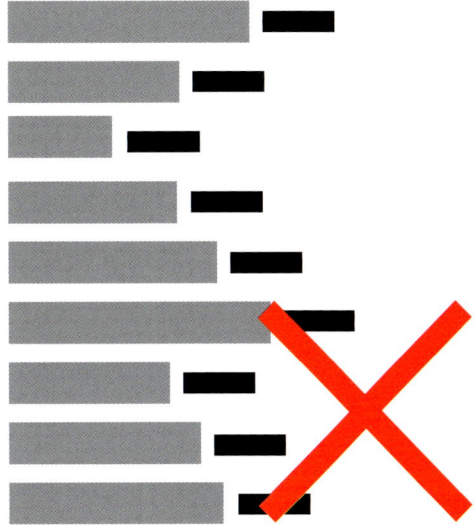

I have had many a debate on this and, yes, I should "get out more," but I (and many others) see no reason for hyphenation when the body text is ragged right. Yes, line endings should certainly be tidied up, short words taken over, and orphans and widows dealt with. But the natural line breaks that appear with flush-left/right-ragged negate the need to apply hyphenation. It is an additional element that, when added, actually hinders the reading process and doesn't look very good. **PD**

---

* See page 88 for exceptions in certain cases (like this book).

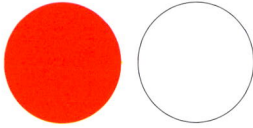

# DON'T be scared of our useful little friend, the hyphen

I'm not entirely sure why this is the case, but there's something going on which has set designers against hyphens. I'm going to make a bit of a distinction here as you see hyphens used to good (and often atrociously bad I grant you) effect in newspapers and magazines all the time, but for some reason books, corporate brochures, and packaging featuring justified text seem to have become hyphen 'no-go areas'. The flip side of this is that the same books, brochures, and packs have simultaneously become safe havens for bad word spacing, which really does defeat the object entirely. The answer is, if you're really that scared of using hyphens don't justify text, set it ragged. On the subject of ragged text, there's nothing to stop you hyphenating that either if you're having to deal with short measures and long words. Hang on a minute—I can hear a wail of dissent getting louder and louder. I think I may have taken this argument a bit too far!

I'm not entirely sure why this is the case, but there's something going on that has turned designers against hyphenating at the end of lines. I'm going to make a bit of a distinction here, as you see hyphens used to good (and often atrociously bad, I grant you) effect in newspapers and magazines all the time, but for some reason, books, corporate brochures, and packaging featuring justified text seem to have become no-go hyphen areas. The flip side of this is that the same books, brochures, and packaging have simultaneously become safe havens for bad word spacing, which really does defeat the purpose entirely. The answer is, if you're really that scared of using hyphens, don't justify text, set it ragged. On the subject of ragged text, there's nothing to stop you from hyphenating that either, if you're dealing with short measures and long words. And before you say it, yes, I know I'm contradicting the advice just given on page 87. Hang on a minute, the wail of dissent is getting louder and louder. I think I may have taken this argument a bit too far! **TS**

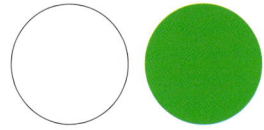

# DO embrace the use of Web font embedding services

```
<link href="https://fonts.googleapis
.com/css?family=Source+Sans+Pro"
rel="stylesheet">
```

Anyone involved in designing for the Web in the not-so-good old days will remember the frustration of being limited to a narrow selection of Web-safe fonts, or, in other words, the fonts installed as a default by Windows or OSX. Today, the choice of fonts a designer can use confidently, knowing a site will appear exactly as intended, is vast thanks to Web font embedding services. Google Fonts is arguably the most widely used service of this kind (plus it is completely free, which helps explain why) and features hundreds of good-quality fonts in its directory. Typekit from Adobe is another excellent option; it is included as part of their Creative Cloud subscription, and, as one would expect from Adobe, all fonts in their directory are of professional quality. If you don't have an Adobe subscription, they also offer a free service, Adobe Edge Web Fonts. Using a font embedding service is very simple; a JavaScript tag that can be added to the <head> of a website is provided for each font. Job done. **TS**

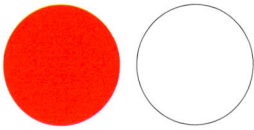

## DON'T underline text for *emphasis*

# Instead of using an <u>underline</u> to emphasize words—*use italics.*

Using an underline, or an underscore, to emphasize a word isn't a total no-no, but there's a much better way—use italics. The term *underscore* derives from the name of the individual character that typists would apply to words by backspacing and retyping an underline, and underscoring for emphasis is a bit of a "typing" thing rather than proper typesetting practice. Italics, particularly when used in running text, present a much more elegant solution and provide the required emphasis without interrupting the flow. This means emphasis is achieved invisibly without jolting the reader's attention away from the fluid run of the narrative. If you're designing an application form or diagram, for example, the rule doesn't apply so much—it's more appropriate for larger blocks of body copy. There's another good reason for not using underscores: online they denote a hyperlink, and any text that will be repurposed from a print project ideally shouldn't contain any underscores at all. **TS**

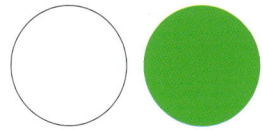

# DO use true typographer's quotation marks

These are sometimes called smart quotes, which seems a bit over the top, since there aren't any other kinds of quotes you can use correctly. Whenever you need to highlight a quotation or utilize an apostrophe, please use the proper quotation marks that look like miniature floating pairs of sixes and nines. The marks that don't have any curly bits are called straight quotes, and they specifically denote feet (single prime), inches (double primes), minutes (single prime), or seconds (double primes), so this isn't just a styling issue. The sixes open a quotation, and the nines close a quotation and double as apostrophes, providing added value at no extra cost, except for my dental bills that is, as seeing primes used incorrectly in place of quotation marks makes me grind my teeth, so spare a thought. **TS**

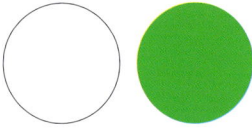

# DO use correct accent marks

á ê í ó é ō ç ö ú ñ ü

Despite our general assertion and expectation, the rest of the world doesn't do everything in English. They even have the nerve to add little squiggles, dashes, and dots over some of our precious letterforms. How dare they! It seems like some of these have a basis in how these people talk, you know, with those funny sounds that come out where we would have plainly said an *o* or an *e*. It might seem humorous until you realize that we could use the same system just to help Northerners and Southerners understand each other. The reason we have printed matter at all is as a substitute for a person actually being there to say it in front of us. If they were standing there pronouncing words as they occur in their natural environment, then we would respect those sounds. If this means mastering some of the keyboard shortcuts and special characters, well, we are learning something, broadening our horizons, and showing respect at every level. **JF**

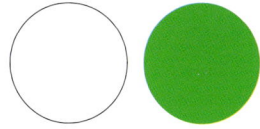

# DO use correctly formatted fractions

1/4  1/2  3/4  1/3  2/3  1/8  3/8  5/8  7/8

¼  ½  ¾  ⅓  ⅔  ⅛  ⅜  ⅝  ⅞

If you have the advantage of reading the copy before beginning a layout project, especially if you expect to be dealing with financials or some form involving numerical breakdowns, I strongly advise that you start by choosing typefaces that have extensive character sets and, better still, typefaces that include specific characters for fractions. This is a place where taking a shortcut will make for a very awkward piece of typesetting. There are few things as clunky as two numbers separated by a slash, when a proper, tight fraction is available. Think about it in the sense that a fraction takes up the equivalent visual space of a single character, less than if it were a series of full x-height numbers, and you get the idea pretty quickly. Like the proper use of small caps, this treatment instantly indicates to the reader that this is the work of an experienced designer with a sophisticated ability to deal with type. **JF**

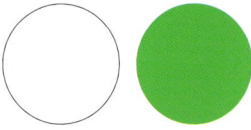

# DO use an en dash to indicate a range of values

# 1969–2011

The use, or misuse, of en dashes is a common problem we see in the written content we receive. An en dash should be used when numbers or words that denote a range need to be linked together or to signify an open range. For example, 1939–45 and 100–200 BCE are examples of the en dash being used in a closed range. Note that there is no space on either side of the en dash.

When typesetting these figures, and if one is using nonaligning numerals, it is worthwhile to kern a little space between the figures and the en dash so that they don't appear as if they are colliding. An open-ended range would be set as: 2011–. Words that are communicating a range would look like this: January–December 2011. **PD**

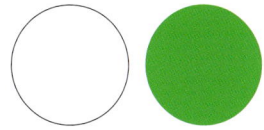

# DO use an em dash to indicate a conversational break

Although used as often as its cousin the en dash, the em dash is the correct punctuation mark to insert into a sentence when a conversational break is required. The em dash, being more significant in presence than a comma, provides greater emphasis in setting apart an aside in a sentence. At the same time, it is not as aggressive as a full stop, so the subject and intent of the sentence is carried through. For example, "Despite the disapproval of his friends—they thought he had forsaken his values—Peter decided to use Comic Sans." In addition, it can be used to signify an emotive interruption into a sentence: for example, "I can't believe it's—," which works better than a full stop and signifies that the speaker is left hanging. Its use seems to be waning, which I think is a shame. That said, be careful not to overuse the em dash; it can be somewhat overpowering. Everything in moderation. **PD**

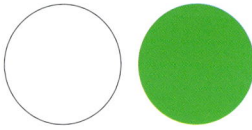

# DO tuck full stops and commas inside quotation marks only in the United States

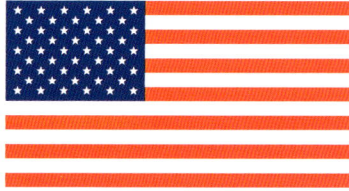

## "Only in America."

No one is quite sure when it happened (maybe it was linked to that little "independence" dustup), but when British conventions were sent across the Atlantic, a few of them seemed to have fallen overboard, leaving the Yanks to make their own decisions. While Americans have removed the *u* in *colors* to reflect their pronunciation, other decisions are more closely linked to modern typesetting. The placement of punctuation in regard to quotation marks was formed at an earlier time, founded on basic needs—namely, that punctuation signaled the end of a sentence. Therefore, of course it fell outside the quotation mark. However, American typesetters noted the awkward space it creates and, as one of many adjustments, experimented with placing punctuation on the inside, creating a tighter space. This was soon adopted as the correct way to position full stops and commas. **JF**

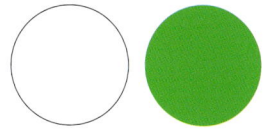

# DO place full stops and commas outside quotation marks everywhere but the United States

# "Outside America".

While American typesetters would surely tell you that they have reengineered the fuddy-duddy old-world ways for the better (and in this case, it is hard to argue against the more appealing visual white space left by tucking the punctuation inside the quotation marks), that doesn't necessarily mean that we can expect the thousands of years of the written word to instantly abide by their new rules. The placement of full stops and commas is based on the intended use of the marks, to signal the end of a thought. Following that line of thinking, full stops and commas have to come after all other elements of that segment. While figuring out the differences in spelling certain words can occupy a lot of your time when trying to make a layout for audiences in several countries, this variation is the most difficult practice to go back and forth on. **JF**

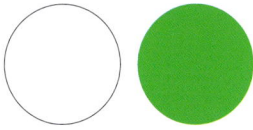

# DO hang quotation marks outside the paragraph margins

"

"Reminds us that the struggle for justice is also the struggle for truth, then as now."

—*Khalil Gibran Muhammad, Harvard University*

In order to achieve a smoothly aligned left edge for a pull quote, it's best to "hang" the quotation marks. This involves repositioning the opening quotation mark out to the left so that the initial letter of the text is aligned with the initial letter of the subsequent line. It's a simple task to do; if you are using a software package such as InDesign, there's a feature under "Story" with a panel window containing a checkbox called "Optical Margin Alignment." There, you can key in the point size of the text you are using, and it will refine the alignment and hang the punctuation for you. However, I always find that it is never quite enough to key in the exact match of the text size you have styled, so I always key in a size 20–30 percent bigger to ensure a crisper alignment. **PD**

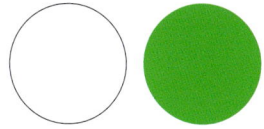

# DO add a full stop after an ellipsis at the end of a sentence

graphin....

When an ellipsis is employed within the text, it can be used in a number of ways: dramatically, to create a pause in the middle of a sentence, or at the end of a sentence, almost as if the writer has faded away, lost in thought. However, a common mistake is to leave the ellipsis at the end of a sentence unfinished. I understand that there was great debate about this in the past, so whether this entry adds fuel to the fire, who knows? In my professional opinion, however, it needs the full stop in order to provide closure to the sentence. The house styles of some publishers may specify the three-dot option (i.e., without the full stop). In the absence of any such instructions, you should go with the four-dot treatment. **PD**

# Layout & Design

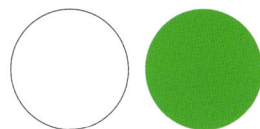

# DO learn about the golden section

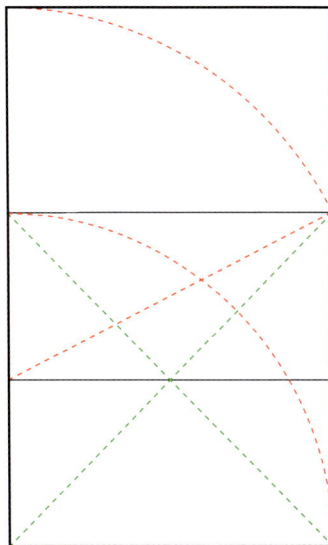

Back when the idea of the printed book was relatively new, type was generally set in a single justified column and placed symmetrically on a spread with the outer margins wider than the inner, and the bottom margin deeper than the top. The proportions assigned to the text area were invariably worked out using a geometric construct, the most highly regarded of these being the golden section. Measurements don't need to be specific, as the resultant golden rectangle can be drawn without a ruler, using a set square and compass.

The only important measurement is the ratio of short to long side, that being 1:1.618, which in itself doesn't really mean anything unless you're into ratios. This ratio occurs many times in art and architecture, so it was a natural choice for the basis of book layouts. The page's margins were often worked out using the Fibonacci sequence (0, 1, 1, 2, 3, 5, 8, 13, 21, etc.), which you can find out about by reading *The Da Vinci Code*. The explanation is quite near the start, so, fortunately, you don't have to read the whole thing. **TS**

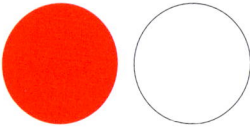

# DON'T be intimidated by a blank page

This is it. Everything you have trained for, all of your dreams and desires, the full realization of your creative potential awaits you. So why are your knees buckled and your hands shaking? It is just a blank page before you, a barren canvas for your skills to shape to your liking (or even better still, to the client's liking). Yet, it stands out as one of the most intimidating forces that a desig- ner can ever face. No guides to go by, no style sheets deciding our typefaces and sizes for us. No corporate color palette already set out. No images already selected for inclusion. All of the decisions have been left up to us, and the pressure has left all parts of our body paralyzed. Pull it together!!! The opportunity for greatness lies before you. You are ready for this. I just know it. Look that blank page square in the eye and announce to the world that you are an incredible designer. Ready. Set. Go! **JF**

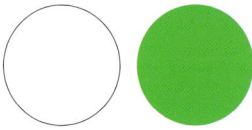

# DO triple check your document size before you start your layout

In the three decades I've been working as a graphic designer, I've heard a number of horror stories about designers having worked with an incorrect document size (the client, too, has gotten it wrong on occasion!). It's discovered at that crucial stage during final approval after months of labor or, worse, when it's at the printer. This can, of course, be fixed, but it will cause a lot of stress: the client will be angry, and there could be a cost issue or a missed deadline. Also, the beautiful design that you have worked so hard on will have to be revised hurriedly into shape, which could result in a poor-quality final product. Be as certain as possible from the start: confirm with the client the document size and get it in writing, either in a contract or confirmed by email, to ensure avoiding such problems. **PD**

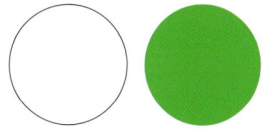

# DO utilize master pages

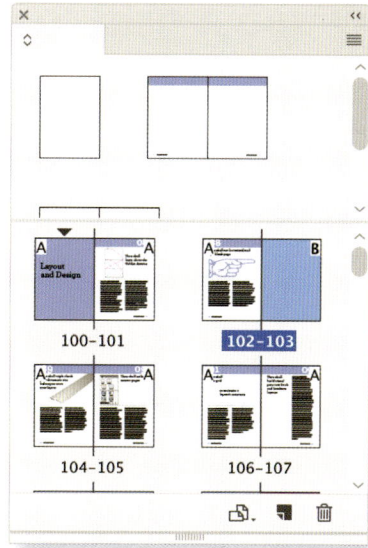

One of the huge advantages of using desktop publishing software, such as InDesign or QuarkXPress, when laying out large documents is the master pages feature. With master pages, you can preset all the consistent and repetitive elements that would appear on a page (running head, folios, heading boxes, text boxes, etc.) to avoid having to re-create them every time you add a page. In addition, any alterations made to the master page will automatically be adjusted on all the pages you are working on, saving hours of labor-intensive activity and ensuring there

are no errors. As soon as you drop the master pages onto your "pages" palette window, you can be sure that the elements you need will be there, allowing you to concentrate on the layouts. You can also create different masters for alternative grid designs within the same document and automatically renumber folios if you move spreads around. Even better, controlling your artworks with a "book" file allows you to update master pages between different files without even opening them. Don't ignore them: they'll save you hours of work! **PD**

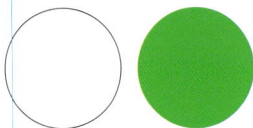

# DO use a grid to maintain a layout's structure

Many designers rebel against the idea of using grids. They argue that the grid is there to punish them, limit creativity, and restrain freedom. In fact, the opposite is true. Grids celebrate harmonious proportions. They exist to create consistencies in negative and positive space. They allow the reader to understand where to look for specific types of information. They exist not to restrain the elements but to create harmony. Consider a grid to be the same as the I-beam structure of a skyscraper.

I-beams give the structure strength, and allow for windows, doors, and individual rooms to connect to each other. In design, the grid is the invisible structure that unifies a poster, book, or website. Without a grid, any design solution becomes a hodgepodge of discord. There is one caveat, however, for those who are experts at grid usage. Grids should be like spiderwebs— pristine, elegant, and strong. And they are activated when one thing interrupts them. **SA**

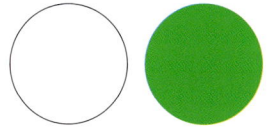

# DO build visual pace into book and brochure layouts

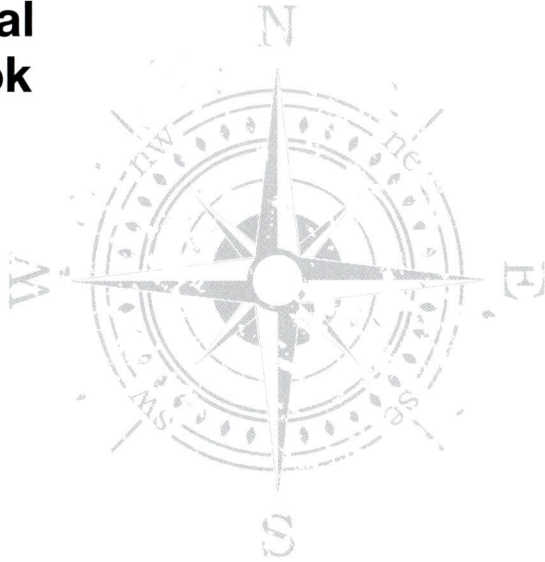

If your next assignment is a sixteen-page brochure, visual pace won't be such a big priority, but if you're designing a 256-page illustrated book, this rule is for you. There are some types of books or brochures (or websites) that demand that certain elements appear consistently from one spread to the next. For example, instructional books with illustrated tutorials (or perhaps books of graphic design rules) are likely to feature repeat page structures to aid navigation. However, for publications with content that varies throughout, seeing the same size image with the same amount of text and a caption in the same position every time could become very monotonous by the time you get past the first dozen spreads. Try to vary a layout from one spread to the next so images change size and position, thus allowing the flow of the text to meander and interact with the imagery in a more random fashion. Be careful not to lose navigability—the text and images must maintain a cordial relationship—but always build in as much intentional pacing as the material will support. **TS**

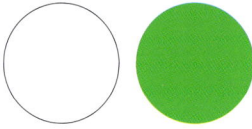

# DO understand how to design with a modular grid

We are going to learn an awful lot about designing with grids during our days doing layouts, but one of the most useful to work in is the modular grid. Like many things the Swiss masters brought into vogue, it is simple yet deceivingly sophisticated and incredibly intelligent. Formed using consistent horizontal divisions from top to bottom, in addition to vertical divisions from left to right, it determines where various elements and blocks of text line up. The result can be very simple, or it can become terribly complex. The joy is that it will hold together through limitless variations. Sticking to the grid will create an invisible sense of balance among all elements on the layout, even if an image runs the width of three columns of a block of text the height of four columns. Even though the lines aren't visible in the final product, they pull it all together, and the viewer just feels comfortable interacting with your work. **JF**

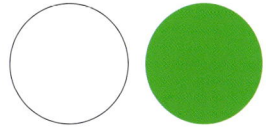

# DO break out of the grid if the layout prescribes it

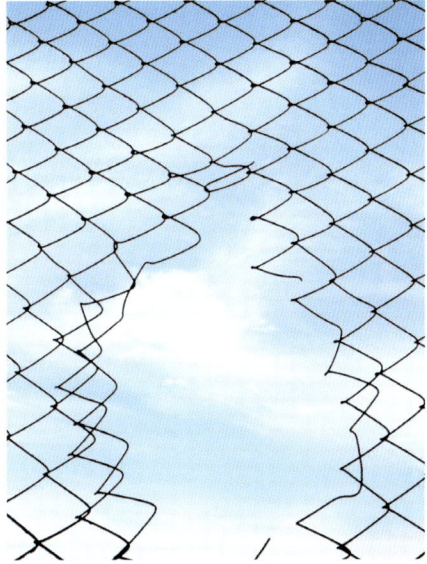

Grids are things of wonder to us designers, especially when they go all multicolumn and modular. Exciting stuff! Like the saying "Behind every great man there stands a great woman," behind every great layout there stands a great grid. If not for those grids, our layouts would stay out late, drink too much, and end up lying facedown in a gutter covered with messy typography. But hey, it's good for a layout to let its hair down every once in a while and give itself a break. Grids provide layouts with a stabilizing influence, but a layout should take its grid out on the town every so often to say thanks for all that good advice. It's at times like these that the combination of perfect grid and flexible layout can make the grandest of statements. Without them, the life of a layout can become so passé, if you know what I mean. **TS**

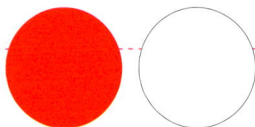

# DON'T automatically use the default margins in your layout program

The title "designer" says it all! You need to design, which means considering every minuscule aspect of any project you work on, including the margins. When considering the page layout, and how the content is going to be organized and structured within it, a part of your design process will be to develop a grid that works harmoniously with the page size. One of the grid's many structural components will be the margin area, and you should consider applying a principle such as the golden section, described earlier on page 101, when deciding on its size and proportions. The default margins for new documents are a standard border of .5 inches—almost a safety area for the complete novice—and have no design or structural merit, so think creatively and independently! This book uses inner and outer margins of .7 inches with a top margin of 80.5pt and a bottom margin of 65.5pt. **PD**

½"
12.7mm

½"
12.7mm

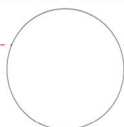

# DON'T place content too near the trim edge or gutter

Apart from an improvement in the tolerances involved, the technology used to trim and bind printed publications hasn't really changed much for decades. Even the best bindery plant has to account for some leeway when trimming finished copies of brochures and books, and for this reason it's advisable not to place content too near a trim edge. The fact that it might get guillotined off during the binding process is only half the story. It's harder to detect small changes in the gap between the text area and the trim if said gap is generous enough to absorb a slight variance in width or height. Slight discrepancies that result from trimming and finishing will "jump" out at the reader when the pages of a book are thumbed through rapidly, so try to allow at least .25 inch for small items like folios and at least twice that for large text blocks and images. Consider the gutter margin, too, as bunching may occur in publications with a large page extent, swallowing content that can otherwise be seen only by breaking the book's spine. **TS**

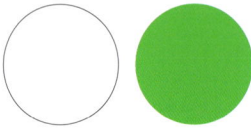

# DO design books and magazines as spreads, with facing pages

Walk into your closet and choose a shirt with a pair of pants you are going to wear later in the week. Obviously, you are going to want them to look good together. Take just the shirt out and place it on the bed. A few hours later, walk into the closet and find a pair of pants that matches the shirt you wore yesterday. Lay those pants next to the shirt you laid out earlier. You know what doesn't match? This random, hideous outfit! You would never dress this way, so why would you design a page in printer's spreads (already imposed) or worse, independently? You know that the left- and right-facing pages will be next to one another for the final viewer, so start from that perspective when designing. Always consider what will appear on the opposite side to the page you're designing. **JF**

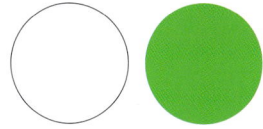

# DO design spreads with crossovers in mind

Now that we have decided to design with our pages facing each other (as anyone with common sense would), we have to consider the work that needs to be done after we have finished. Oh, right, the poor printers who have to realize our vision on paper and bind the pages, allowing for pages to be turned and enjoyed. We know that the viewer will experience the pages side by side— as a spread—so we design with that in mind. We also know that the pages aren't actually organized that way, that except for the center spread, none of the facing pages actually exist that way for the printer (thus, the designation "printer spreads" for the formation post-imposition). So we have to remember that letters that cross over from page to page will likely be cut off and out of alignment, and images with specific detail may suffer the same fate. Some printers are better than others, but the onus is on us as designers to make it look its best. **JF**

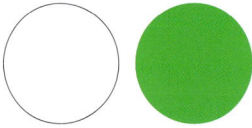

# DO create a focal point for every layout

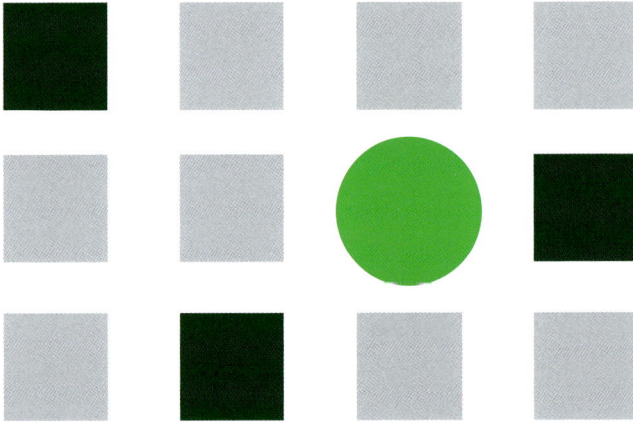

In most cases, a layout will contain a piece of information, such as a headline, that should be the first thing the reader looks at. In Western culture, the focal point is normally the top left corner of a page or spread, so it's no surprise that that is where a heading is usually positioned. Placing it anywhere else will fight against the natural instincts of the reader to look at the top left corner first. If you want to break away from this convention, and it's good to break the rules sometimes, the focus must be achieved using a visual device such as color, font size, or a strong graphic element. Bear in mind that readers tend to react in a different way to text and images. We're naturally inclined to gather information about what we're looking at, and a well-positioned headline will often trump an image in terms of a hierarchy of focus. **TS**

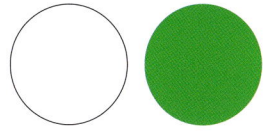

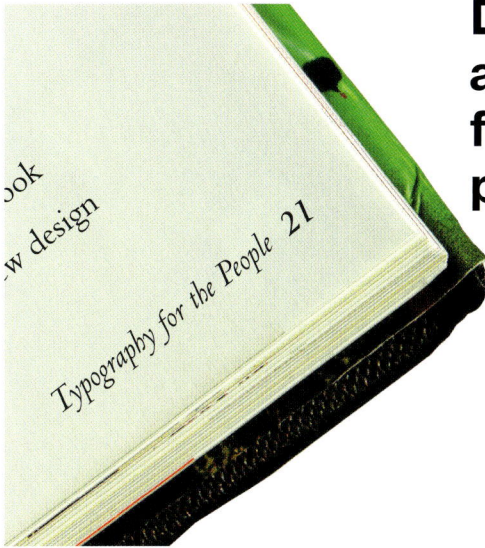

# DO always have at least one folio showing per spread

When you are deep in a design, it can be easy to lose sight of the final viewer. This can lead to a number of different decisions, but one of the easiest to shed is the tiny, harmless little folio often at the bottom of the page. It's not really disruptive, but my spread would look so much nicer if it had a clean section of deep color at the bottom left corner. Over here to the right seems to beg to go all white, and, well, can't we just eliminate them for a spread? Certainly this works in isolation when designing a single spread, but if we give in once, we are sure to do so a few more times before finishing. Now, the viewer doesn't interact with a single spread. They have the entire thing, possibly well over a hundred pages in their hands, and they would want to know where they are as they flip through. You see what I am hinting at? Folios don't need to be on every page, but there needs to be at least one on a page of each spread. **JF**

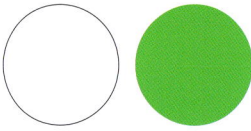

# DO periodically check a printed laser or inkjet printout rather than viewing a layout solely on-screen

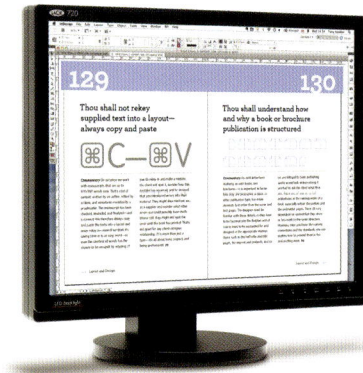

Despite the amazing quality and resolution of modern screens, whether standalone or as part of the computer, there's nothing better to judge the quality and detailing in your design than viewing it as a printout at actual size. I always insist, when reviewing early stages of a work at my studio, that we do it with laser prints. Only then can we most accurately understand how the design is progressing, check the balance and structure of the layouts, the detailing, and the sizing of the typography, and confirm that all the content required for the page has been included. We still always start a design with paper and pen. When you design on a screen, a majority of the time, your mind is concentrating on the mechanical aspects of using the software rather than the creative aspect of working the layouts. Only printouts will really reveal how effective your design is. **PD**

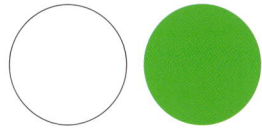

# DO consider how a layout looks at full size and as a thumbnail online

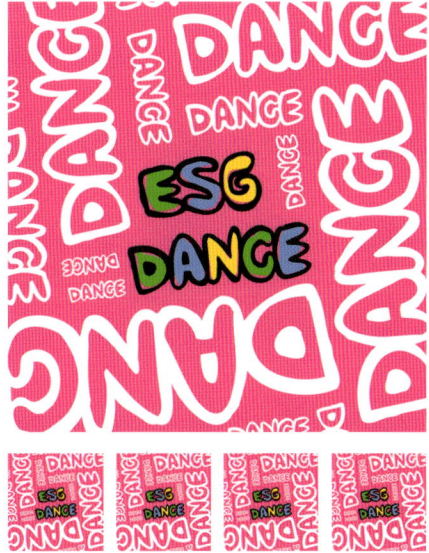

I like small type as much as the next guy. All things being equal, I like it more than the next guy! I love a detailed and nuanced illustration or photo as well, something that truly rewards closer inspection. I have come to realize that there is a time and a place for this type, but often that place is not in commercial products, even if it is a piece of music packaging that is only manufactured in a limited edition of a few hundred—certainly not on a book cover that will sell all around the world or a can of soda that will be produced in the billions. Why, you ask. Why can't those layouts have little bits of important type? Because more often than not, they appear online, and that means that most consumers will first interact with the design in an already reduced, tiny form. Be sure that it works both on-screen and in person. **JF**

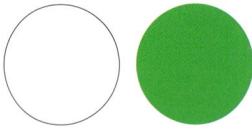

# DO use a baseline grid for body copy, especially in books and brochures

Let's quash a vicious rumor once and for all—baseline grids are not dull devices that restrict creativity. It's true that the why-not-just-place-everything-where-it-looks-right approach can work perfectly well for many projects, but if you're designing a book, magazine, or brochure, a baseline grid is an incredibly good idea. If you've not used one before, you should give it a go. A baseline grid extends the standard row and column grid that most designers use to guide the placement of larger elements in a layout, providing a modular system that works both horizontally and vertically. Baseline grids encourage consistency because they help you make decisions about where to position type and images throughout the pages. Your layouts will look much more professional if repeat items, such as page headings, align properly throughout. **TS**

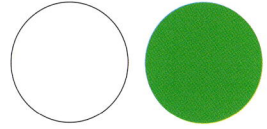

# DO take care to align baselines of type in adjacent columns

# baseline baseline

You spend hours picking out just the right suit, spending a small fortune. You decide you can save a little bit on the tailoring, so you go to a discount place around the corner. The day of the big event, you hustle back to get dressed only to discover that something looks a bit off in the mirror. Could it be that they have hemmed the trouser legs a little higher on one leg than the other? You look at every angle, and it certainly appears so. Nothing major, you think: who would notice such a thing, anyway? You set off and soon find yourself standing outside the dance floor. A very attractive woman comes up and asks if you are "able to dance." You flash an uneasy smile and reply, "Don't you mean would I like to dance?" "No," she says. "I meant are you able? On account of your legs being two different lengths." **JF**

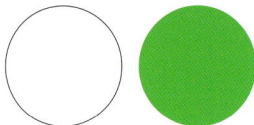

# DO align the bottom margin with the baseline grid

## One of the worst possible layout errors, the slight misalignment.

This is one of my favorites when it comes to rules that should never be broken (yep, there are some unbreakable rules). That doesn't stop designers from doing it though, and when they do, it highlights one of the worst possible layout errors, the *slight* misalignment. Here's the scenario. The margins are set, and the baseline grid is added with a start point at the top of the text area. All good to go, you say, but wait—the final baseline and the bottom margin don't quite line up because the margins are in inches, and the baseline grid is in points. This is such an easy thing to put right, as all you have to do is measure the final baseline to trim distance in either of those units and set that as your bottom margin. But many folks don't bother, and it looks really messy when you try to align an image with the last line of text. The funny thing is, slight misalignments really stand out, while whopping great big ones don't because they look intentional. Please avoid. **TS**

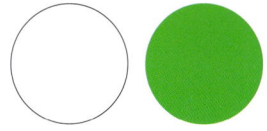

# DO align layout content harmoniously

Alignment considerations should extend to all elements of a layout taken as a whole.

Alignment considerations should extend to all elements of a layout taken as a whole rather than simply images with images, text with text, and so on. Furthermore, the alignment of the text itself should be considered alongside the positioning of images—an image centered on a page might benefit from a centered headline beneath it to avoid mixing elements and producing a visually incoherent layout. If you want to draw the reader's attention to a premium image positioned to the right of a brochure spread, consider using flush-right text aligned down the left edge, but be careful not to propel the reader's eye off the spread altogether. The way elements align within any layout influences the structure just as much as the grid dictates where content should be placed, and as long as the elements don't fight with one another while jostling for position, a layout will generally work perfectly well. The harmony in a layout stems not from the fact that alignments are right but from the fact that they're not wrong. **TS**

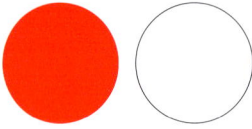

# DON'T always attempt to align captions to the same baseline as body copy

French arc
followed an
with empha
A growing
but one mus
In the Dord
with much
but of finer
neighboring
pioneer of th
Several fact
and it is not
natural sto
pale colours

*Examples of unspoilt medieval architecture can be found throughout the Limousin region of central France.*

It's a common error among inexperienced designers, as they try to get a grip
on the rules of using page and baseline
grids, to become obsessed with locking
everything to grids, including captions.
This doesn't need to be the case. At
the start of a project, as you evaluate
the content and decide on the styling
requirements, you will have to decide
which text elements should be locked to
the grid. As your body text is larger
than the captions, the leading applied

to it (which your baseline grid has
been set to) will be too great for the
captions. This will result in them
looking aesthetically poor and loose.
You can, however, set the first line
of the caption to lock to the baseline
grid to align it with the top line
of the body text. With this done, it's
simply a case of applying an appropriate leading to the caption and letting
it hang. **PD**

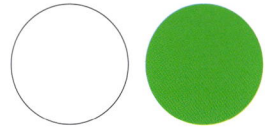

# DO use alternative baseline grids within caption boxes

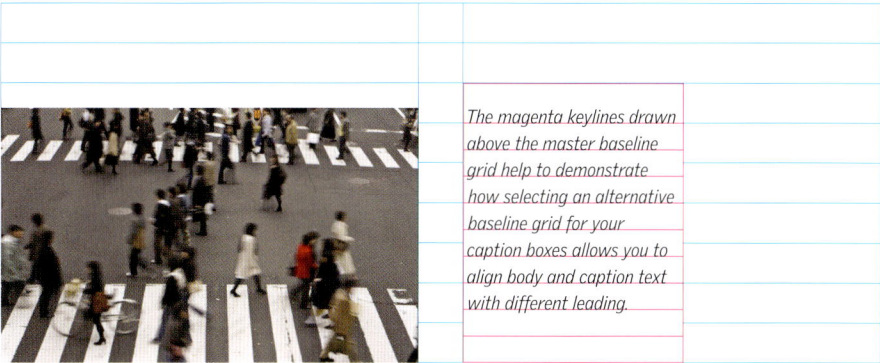

*The magenta keylines drawn above the master baseline grid help to demonstrate how selecting an alternative baseline grid for your caption boxes allows you to align body and caption text with different leading.*

An alternative to the technique outlined on page 122 is to create your own custom baseline grid for captions. This is particularly useful when your page layout has multiple captions (such as annotation) spread across the two pages. Desktop publishing software, such as InDesign, allows you to create adjustable baseline grids within the caption boxes, independent from the baseline set on your master pages. This allows you to ensure alignment between captions if the boxes are positioned correctly. It also allows you to create a ratio between the two baseline grids so you can create a proportionate leading between the two text styles. For example, say your page leading is set at 15pt with 10pt body text. Your captions can be set at 10pt leading with 7pt body text, giving a multiple of three lines for every two from the master baseline grid. If you align the first line of your caption text with any line of the body text, your typography will look so much sweeter! **PD**

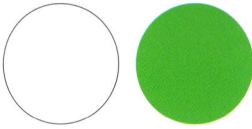

# DO use rounded numerical values when placing elements on your layout

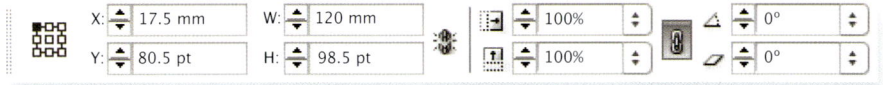

| X: | 17.5 mm | W: | 120 mm | | | 100% | | | 0° | |
| Y: | 80.5 pt | H: | 98.5 pt | | | 100% | | | 0° | |

"Graphic designer" and "typographer" should be bywords for precision, and a compulsion to be accurate is essential when working with type and layouts on a computer. After all, your project will be printed or published online for everybody to see. One of my major pet peeves (and it REALLY drives me mad!) is the inaccurate laying out and positioning of elements for artwork, such as employing random and inconsistent measurements throughout. For example, a picture box positioned .412 inches from the top of the trim edge—what's wrong with .5 inches? A picture scaled to 86.428 percent—why not 86.5 percent? Headlines at 30.697pt—where did that figure come from? I understand we all have a lot to think about and a lot to remember (the many rules in this book are prime examples). Invariably, with a deadline looming, the pressure is on, but taking care with your work brings more quality to it and will make you the better designer. Phew! Okay, rant over. **PD**

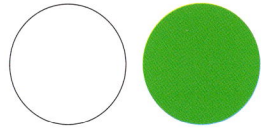

# DO ensure spacing
# is consistent throughout
# a layout

*Visit our private beach*

*Relax in style*

*Check out the surf*

*Remember a good book*

Rigor is part of the job of being a good designer. It is the difference between a world-class designer and a hack. Sloppy and inconsistent spacing is the first clue to identifying a careless designer. First, use a grid to maintain consistent line length, rule width, and image sizes. Second, use the guides to ensure uniformity in the position of text and images. Third, specify a comfortable distance between the baseline of a caption and the bottom of an image. Adhere to this spacing on all images. Fourth, create rules (stroke size) as part of the paragraph style of the text. This will maintain a consistent spacing between the baseline of the typography and the rule. It may be tempting to optically determine these spacing issues, but you are not that good. Do it mathematically and consistently. **SA**

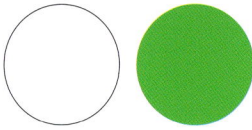

# DO be certain to stay consistent with use of type and color throughout a project

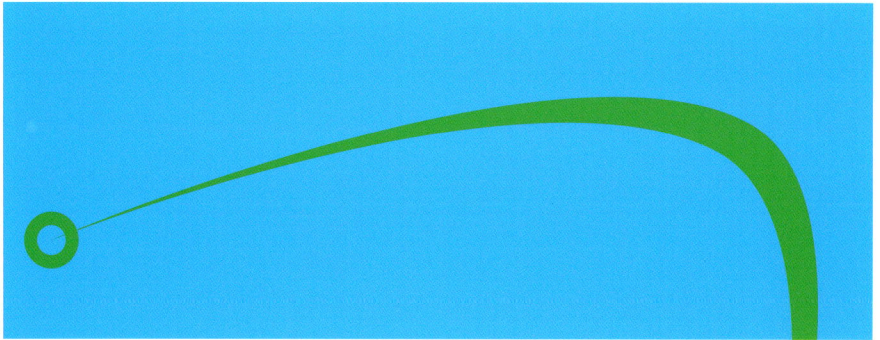

There are two schools of design. At one extreme of the spectrum are designers who believe that self-expression with no regard to the client problem is "good design." At the other end of the spectrum are designers who believe that the individual designer's style should be invisible and only the client's problem should be relevant. Many designers work somewhere between the schools, solving a problem while exercising self-expression. Unless a designer is only interested in self-expression, with no regard to communication, consistency of typographic style and color palette are required. Basic compositional rules dictate that a color palette be of a family and that each color is echoed somewhere in the project. If a design solution calls for a large red circle, echo this color elsewhere, so it does not appear to be an alien object. The same is true with typography. If Univers is the typeface on the cover, use Univers inside the book. Otherwise, it will appear that two unrelated designers designed the cover and interior. **SA**

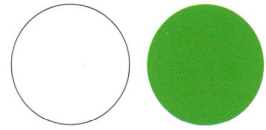

# DO establish a visual hierarchy that leads to the most important information

## Hello. I am Important.

**I am also important. Not as important as the item on the top though.**

*I am required reading but not essential.*

I am secondary information that would be nice if you read me and comprehended my deeper understanding of the subject matter.

- I am bulleted text. Highlighted.
- I am also bulleted text. Highlighted.
- I am also bulleted text. Highlighted.
- I am still bulleted text. Highlighted.

Assembling all of the components for your design is the easy part. Making sure to get the main point across is much more difficult. The first and most important step is to establish what that point is with your client. Once you are on the same page, set up a hierarchy—the sooner you start, the easier time you will have in creating a successful solution. There is always a star or hero—the most important bit of information that the viewer should take away. Be sure that your layout, right down to your font selections and type size, all reflect this goal. It can be as simple as size or placement, but often you will need to dig into your toolbox for color and other graphic devices. Then determine what is the next most important bit and so on and so on. Using everything you know about type and image, set up the layout so that the viewer has access to all of the needed information. **JF**

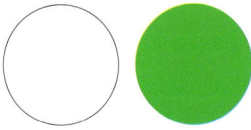

# DO experiment with paragraph layout only for conceptual emphasis

This was the point in the story
when an INTENSE flash took
him over and sent things
*sprawling, falling, crawling,*
seemingly all was lost
as he began to

choke.

The other side,
*reaching* out, was
a light. Dim, then brighter
and brighter still. Until he
knew that he had properly
laid out the paragraph.

After all of this talk about rules, it is probably starting to feel like all we are only telling you what you can't do. The man is literally keeping you down. Didn't we all get into this to be creative? Well, here is a bit of freedom of the highest order. Now that you know the rules, you can finally break them wide open. Nothing makes a bigger impact on a reader than an experimental layout of a paragraph, or set of paragraphs.

The key is that it has to be intentional and with purpose, or else it just looks shoddy and unprofessional. A layout about a dense forest gets six tall, narrow columns of type nearly side by side? Worth looking in to! A story about reaching a mountaintop is laid out in a cone of type widening with each line? You know it works. Just be sure to do it only when really and truly appropriate. **JF**

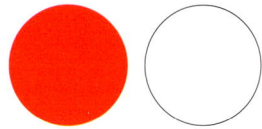

# DON'T ignore the advantages of visual grouping

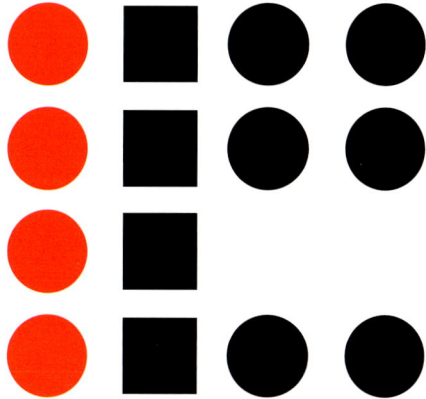

Imagine if you could take a layout and physically pull it apart in several different directions. If there's no strong relationship bonding the elements that make up the layout, it'll split and pull apart, but if you've used visual grouping effectively, the layout will spring back together like elastic when you let go. It's a slightly odd analogy, I know, but think it through and you'll see what I mean. Using visual grouping will provide structure for a layout that might otherwise appear as a collection of free-floating objects. Grouping anchors objects together with invisible threads, which our eyes then fill in for us, and allows for easy navigation by drawing the eye through a layout in the correct order. Grouping can be achieved through the use of borders, panels, rules, or even typographic hierarchy, as well as the obvious idea of using proximity to form distinct groups of content. Take care not to create areas of trapped space between groups by watching what's happening around the edges of your layout. **TS**

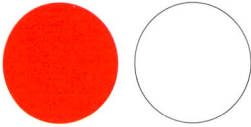

# DON'T group white space in the middle of a layout

When designers talk about white space, what they really mean is blank paper. If you're a newcomer to graphic design, you might find that you feel uneasy about white space, seeing it as a missed opportunity to add another image or some more text. The thing is, the white space between items is integral to a layout's structure for two reasons. First, it provides a frame for objects or groups, setting them apart from other elements. Second, it helps to create better visual navigation by drawing a reader's eye through a layout in the intended sequence. For both these reasons, you should try to avoid creating blocks of white space that are surrounded on all sides, as these areas of white space act like holes in a layout that the reader can fall into and get stuck in. Try to give your white space room to breathe; don't pen it in, or it'll turn on you and do bad things to your layout. **TS**

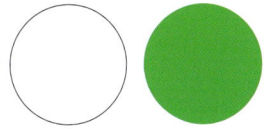

# DO use only as many columns as you genuinely need

A document grid exists to make it easier to create accurate layouts with correctly and consistently positioned content, so it makes sense to keep grids simple. A good grid will also be flexible, of course, as you don't want to be restricted in what you can do with the content, and the number of columns you use exerts considerable influence on that flexibility. Grids with odd numbers of columns can be particularly useful, as they allow images to break into columns of text, and you can vary the measures for running text, captions, and so on without departing from the grid itself. However, try not to get carried away with the number of columns you introduce. A twenty-seven-column grid is all very well, but it's very hard to keep track of consistency with that many active columns, and you're likely to end up with columns that are as narrow or narrower than the gutters. Start with fewer columns and add as required, or use guides to create subcolumns if you need them. **TS**

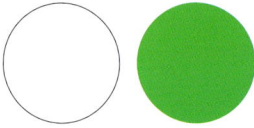

# DO persevere with InDesign's table functionality

Early in my career, I worked for a design firm that did a lot of work for the tourist industry, and that meant designing brochures with lots of complex price tables created "by hand" in Quark-XPress. All the rows and columns were separately drawn rules, and all the text was tabbed by hand or a series of individually linked text boxes. Boy, was it difficult and time-consuming work—but what a sense of achievement when you completed a table with all the footnotes and extras! Until, that is, the client calls to ask for a change—

"we need to add three weeks to the season, and, oh, by the way, we secured rooms in two more hotels." Without table functionality, it's start again from scratch—you'll need to redo the whole table, so no going home for you tonight, my friend. With table functionality, just "insert two columns" and "insert three rows" and adjust the size a little, and you're off to a bar for a well-deserved beer. It's not that intuitive a process, to be honest, but it's worth sticking with, in case you ever get that call. **TS**

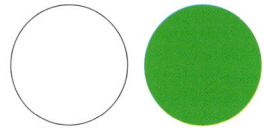

# DO use footnotes[1] only where they best serve the editorial content

While you are considering typographic styling for a book, the author or client may also request the use of marginal annotation. If so, stop and consider what type of book or publication it is and what the comments are communicating. If working on a technical or academic title, it will be useful to employ the annotation as footnotes (at the bottom of the page) to aid the reader and expand on their understanding of the material. If these footnotes are more reference-based (for example, a list of third-party reference material), then these could be placed at the back of the book as endnotes. Similarly, if a large number of footnotes exist and the title is more narrative, like literature, then an abundance of footnotes placed at the bottom of the page can look unsightly, be intimidating, and significantly break up the flow. Better that these be placed as endnotes. **PD**

1. An ancillary item of text providing additional information that is printed at the foot of the page.

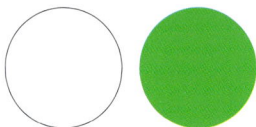

# DO remember that one does not have to fill up every section of a multicolumn page

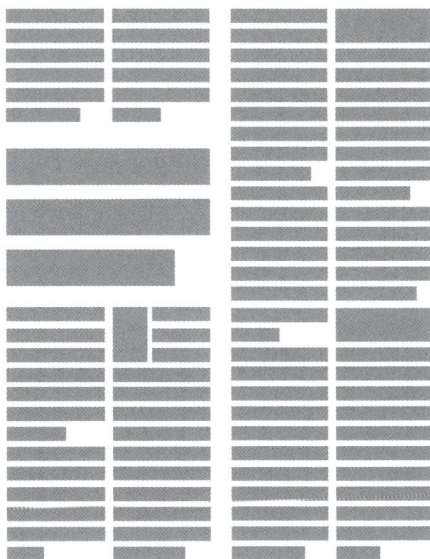

White space is your friend. Say it with me. White space is my friend. Like in music, it is often the notes that you don't play that resonate the most with the listener. Far too many layouts suffer from crowding out, filling every last nook and cranny with elements or text. Say you have a multicolumn layout before you, and the text holds to the style of the rest of the document. But paired with the photo and caption on the page, it leaves enough space for two more paragraphs. The compulsion, then, can be to increase the size of the photo until it all fills out the space perfectly. Or worse, you may want to start adding in extra spot illustrations or pump up the size of a pull quote to force the issue. All of that takes away from the original intent and ends up making the layout uncomfortably crowded. The grid already has the page organized, and less is often more. **JF**

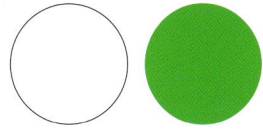

# DO consider a hang line when given inconsistent columns of text

| | | | |
|---|---|---|---|
| This is one column of text that you need to deal with. Factor in the length and start planning. | This is one column of text that you need to deal with. Factor in the length and start planning. How you decide to use this, now that you know it will be longer, determines a lot. | This is one column of text that you need to deal with. | This is one column of text that you need to deal with. Why not try a hang line? |

One of the most maddening things can be when a designer is presented with inconsistent amounts of text, such as paragraphs of various lengths, that need to work in a multicolumn document. But a little perspective helps soothe the nerves and find a solution. When you are given a stack of framed prints to go across a wall and they all differ in height, what do you do? You make a horizontal line where the tops of each piece start at the same distance from the ceiling so that you have a clear visual organization that celebrates the difference in scale while still keeping the wall from feeling cluttered and all akimbo. The same is true in a layout. Creating a hang line, you organize the vertical columns with a horizontal line in your grid. You can even have certain elements only exist above the line, for example. It is referred to as a hang line because the columns of text "hang" from a common line invisible to the viewer. **JF**

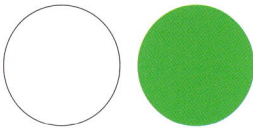

# DO use layers to organize type, color, and imagery

It's an absolute no-brainer to organize and distribute content into separate layers, which can be color coded and labeled. I think the feature is one of the best things ever introduced into layout applications. Therefore, it's a mystery why anyone wouldn't use layers, instead choosing to dump everything into one default layer. What happens if you want to select something that appears behind another object? Lots of fiddling about and multiple clicking—that's what. Sure, it's not essential for simple layouts that are only worked on by you, but what if you work with a team or have files that third parties need to edit? The ability to add all the text to its own layer and lock up the color in another so it can't be moved or deleted accidentally is pretty compelling. Try to get into the habit of using at least one extra layer for all your text, and it'll pay dividends in the long run. **TS**

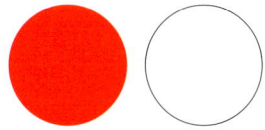

# DON'T use multiple layers of content unless they provide a benefit

First, let me define *layers* here. This is not the good type of layer a designer uses to organize information using Adobe Photoshop. This is the result of reckless layering of objects, images, and typography to create interest. Interestingly, this same technique of layering images on top of other images, or pieces of typography, was an afternoon hobby of upper-class women in Victorian England and the United States in the nineteenth century. Hopefully, a century of technological advances, aesthetic movements, and educated designers has discarded this technique in favor of clear communication. Unfortunately, there are still designers who are under the false assumption that they have invented a unique and revolutionary style with layers on layers of found images, odd squiggles, and distorted typography. Too often, when faced with a project that isn't compelling, a designer decides that adding another element will help. This is wrong. This is the same as putting more icing on a badly made cake. Go back to square one; the original idea is probably flawed. Adding to it is only ignoring the reality of a bad idea. **SA**

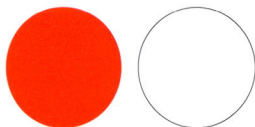

# DON'T use Microsoft Word for layouts

If I had a dollar for every client who, seeing themselves as something of a designer, has used Word to lay out a document, I would be a rich man! So why not use it? Well, Word provides little flexibility for a designer to work with, as it is set up for writing letters, making lists, or laying out text-based reports. The clue is in the name: it is great for writing text, not designing layouts. For the graphic designer, Word's very limited page layout and typographic features do not allow any flexibility or the precision to craft and create designs. In addition, Word has no prepress ability, nor does it have industry standards, such as Pantone color systems, built in. You should be using dedicated design software, such as InDesign or QuarkXPress, for your work. You wouldn't use a saw to hammer a nail into wood, so don't use Word to design your layouts. Ever! **PD**

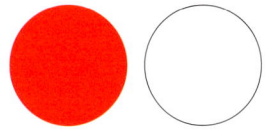

# DON'T design in PowerPoint

You might think I am crazy for even making this a rule, but trust me when I tell you that sooner or later, a client will ask you to design something in PowerPoint, while swearing up and down that it is the most creative application ever created and that you just haven't tried to appreciate its abilities. Now, we can acknowledge that PowerPoint may, indeed, be the most creative application that THEY have ever worked in. But we have other tools at our disposal. PowerPoint is good at one thing and one thing only: making incredibly basic slide shows. And even there, in layout terms, it is extremely limited. What it has in its favor is that it is used everywhere, thus the push from your client. Frighteningly, its tools seem to have been set up to encourage crimes against design, particularly when it comes to scaling type and images vertically. I shudder just thinking about it. Don't encourage it, and certainly don't do it. **JF**

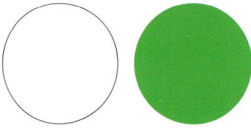

# DO learn how to thread large quantities of linked text correctly

Let me paint a picture here. A designer receives copy for a publication. He or she places the copy into the Adobe InDesign document. The designer then copies and pastes each paragraph into place. So far, everything seems okay. The client reviews the proof and changes the order of the pages. The copy is now no longer in the same order in which it was first supplied, and the designer has no idea where each paragraph should subsequently belong. This is bad. Alternatively, once copy is placed in the document and organized as linked, or threaded, text, the order will always remain clear. By selecting "show text threads," handy arrows appear. The arrow identifies each text block and the order of subsequent text blocks. **SA**

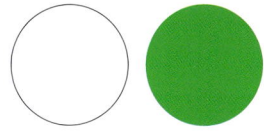

# DO create text threads for stories or chapters at the planning stage

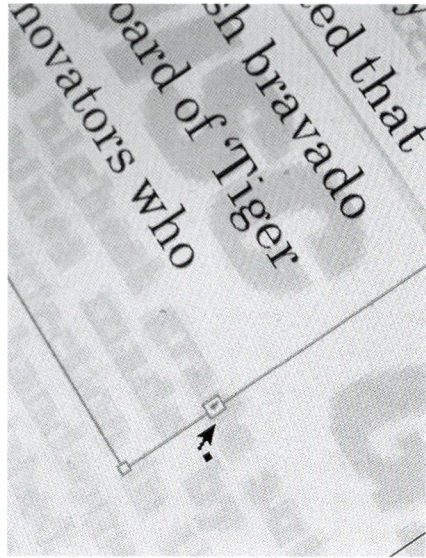

When you are first supplied with the copy for a multipage layout, you are usually forced to break it up into parts to a certain degree, but large portions can usually stay intact. It is best to keep stories or chapters as a single chunk of copy by first importing the text into a series of threaded text boxes. The small signifier at the bottom right of the first text box can be clicked to load the cursor with any overmatter, allowing you to create as many extra text boxes as needed to view the complete linked text chain. Once all the copy is styled, you will know how many pages are needed and be able to start making some design decisions pretty quickly. Why is this preferable to creating separate text boxes and cutting and pasting each item of copy as you go? Because subsequent edits will affect the entire flow of the story or chapter, and losing that connection is the quickest way to misplace a portion of text in your final file. **JF**

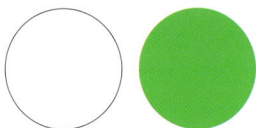

# DO use spell-check, especially when text is supplied

# spell-chcek

Many designers believe that they are visual people, and reading is for uptight academics only. Or they are convinced that the spelling format used in the texting world is correct. This is wrong. *You're* is not spelled *UR*. The mark of an ignorant and careless person is most clearly illuminated by mis-spellings. Nothing is more detrimental than spelling errors in a proposal, email, or presentation. A misspelling on a CV is, frankly, a career killer. In the past, a keen eye and superior education eliminated this issue.

Today, spell-check is the solution. The same rules apply to copy supplied by the client. The initial contract should make clear that all copy proofreading is the final responsibility of the client. However, once a project is printed or published online, a misspelled word remains a sign of carelessness. The designer may be assigned the blame, as he or she typeset the copy. Once again, spell-checking the copy, regardless of the source, is the easy and preferred solution. **SA**

# DON'T
# rely solely
# on spell-check
# to pick up
# every text
# error

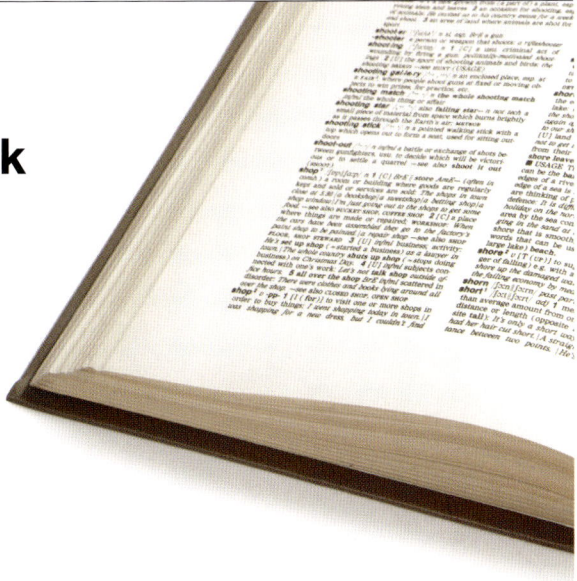

Every designer should possess a dictionary in support of any computer-based spell-checking software. It's a must! Spell-check applications are far from perfect, and they will not highlight words that are spelled correctly but out of context, as illustrated in this rule. Foreign spelling also creates issues.

Because many words can have more than one acceptable spelling variation, it is always worthwhile checking with the client to see which style they prefer to use for their publications and wheth-er they can provide style guidelines for copy. **PD**

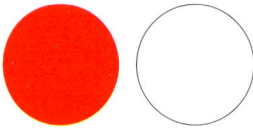

## DON'T rekey supplied text into a layout—always copy and paste

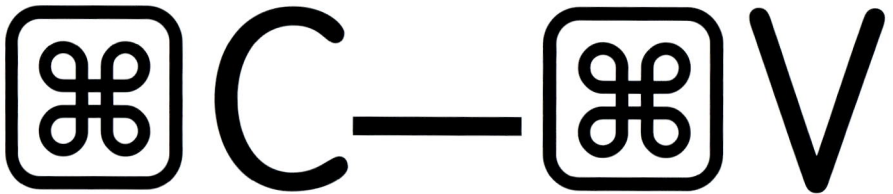

⌘C — ⌘V

On occasion, we work with manuscripts that are up to a hundred thousand words long. That's a lot of content written by an author, edited by a client, and sometimes revisited by a proofreader. The manuscript has been checked, amended, and finalized—and is correct! We therefore always copy and paste the texts into a layout and never rekey in—even if we think it's saving time or is an easy word—as even the shortest of words have the chance of being misspelled in retyping.

If you rekey and make a mistake, the client will spot it, wonder how this mistake occurred, and be annoyed that you introduced errors into their material. They might then mistrust you and wonder what other errors you might have introduced. Worse still, they might not spot the error until the book has been printed! That's not good for any client–designer relationship. It is more than just a typo—it's all about trust, respect, and being professional. **PD**

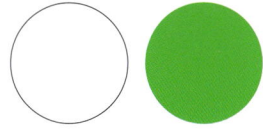

# DO ~~recommend~~ suggest copy changes if they ~~can~~ improve clarity and help the layout

There are many ideas about the purpose of design. Some claim that it is in service of commerce; others postulate that it be used for social change. One side of the industry supports personal exploration, while the other side encourages an impersonal approach. In any case, communication is the most basic requirement. Clear communication is a result of legible and understandable visual forms. Designers are not "type maids." It is not the designer's job to take someone's messy content and clean it up. A good designer clarifies the content with visual form and copy. If the copy is unclear or just plain wrong, suggest changes. If the problem is extreme, suggest hiring a copywriter. The final product in its entirety reflects on the designer. Saying, "I didn't have anything to do with the copy" will not enhance a designer's reputation. **SA**

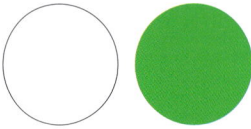

# DO design responsive website visuals at various screen proportions, starting with phones

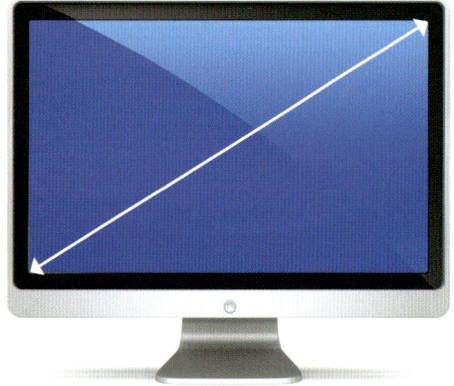

In the early days of the Web, one only had to consider a typical range of desktop and laptop screen sizes, but today all successful websites have to be responsive to ensure that they work properly on phones and tablets as well. In fact, given that people are increasingly using their phone before their laptop to view online content, it is arguably more important to follow a mobile-first policy when designing any website. This approach is not especially new: a similar thing happened when the music industry began to switch from vinyl to cassette tapes and then compact discs. Designers realized that it was better to work on the focused layout of the smaller space before expanding it to the larger area of a 12" vinyl record. Therefore, try to consider the layout of a new site with the current range of phone screens in mind first before scaling it further for tablets, then laptops, and finally large desktop screen sizes. **TS**

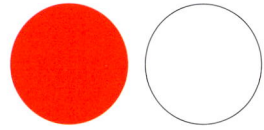

# DON'T employ a Web developer who has a bad website

_Contact Us_

When we start to assemble a team for a project, we often don't heed our own advice. We expect that our clients will have done their homework and researched various designers to determine the best fit for their particular project before giving us a call or emailing us (because we are, indeed, the perfect fit for them). When this doesn't happen, we are the first to throw a little fit. However, when we look for a writer, we often don't read their sample texts, and when we choose Web developers, it's based on their price and availability, neglecting that they are going to be a creative partner in realizing our vision for the client. Imagine you are putting together a band. If you play hard rock and need a bass player, you don't hire the guy playing in the horrific calypso band at the shopping center just be-cause he is free on Saturday nights. You already know he has bad taste. Be as selective with your own teammates. **JF**

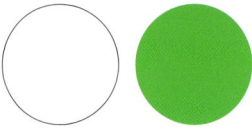

# DO remember that type legibility differs wildly from print to screen

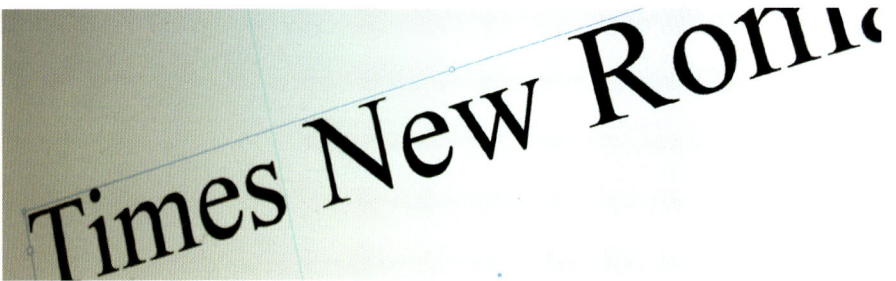

It seems like an obvious thing to say that what works in print won't necessarily work on-screen, but let's say it anyway. A typeface like Times Roman is generally accepted as one of the most readable serifs in print, even if it lacks a little in style. However, it is an absolute failure on-screen, with its forms distorting and being generally difficult to understand. Screen legibility is strongly influenced by a typeface's x-height: a larger x-height is likely to improve legibility, so keep that in mind.

Times New Roman has been adapted with a moderate x-height and works much better on-screen. Certain typefaces like Georgia and Verdana have been constructed specifically with an on-screen application in mind, and we find them lacking in most respects in print form. The most important part of the equation is figuring out where your text is going to be read and designing with that foremost in your mind. **JF**

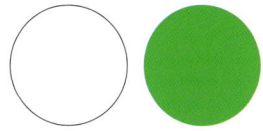

# DO always use typographic style sheets in long documents

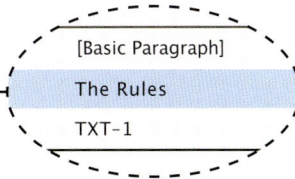

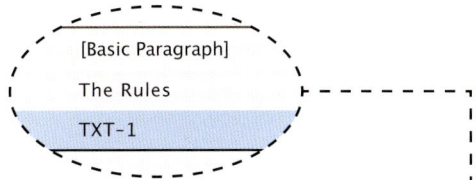

[Basic Paragraph]

The Rules

TXT-1

[Basic Paragraph]

The Rules

TXT-1

Style sheets are a thing of beauty and, when used correctly, will enhance your life and make you a better person! Well, maybe I'm going a bit far, but what they will do is provide exacting consistency and ensure that a number of fail-safes are in place when you are typesetting a long document, such as a book. First, simply create the style sheet, incorporating every facet of styling needed—typeface, size, tracking, and so on. Highlight the text, click on the desired style in the Paragraphs style palette, and, presto, all done! Consider the following situation: you're nearing the end of the book and the client asks to see the B-Heads one point bigger. It's a change you are happy to make, as it's a single adjustment to the type style! The hundreds of B-Heads in the book are instantly restyled, saving you the pain of doing each one manually. Joy! **PD**

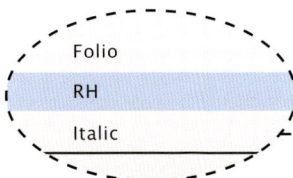

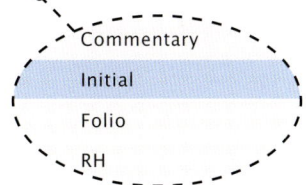

Commentary

Initial

Folio

RH

Folio

RH

Italic

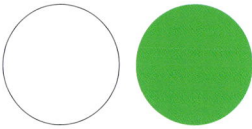

# DO always use object styles when working with long documents

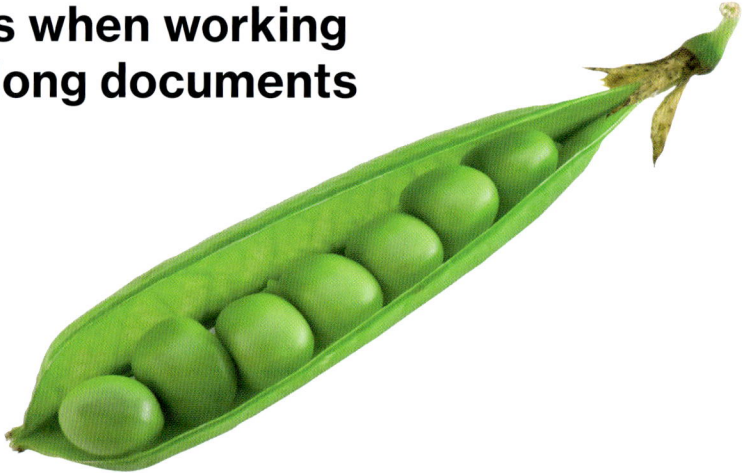

As designers, we tend to concentrate on the things we see directly in our layouts: the type, color, images, and so on. What we don't always prioritize correctly are the properties of the frames that contain those items and the various rules and borders that make up the page "furniture," or elements. Master pages are great for adding repeat elements to the pages of a long document, but a lot of additional content is added along the way. Object styles containing information about a frame's color, the stroke thickness, and the text can be applied in the same way that character and paragraph styles are applied directly to selected type. This, naturally, helps to speed up your workflow and, as a by-product, helps to ensure consistency. It's all too easy to start a project with .5pt rules that accidentally become .3pt rules halfway through, and these small details are very difficult to spot on-screen. You can bet you'll spot it straight away when you see the printed item—use object styles to achieve perfect consistency, just like peas in a pod! **TS**

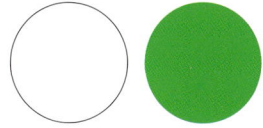

# DO seduce your audience with your layout

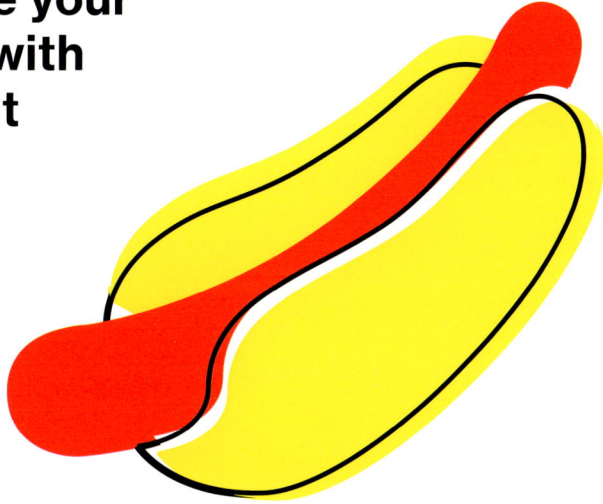

The opposite of seduction is repulsion. When we seduce in a bedroom, we use soft lights, play 101 Strings Orchestra albums, and offer alcohol. Turning on the overhead fluorescent lights, playing Anthrax, and offering heroin may be repulsive, depending on the date. Design is no different. Good design seduces the viewer. The message may be complex, controversial, or challenging, but the design encourages the viewer to look at it. Work that is impossible to access and repulsive to everyone at first glance is a failure. Seduce the audience. Utilize pleasant colors, legible typography, and clear imagery. Consider Andy Warhol's Electric Chair series. Silk-screened with vibrant and optimistic tones, these paintings hang on walls above sofas. They look beautiful, but they are a discourse on death and execution. This does not mean that every project should be pretty—we can be seduced by strong images and dark tones. Confused and impossible-to-access work will repulse. The viewer has limited time and will instantly decide which solution to engage with or ignore. **SA**

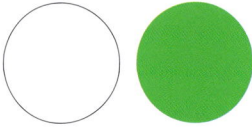

# DO follow Coco Chanel's advice: "When accessorizing, always take off the last thing you put on."

Too much of a good thing is still too much. You may own beautiful Rolex, Cartier, and Tiffany watches, but wearing them all at once does not increase the overall effect. Designing a poster, book, website, or any other item is the same. More is not more. If an element is purely decorative and serves no purpose, then it serves no purpose. It is a distraction at best.

Good design is purposeful. Each typeface, image, ornament, shape, and color must be applied with intent. When we fall in love with our own design, it is easy to ignore the extra, unnecessary items. A good practice, like Coco Chanel's advice, is to remove one element when you are finished with the design. **SA**

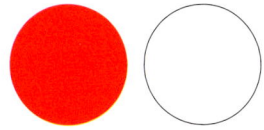

# DON'T assume small adjustments will improve a bad layout

The core of good time management is understanding how much time is needed to complete a task and stopping when it is finished. Long hours and all-night sessions are typically the result of repeatedly adjusting small elements in a layout. Refinement is a different issue. When a designer refines a design, he or she finely crafts the typography, color, and form. The goal here is to create an immaculate solution, free from sloppy technique.

Small adjustments, shifting a line of text up 1 pica, down 1 pica, and back repeatedly are done to attempt to solve a larger issue. This issue is probably a bad fundamental idea. If the basic concept is flawed, endlessly adjusting elements will not correct it. A great concept can withstand any layout issues. When a designer is making these tiny adjustments all night, he or she should stop and ask, "Am I simply adding lipstick to a pig?" **SA**

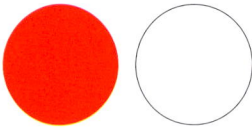

# DON'T use random squiggles and lines unless they have meaning

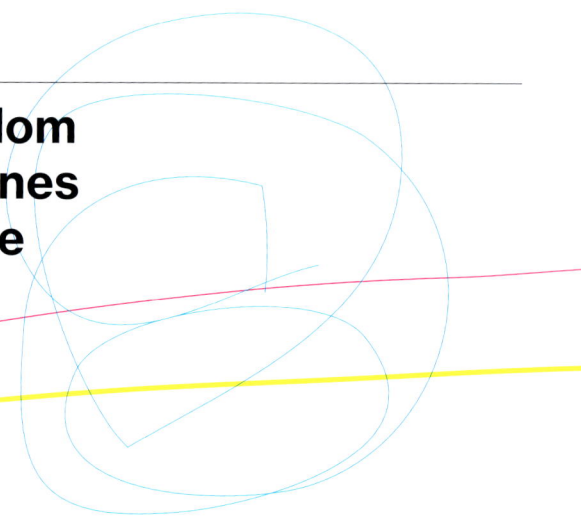

Similar to the error of making small and pointless adjustments to a layout is the issue of additive thinking. This is the scenario: the solution seems dull and bland. The designer adds several lines. It still is tedious, and the designer adds random hand-drawn squiggles. The dullness doesn't abate. More lines and squiggles are added. This process continues until the solution is, at first glance, "hip and now" but in reality is a mess. It is all icing on top of a hollow cake. Today, this can be passed off as avant-garde design. It is not. True avant-garde work challenges our perceptions and ideas. Meaningless form is meaningless. **SA**

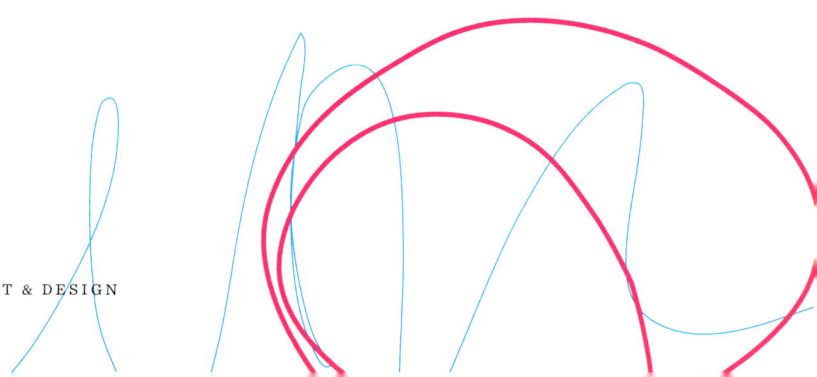

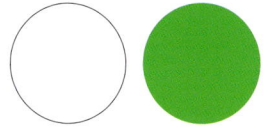

# DO use borders with a purpose, not simply for decoration

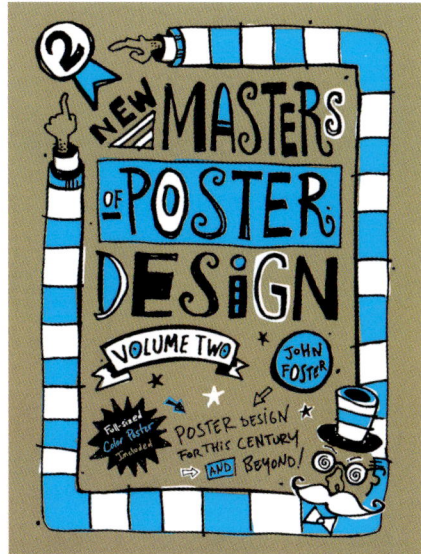

Borders can be a wonderful element, but they are not to be used without thoughtful consideration. They come in so many variations: thick and thin, ornate and ragged, rough versus clean. They can allow the designer to convey so much, simply highlight a bit of important information, or liven up a dull image or layout. Borders are our friends…when we use them properly. When we toss them in just for decoration, they often do more harm than good. If you have a garden that rabbits are savaging (curses to you, long ear!), then a pretty pink fence with widely spaced slats certainly isn't going to keep them out. What's the point of dressing up a patch of garden that's now a field full of holes and half-eaten carrots? The same holds true for your borders in your layout. **JF**

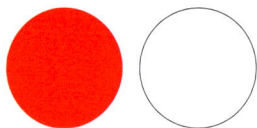

# DON'T use retro-style graphics gratuitously

*Thank You*

For some years now, retro graphics has endured as one of the most popular styles in many graphic design circles. The theory goes that the whole handmade trend is a reaction against all the pixel-perfect imagery that became so de rigueur with the evolution of the digital design age, and retro styling provides a great excuse to use some inked texture or some grubby colors with headlines set in a bold calligraphic script. There are even dedicated apps and Photoshop plug-ins to help you turn pristine artwork into a misregistered screen print or a facsimile of a cheaply printed comic book. Personally, I love the whole retro deal, but I sometimes have to stop myself from justifying the use of retro styling at the center of a concept. If you're designing an indie poster for a band or a book jacket for a cool new collection of urban fiction, then retro is right on the button, but an attempt to bang a square peg of style into a round hole of appropriateness is probably not going to work. **TS**

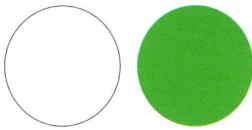

# DO design signage layouts to be read, not just seen

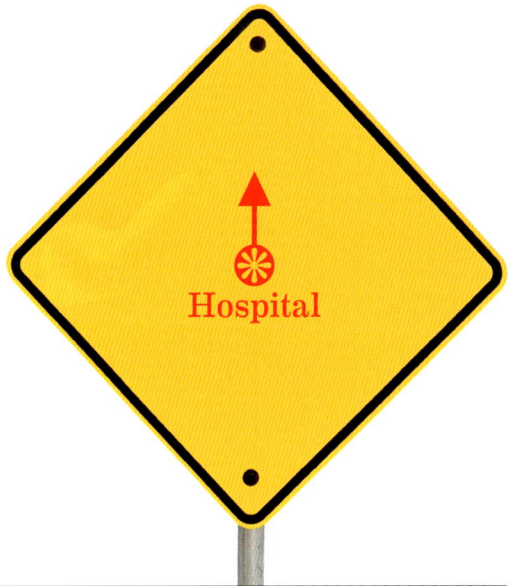

Hospital

There are few designers who do not like small type. Rarely do clients ask to make the type or their logo smaller. Smaller type appears more delicate and provides more negative space. The result is aesthetically appealing. But, when it is too small, it is not functional. Signs are a perfect example of this problem. Signage must be read, not simply be aesthetically appealing. In the middle of a fire, the viewer, even a designer, will not stop to appreciate the delicate typography and refined white space of the evacuation map.

He or she will need to quickly determine where to find the stairs. This requires typography and iconography large enough to be read quickly, and from a distance. The contrast of the message to the background must be strong. The letterforms need to be sharp and clear. Do not use degenerated, decorative, or overwrought typefaces. And the type size will always need to be larger than you think. There is a good reason why street signs are not set in Curlz. **SA**

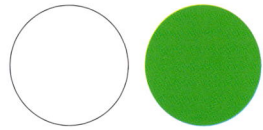

# DO design book covers with title legibility as a priority

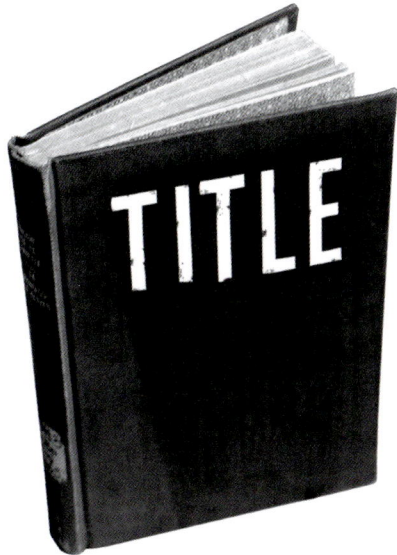

The best book-cover designers will all readily acknowledge how important it is to keep readability intact. Many spend days judging how much of a distressed look they can apply to their type solution while still retaining legibility. They will always err on the side of comprehension. With music packaging, people have additional interactions with it; even major and minor brands of food and beverages have consumers tasting and experiencing their product. With books, people read: it's as simple as that. That's not to say that you can't take chances—by all means, be creative. But always keep in mind that the title and author name need to be clear; and in this age of digital sales, they need to be legible at a very small scale on the Amazon website to sell enough copies so that the publisher can afford to pay your design bill. **JF**

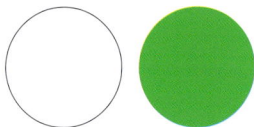

# DO design logos that have mnemonic value

We remember by recognizing shape and color. This is not an accident. As an evolutionary tool, remembering that the blueberries are poisonous but the oval red berries are good was invaluable to hunter-gatherers. We use this trait now to recall the items we need. Rather than berries and fruits, the viewer now identifies products. Successful logos take advantage of our ability to recognize shape and color. If a form is too complex as an illustration or disjointed set of elements, it will be difficult to recall. If a logo uses a banal color palette or colors difficult to identify, such as puce, it may be unsuccessful. Simple and clear forms with a distinct shape and color, therefore, have mnemonic value. Consider the Apple, FedEx, and McDonald's logos. Each of these has a distinct shape: a circle, rectangle and arrow, and an arch. Each of these also has a distinct and simple color scheme: gray, purple and green, and red and yellow. **SA**

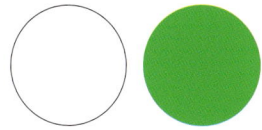

# DO design logos that can adapt to a company's changing needs

In 1956, Paul Rand designed the IBM logo, and IBM continues to use a version of the same logo today (updated by Rand in 1967 and again in 1972). In 1956, IBM, known previously as International Business Machines Cor-poration, produced computers and other business machines. Today, IBM is engaged in a range of activities from training and consulting to digital technologies. A neutral logo allows a company to shift direction, change products, move into other categories, but still maintain its identity. A logo that is too specific to a product or activity presumes the company will never change. Good logos don't describe a company's activities; they identify its values. **SA**

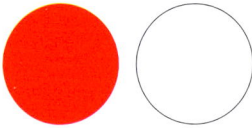

# DON'T ignore a client's corporate standards

Before the cultural revolution of the 1960s, people went to work in accounting, law, insurance, and manufacturing, and did their job. They didn't consider themselves to be artists. Today, everyone is told to be creative, to be unique and express themselves. This works well when choosing ties but is a recipe for disaster with corporate standards. These standards exist to maintain a clear, cohesive, and proprietary voice for a client. They are not created to restrain creativity simply as a measure of cruelty. In any company, there will be people who will want to ignore the standards and make their own logo or add purple because it is their favorite color. As a designer, you are collaborating with the enemy if you do the same. Reserve the creative expression for the concept, and leave the logo, color, and typeface alone. **SA**

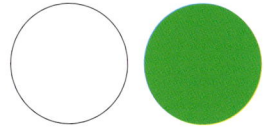

# DO create logos your client can use anywhere

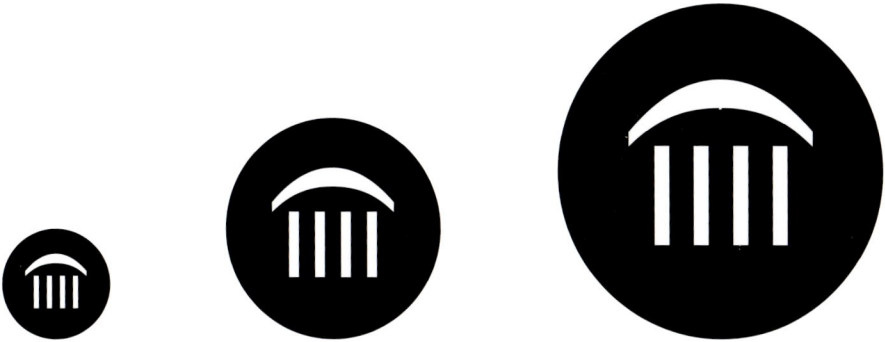

A well-crafted logo is something that is built to last. It is crafted so that it can be applied to every application imaginable for the business it represents. Don't produce something that your client won't be able to use anywhere other than on their website. Logo designs that incorporate bitmaps are restrictive, as they do not allow for unlimited scaling. While this excludes a feathered drop shadow from the discussion, I think we can all agree that is for the better. (Flip through the portfolios of the logo masters, and let me know when you come across a drop shadow.) The reason that you need to try to avoid bitmapped logos at the onset is that even if the client may never need it, a wise branding exercise will be prepared for anything that comes in the future. Logos built with vectors can be scaled infinitely with no loss of quality. Logos that contain bitmaps cannot. If you need your logo properly embroidered on shirts, you need a vector version. If you need it silk-screened on recycling bins, you need a vector version. If you need it eight stories high on the side of a building, vector. **JF**

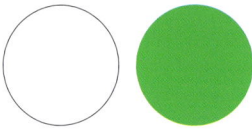

# DO understand the figure– ground relationship in logos

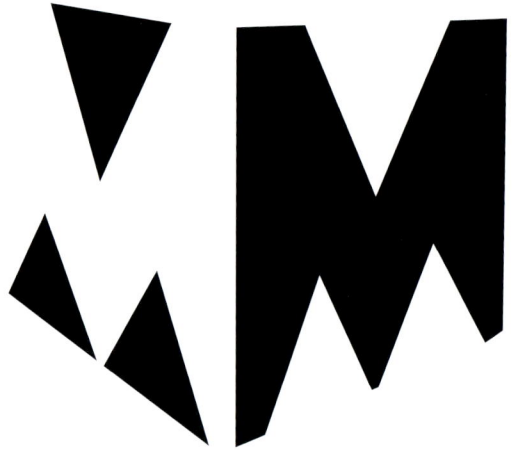

Logos are a two-dimensional exercise, and with anything two dimensional, one must take into account the figure– ground relationship. Because, in most cases, it is centered on a single strong image, it has on a heightened impor- tance in logo design. The figure part of the equation is essentially the object that we see, and the ground is the sur- rounding area. Applying contrast to make this relationship as obvious as possible, the designer can make the image clearer. The designer can also use the negative space to create secondary objects, exploiting a reversal in the figure–ground relationship. Graphic designer M. C. Escher is a good example of someone who experimented with this process to great success. More directly, many logo designers have seen fit to use this space to their advantage, like the "arrow" between the $e$ and $x$ in the FedEx logo. It is one of the most important lessons to learn in design, that the space between forms is just as important as the forms themselves. **JF**

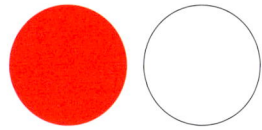

# DON'T make everything on a page the same size

Good composition is a mix of scale, shape, and color working together dynamically in harmony. A good trick to create dynamic composition is to think of the page or screen not as a flat surface but as a window into a three-dimensional world. The closer an object is to the viewer, the larger it will be. The more distant objects will be smaller. If all objects are the same size, they will appear to be static and on a single plane.

The use of multiple sizes creates an unexpected composition. Unless the goal is to bore the viewer, the scale must not simply differ slightly but have extreme scale changes from tiny to huge. Combine giant type with small lines of text. Mix a small set of images with a large one. Use an extreme close-up of a face with a distant background. **SA**

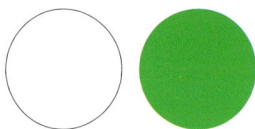

# DO respect the safety when placing vital type and images

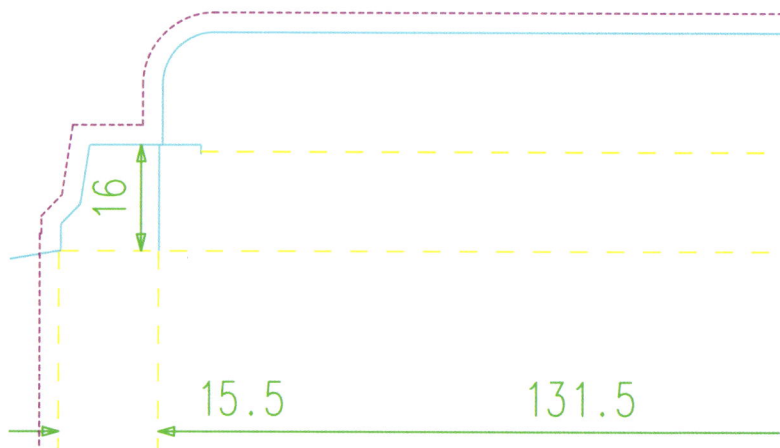

16

15.5     131.5

When your parents told you not to play in the middle of the road, it wasn't so that they could boss you around and show you that they were in control. It was because they knew that if you were playing football or drawing on the pavement in chalk, eventually a truck would come along and make a kid-shaped pancake out of you. And while they might have gotten out of paying for college, they probably didn't have a spatula big enough to pry you off the road—AND they likely actually cared about your well-being. The same is true of the people who make your production templates. The safety is there for a reason because, if you flirt with it often enough, the production process will eventually burn you and trim away vital copy and images. Respect the invisible line. It's for your own good. **JF**

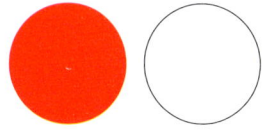

# DON'T silhouette and drop shadow every last image

The computer allows designers to create forms that were previously extremely difficult to make. Twenty years ago, hand-cut film created a silhouetted image and a photographer created drop shadows with light and film. Today, the tools in Photoshop can create a silhouette and drop shadow in moments. This may seem like a modern miracle, in the same league as antibiotics and mobile phones, but it is not.

As the saying goes: "Just because you can do something doesn't mean you should." Creating a silhouette is the appropriate solution at times. Adding a drop shadow digitally may also be necessary in certain situations. Like eating pastries, these things should be done in moderation. Too many images with silhouettes and drop shadows will make a project look like an advertisement for a stock-image company. **SA**

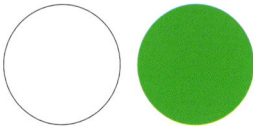

# DO return to the creative brief numerous times during the creative process

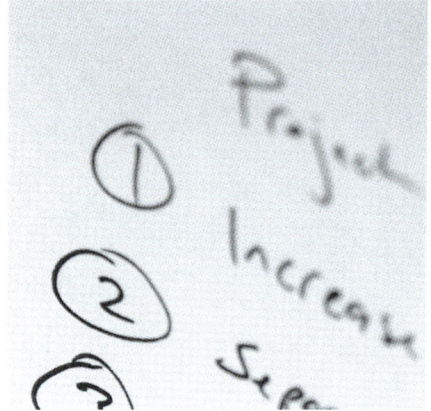

I cannot stress enough how important a creative brief is to a project. It doesn't have to be extensive or too involved. Actually, I prefer that it be simple and short. It is a brief, after all. Take the time to talk through your project with your client, establish the priorities they wish to see accomplished, and then rank them in the order of importance. The focus should always be on the top two or three items on your list, with anything else accomplished a bonus. When you both agree on the list, type it up and share it, and agree that you will both keep it close. If you refer to it often while designing, it will surely help you accomplish your goals. For the client, referring to the brief removes a lot of the subjectivity and keeps everyone focused on what is best for the project. A win-win. **JF**

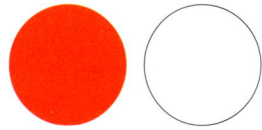

# DON'T project a personal style at the expense of the client

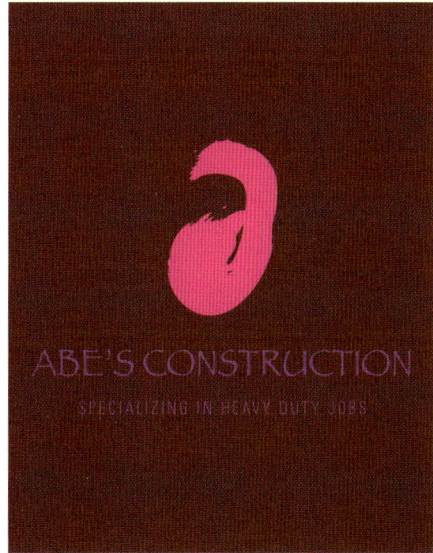

Every city has at least one design firm that becomes famous for the wrong reasons. It is not because they are helping clients reach unexpected success or financial windfalls or helping change the world for the better—it is because they have a recognizable style. They use the same layouts and fonts whether they are selling swimsuits or houses, saving the seals, or filling theater seats. It is depressing because it is unfounded attention—but it is generally short-lived once the clients realize that not only do their materials look like everything else that the firm has designed but that they have been left in a precarious position in which competitors can steal their branding just by using the same colors and fonts. Style can be a quick fix, but true solutions that provide value to all involved require a great deal more work. We all use our tools in certain ways, and prospective clients should be able to see how we problem-solve while also knowing that the final result will be unique to them. **JF**

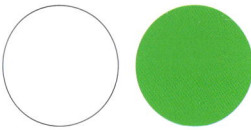

# DO understand designing "above the fold" in both print and online

Designing a layout on your screen is far from how it will ultimately be used, whether it is a publication or a website. You have the ability to zoom in and out, controlling your perspective, and usually keeping it at a size and position that looks best to you. You might revel in a tiny detail at the bottom of a magazine cover or your ability to find room for some fund-raising information toward the lower right on a website front page. Thinking it's a job well done, you will be quickly disappointed when you go to the supermarket only to see the racks covering up your beautiful work or when you catch your better half clicking past the website or page before ever scrolling down. Respect the fold, and you won't pay that dire price. The term *fold* comes from newspaper layout, when the portion you would see in the racks and at your doorstep was the front of the folded final copy, and everything that was vital had to be "above the fold" lest it be missed. **JF**

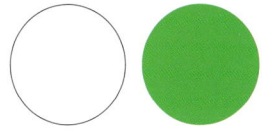

# DO know a good design in one's gut

APPROVED!

Everyone possesses a "gut instinct." At times, this intuition tells us to slow down at an intersection or pause before we scream at the mail carrier. This instinct also tells a designer that he or she has the right solution. It's the idea the designer had and then sketched on a napkin while meeting with the client. Or the solution he or she keeps returning to when walking home at night. It's good practice to explore many ideas and concepts. This should be done without editing oneself—one bad idea may lead to a great one. But the right idea will always feel right. Some designers believe work must be hard. They believe that the only good ideas come from endless hours of suffering and difficult labor. Design does not need to be hard and overwrought. A simple and smart idea that feels good may be perfect. **SA**

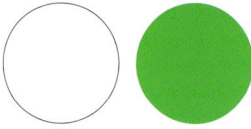

# DO understand how visual "closure" works

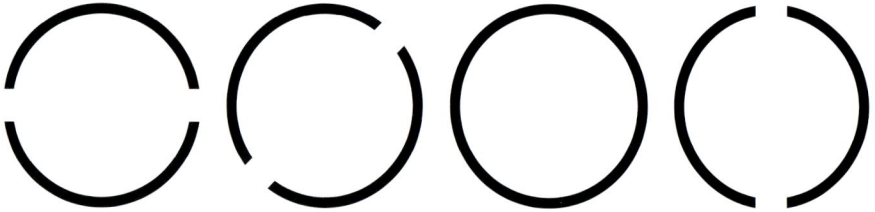

At some point in our lives, we have met someone who wants to show us a visual trick. While looking at a pattern, we scan farther to the side and are shocked to see a red dot when no red dot exists in the pattern—or any number of tricks our minds can play on us. We can all agree that these things are annoying and so are the people who present them to us. However, they play a very important role in our visual practice: they allow us to visualize the remainder of an image when we are given incomplete information, which is referred to as visual "closure." We use this to process and understand concepts quickly without being bogged down by every last detail. Glance quickly at the circles above for a quick demonstration: do you see four complete circles? As designers, we can use the closure to our advantage and help us be sure that vital information is not lost to the viewer. The eye is in the detail, even if some of the detail is left out on purpose. **JF**

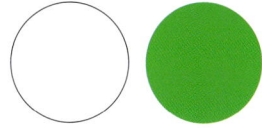

# DO learn
# how to format
# an index
# correctly

On paper, an index seems like it would be the simplest thing in the world to get right, but typesetting the perfect index requires practice. You need to understand how the various levels of indent work for entries that run to two or more lines. Two levels of indent are sufficient for most indexes, with subentries to main topics that run to a second line. If any one entry runs over to a third line, the indent should remain the same until the next unique entry begins. Try to avoid anything more complex than this in terms of indexing levels.

A well-designed index should be easy to navigate. Liberal use of font weights, perhaps a different one for the page numbers, can help to improve the look as well as ease of use. Indexes are usually the last thing that gets done before repro and print, but don't scrimp on the time and effort you put in, since, theoretically, those pages could be the most used pages in the entire publication. **TS**

# Color

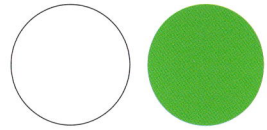

# DO study the
# color wheel

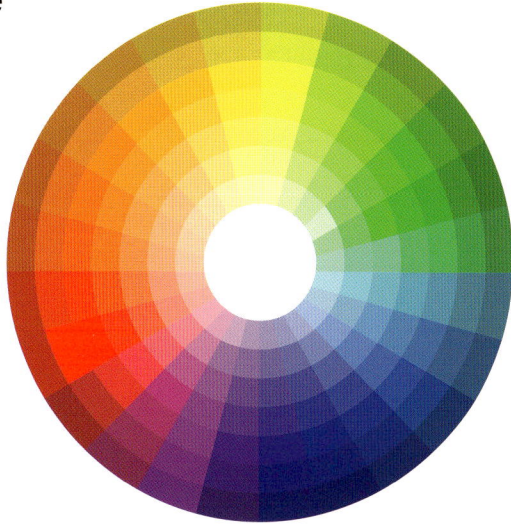

The study of color and how it's used revolves around the simple concept of color wheels, which explain visually how color is created from either light (RGB) or pigment (CMYK) and how the relationship between different colors comes about. We normally represent a color wheel as, surprise, a circle with distinct segments that combine to form 360 degrees. Alternatively, color wheels are shown as gradient tints of merging color, with more saturated colors at the outer edge. It's sometimes depicted as a strip, as in the Photoshop's Color Picker. The important thing to note is how a color wheel is structured: red, yellow, and blue—the primary colors— form the three main spokes of the wheel. These colors are blended to form secondary colors: orange, green, and violet. Blending primary and secondary colors produces tertiary colors, and so on. Complementary colors are those that sit directly opposite each other on a color wheel, for example, primary blue and secondary orange. **TS**

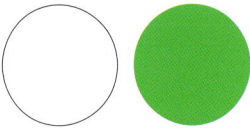

# DO learn about hue, saturation, and value

H

S

V

Hue (another name for color), saturation, and value (or brightness) are the three components that combine to form the colors we see around us every day. Saturated colors are strong or vivid; unsaturated colors are weaker and can be created by mixing either black or white pigment (or more or less light) to pure hues, such as the primary colors. Value is the measure of how dark or light a hue appears compared with black or white. It all sounds a bit scientific until you experience it:

Squint at a standard color wheel. You'll notice that the brighter colors like yellow appear brighter because they already have a higher value relative to black compared with, say, dark violet. Another good way to visualize this is with the Color Picker on a Mac. Saturation is 0 percent (or white) at the center of the wheel and 100 percent at the outside edge. The slider to the right controls the value, with 100 percent brightness at the top and 0 percent (totally dark) at the bottom. **TS**

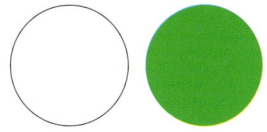

# DO understand the difference between additive and subtractive mixing

This is a simpler concept to explain than some of the other areas of color theory. Additive mixing is all about light, and subtractive mixing is all about pigments. When you look at your computer screen, all the colors you see are the result of additive mixing, with red, green, and blue light combined. Mixing all three colors together produces white light, adding green and blue makes cyan, adding green and red makes yellow, and adding red and blue makes magenta. This is additive mixing. Subtractive mixing happens when printed pigments absorb particular wavelengths of light—what we see on a printed page is actually the reflected light that hasn't been absorbed by the pigment. This is why we use cyan, magenta, and yellow pigments for process printing—they're the colors produced by the additive color model, and this works in reverse when printed. Black is added into the mix for four-color process printing to produce a purer black than would be achieved by mixing solid cyan, magenta, and yellow together. This also provides better control over value (or brightness). **TS**

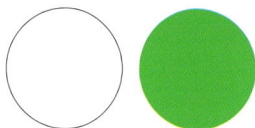

# DO understand the function of different color spaces

Color spaces, when combined with color profiles, are important in maintaining color consistency in a workflow. It's all mathematics, but don't worry, you don't actually have to do the math yourself. The models that most designers will recognize are RGB and CMYK. These are device-dependent models, meaning that they're designed to facilitate color reproduction on devices such as monitors and printing systems. They also have a limited color range—known as a color gamut (which you can read about on page 182)—so some colors produced with these models aren't always true to the original but are governed by the device being used. Device-independent models, on the other hand, mimic the way our eyes perceive color and are technically more faithful to the original. LAB is the most common model of this type and has a much larger color gamut than other models. It's popular with designers who do a lot of color correction because it can separate an image's luminance (or brightness) from its color. **TS**

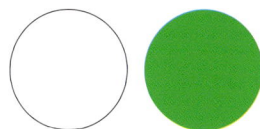

# DO ensure your color settings remain synchronized across all applications

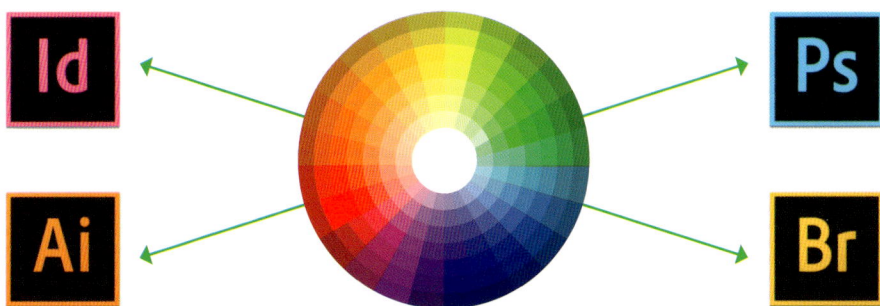

One of the great advantages to using an integrated suite of design tools is the fact that you can create similar (or similar-ish, at least) working environments when switching from one application to another. Adobe Creative Cloud applications are particularly good at this, paying special attention to the synchronization of color settings for different color models or working spaces through a centralized function in Adobe Bridge. It also allows the user to synchronize how applications treat images as they move from, say, Photoshop to InDesign or Illustrator. Why is this important? If you can't rely on consistent color when moving between applications, there's really no point in paying any attention to the colors you specify, as the final results won't be predictable or consistent. It's not a creative process as such, but color consistency is extremely important if you want to see a final output that's a close match to what you've been seeing on your computer screen. **TS**

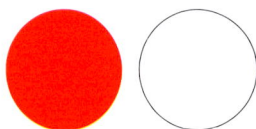

# DON'T ignore the constraints of color gamuts

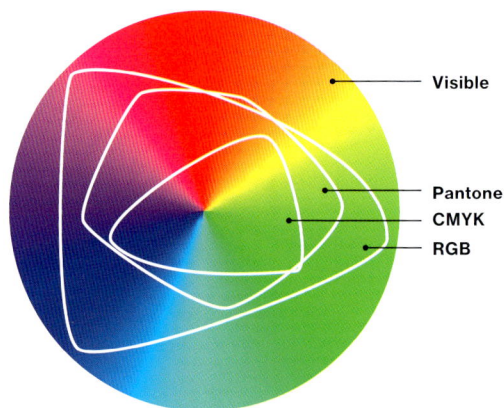

Visible

Pantone

CMYK

RGB

Did you ever wonder why you can create an amazingly vibrant red on-screen but can't seem to get it to print out with the same kind of intensity of color? The reason that it's not possible to translate certain colors from screen to paper has a lot to do with color gamuts. A color gamut represents the complete range of colors that any single color model is capable of producing in print. It also represents the complete range of colors that a device can capture, as with a camera or scanner, or display, as on a computer screen. Screens use the RGB model to display color, and the RGB gamut is larger than the CMYK gamut used for four-color printing. This is why you can't print that amazing red with CMYK—it's outside the CMYK color gamut. Spot colors like Pantones are not dependent on the CMYK color gamut, as they're mixed from pigments, so a much brighter red can be achieved if printed as a spot color. This is true of many colors limited by the CMYK gamut. **TS**

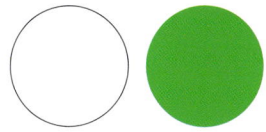

# DO get to grips with color rendering intents

Rendering intents help to address the issue of the RGB gamut being larger than the CMYK gamut by controlling what happens when colors are converted from RGB to CMYK. There are four rendering intents to choose from, and each produces a subtly different result. *Perceptual* attempts to preserve colors by compressing them into the CMYK gamut tend to alter most colors and can reduce saturation. *Saturation* keeps colors that can be produced using CMYK but changes any out-of-gamut colors while attempting to preserve saturation. This can cause significant color shifts and isn't great for color critical imagery. *Absolute colorimetric* keeps colors within the CMYK gamut intact and converts out-of-gamut colors to the closest possible hue at the expense of a little saturation—but it can also produce a slight color cast in the white areas. *Relative colorimetric* is the default for most uses, as it's similar to absolute colorimetric but also adjusts the white point, thus reducing color casts. If in doubt, always go for relative colorimetric. **TS**

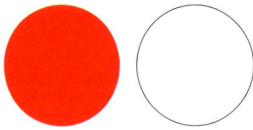

# DON'T neglect the fact that colors change according to their surroundings

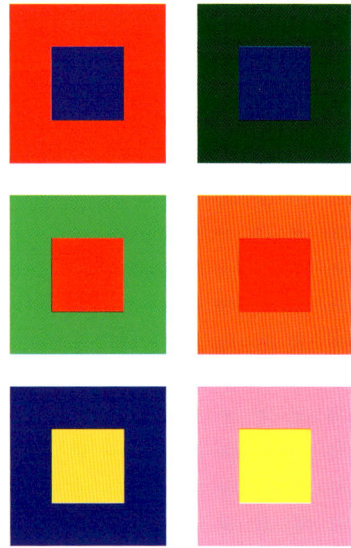

Color is subjective and emotional. It is challenging to convince someone to like pink if they were repeatedly locked in a pink closet as a child. This makes color one of the most problematic elements of designing. In addition to the subjective nature of color is the way we see color. First, we all experience color in our own way. Warm red will appear different to every person viewing it. To one person, it looks orange; to another, red. It is vital to be accommodating when dealing with color. Telling someone they are wrong about a color choice is like telling them they are a bad person. If these hurdles were not high enough, color also changes according to its environment. What seems to be a soft yellow in the designer's office can be an awful yellow-green under the client's fluorescent light. The primary colors, red, blue, and yellow, are the most consistent in different surroundings. Complex colors, such as violet, are more volatile and can easily shift from blue to purple. When showing color options to a client, it is best to explain that color changes in different settings. **SA**

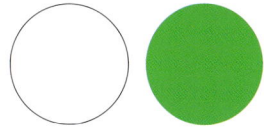

# DO look at what surrounds us for color inspiration

A common obstacle for designers is choosing colors. The swatch panel of default colors in Adobe Illustrator exists for broad gestures of color. It is not a color palette. It is, like the default shapes in Illustrator, ordinary and overdone. A strong color palette is as important as the typeface choices. A good color palette will be unique, seductive, and harmonious. The natural world is a good place to look for inspiration. A poplar tree is not green. It is a mix of blue green, lime green, silver green, light brown, cool gray, and white. The sunset is not red. It is dark blue, light blue, pink, orange, and yellow. A smart process for creating a color palette is to take an image of a natural setting and sample distinct colors from different parts of it. The result will be a system of colors ranging from light to dark and intense to soft. But they will always remain in harmony and be unique to your experience. **SA**

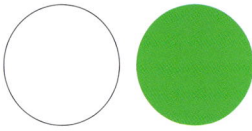

# DO draw color inspiration from great works of art

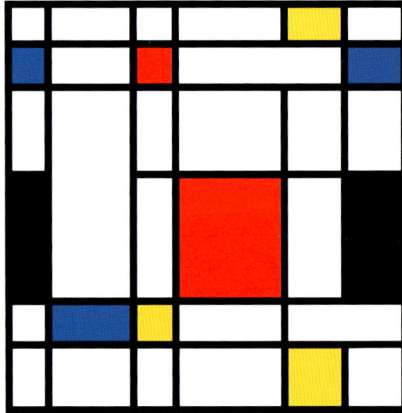

If you're looking for a new colorway for your latest project, there are lots of very useful resources out there in print and online, with thousands of different color combinations or schemes that can be referenced. However, there's another way of looking for color combinations that already provide a real-world view of how colors combine—and provided by absolute experts of color. Look at art. People have been experimenting with color combinations for thousands of years, and it's all out there for us to look at. You can even gear your choice of art to the kind of project you're working on. If you want an earthy combination of blacks and browns, take a look at some cave paintings. If you want rich and luxurious colors, try something by Hans Holbein the Younger. For bold bright combinations, try Vincent van Gogh or some of Mark Rothko's work. If you're not so much into painting but like more graphic work, look at Roy Lichtenstein, Piet Mondrian, or Andy Warhol. The colors are all there for the taking. **TS**

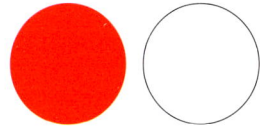

# DON'T use beige to attract attention

**"Hey, Steve! Over here."**

Attracting attention audibly requires the use of loud volume. When you want a friend across the street to notice you, you shout, "Hey, Steve! Over here!" This is also true physically: tapping someone on the shoulder will get their attention. And it is true visually: stop signs are red and have large type. Beige is not loud. Beige, gray, and tan may be sophisticated and classic, but they are not good when vying for attention. Beige is like a silent killer. It will slowly creep into a project. An image may feel too bright, so it is desaturated. A type color seems too bold, so it is softened. The final result is an overall beige tone. Online as a website, it appears beige-green on some monitors and is mundane. On a poster, it hangs unnoticed by passers-by. Do not fear color; do not retreat to the safe, quiet, and deadly world of beige. **SA**

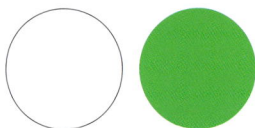

# DO remember that colored type can provide as much emphasis as bolding

# AUDACES FORTUNA IUVAT

There are easy and obvious ways to emphasize type in your layout. That doesn't necessarily mean that they are always the best avenues to accomplish that. Although a highway can provide the quickest trip to your destination, it can also dull your senses during the trip itself. Similarly, when these predictable methods are used too often, they can become a worse option than doing nothing at all. The simple bold may be your default selection when trying to highlight a word or section, but take time to consider color as well. Using a color to bring out a repeated phrase or word can be hypnotic; using a slash of red to create terror over a phrase can add tension. There are so many powerful tools at your disposal; with just a tiny wash of color, you can forever change the viewer's perception. **JF**

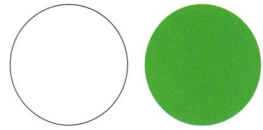

# DO think of white space as a color and use it positively

I find the employment of white space in any design to be a crucial factor in a design's success, and its usage should be a consideration from the outset. I'm not just talking about margins but about factoring in white as a part of the layout so that the elements of the page are separated, framed, and supported. In addition, the positioning and control of white space will guide the reader through the design, quietly hand-holding them through the content. When working on books with mostly photographic content, rather than design the layout with the picture's format as the priority, I think about how the white space can work with each specific picture to present it at its best. Try experimenting with different layouts, using a single image—the extent to which white space can alter the mood, pacing, and presentation of the content may well surprise you. **PD**

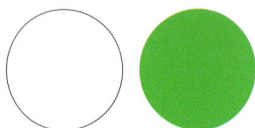

# DO explore color psychology

Psychology generates skepticism among nonsubscribers, but it's not all (ahem) bull. A bull doesn't chase a cape because it's red—in fact, bulls are color-blind. He does it because the matador is waving it in his face* and because he doesn't like the matador very much. Seriously though, designers can use color to invoke a range of emotions and behaviors. Red is particularly interesting, coming from the warm area of the spectrum, and can conjure feelings of warmth and comfort as well as anger, hostility, and danger. Colors from the cool end, such as blues and greens, can be used to calm but can also create feelings of sadness or indifference. It's well worth reading up on how the psychology of color works. It'll help inform your selection of colors for your design projects, offer some context to those choices, and supply you with some ammunition in case your client utters the line: "I can see what you're trying to say, but I don't like blue." **TS**

---

*No animals were harmed during the writing of this rule.

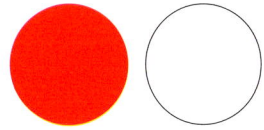

# DON'T follow the rules of color psychology slavishly

There are many rules and theories about color. Psychologically, orange is agitating. Blue is calming. Red is exciting. Pink is restful. Like all rules, however, following them slavishly results in solutions that are expected and rigid. Rules can change. At one time, eating steak was considered healthy; now it's not. Perhaps in a month, it will be healthy again. Orange was once used in fast-food restaurant design to create unease and keep the customer from lingering. Now orange is seen as hip and exciting. It was once a cardinal sin to use red for financial institutions, as it signified the bank being in the red. Today, this rule no longer applies. Knowing the rules is valuable. Then throw them out and use what is appropriate for communication and visual interest. **SA**

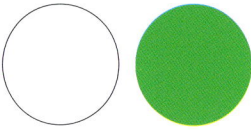

# DO remember that colors mean different things in different cultures

You have spent months perfecting a new brand of perfume that has a name inspired by royalty. Tweaking your glistening crown logo and your type solution filled with flourishes soon gives way to the packaging design. A lush purple finds itself gripping all aspects of the brand. It feels important and expensive while still being romantic and sexy. The line launches to great acclaim, except in Thailand, where the distributor can't even find many outlets willing to give it a chance. The corporate folks can't believe that they are only now learning that in Thailand, purple is considered a color of mourning and worn only by widows. Meaning behind colors is an important consideration when working on international projects. Yellow is a color of courage in Japan, but often linked to cowardice in the United States, and in Egypt burdened with the same albatross of mourning that purple carries in Thailand. It's so easy to use a color but much more difficult (and valuable) to understand its significance. **JF**

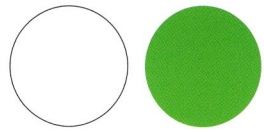

# DO choose colors for a reason rather than simply because you like it

In a lot of ways, this is one of the most difficult rules to abide by and a sign that you have finally given yourself over to 100 percent being the best possible designer that you can be—working *for* your client. We all have favorite colors and those that we avert our eyes from. As much as we have learned to appreciate that a scripty font is not appropriate for a monster truck rally, we need to grasp that our favorite colors are rarely the perfect ones to apply on our client's business design. While it is obvious that branding for an ice company should likely involve blues, it should be just as obvious that the blues be cool in tone, even if you prefer deeper purple-infused blues. Always have a reason for why you selected the elements in your design, right down to the all-important color. **JF**

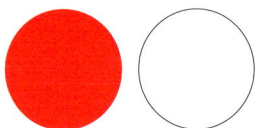

# DON'T be afraid to be bold with your color choices

ars longa vita brevis

A common insult used by eight-year-old boys is to call someone a wimp. Nobody wants to be a wimp. Most people want to feel significant and strong. Design can reinforce a sense of strength and confidence. Bold color choice is one tactic used to communicate power. This is not an endorsement to use fluorescent pink on every project. Bold color can be a relentless palette of pastel colors or a rich combination of dark gray tones. It can also be extremely bright or unexpected. Mix avocado green and bright orange or brown and pink. As long as it is purposeful and handled with courage, it will be right. Wimpy color choices include the predictable combinations such as flat navy blue and medium gray. These colors are appropriate for a job-interview outfit or lunch meeting with grandparents. They may be appropriate for an extraordinarily stodgy insurance firm. They do not, however, declare "We are the s%#t@" in the world of design. **SA**

# DO remember that people like bright things

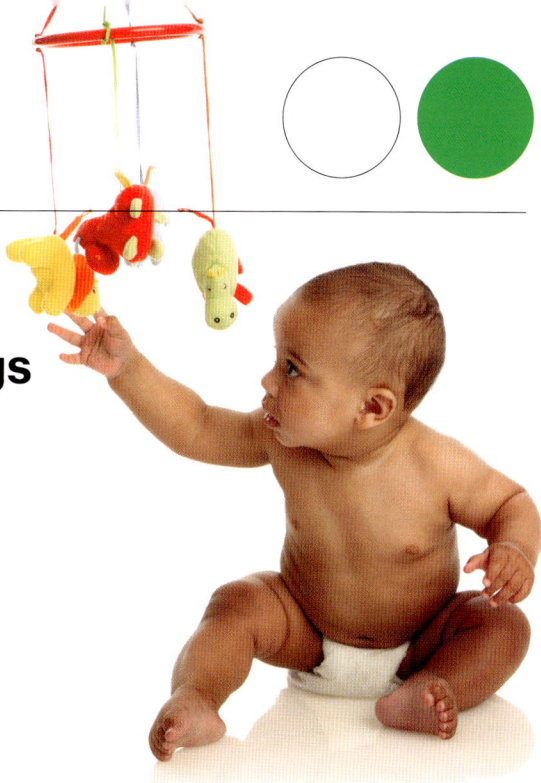

If a baby lying in a cot is presented with two mobiles, one in bright colors and the other in browns, the baby will always grab for the bright one. This doesn't change as people age. As designers, we are told repeatedly that the unpleasant tones are the fashionable colors. Drab greens, browns, and dingy yellows are supposedly sophisticated. When a designer presents a packaging solution with these colors and the client resists, the designer may claim

that the client just doesn't understand good design. This is not true. The client is not required to understand "good design." The client needs to understand his or her own business, the audience, and communication goals. No client has ever requested, "Please design something that will repulse people and make my business fail." The client responds the way 95 percent of the intended audience will. People will always gravitate toward the bright colors. **SA**

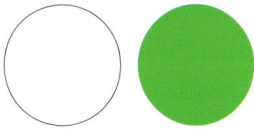

# DO learn how the transparency of a color or ink affects what it overlaps

One of the true glories of the silk-screen explosion of the past decade is that it has exposed more and more designers to the joys of overprinting. As process color has become increasing affordable, trying to do so with spot colors on an offset job via overprinting, duotones, and other tricks seems to be going by the wayside. But you should never forget that you always have more colors on hand than the cartridges of ink would indicate. Seeing inks printed on top of one another—whether it is one of

Bradbury Thompson's famous CMYK experiments or on your current favorite gig-poster artist's work—allows us to see how inks change one another and can create a multitude of effects. There is the straightforward third color that comes from adding two others, such as green by printing a blue over a yellow, or a totally different effect by printing a darker gray over the same yellow, yielding a subtle shift to a deeper gray in those areas. Oh, the possibilities! **JF**

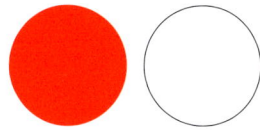

# DON'T use Pantone spot colors in a four-color print job

| | |
|---|---|
| | 000% Cyan<br>010% Magenta<br>100% Yellow<br>000% Black |
| | 000% Cyan<br>100% Magenta<br>080% Yellow<br>004% Black |
| | 100% Cyan<br>045% Magenta<br>000% Yellow<br>000% Black |
| | 080% Cyan<br>000% Magenta<br>090% Yellow<br>000% Black |
| | 000% Cyan<br>060% Magenta<br>095% Yellow<br>000% Black |
| | 100% Cyan<br>000% Magenta<br>030% Yellow<br>005% Black |

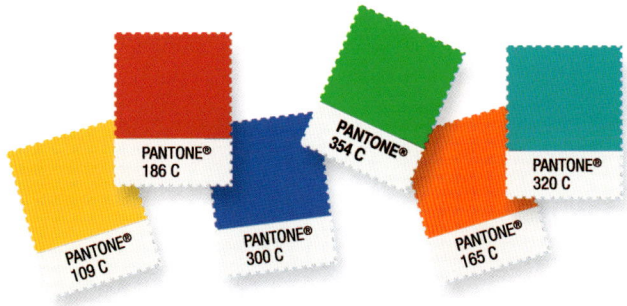

PANTONE® 186 C

PANTONE® 354 C

PANTONE® 320 C

PANTONE® 109 C

PANTONE® 300 C

PANTONE® 165 C

If I had a dollar for every commissioned layout I've ever had in prepress that had a rogue Pantone color hiding within its pages, I would have enough for a night out on the town, at the very least. The use of Pantone, or spot, colors in a project destined for four-color printing is disastrous for a number of reasons. First, a spot color must print as a fifth color, which will increase your print bill, mess up your quote, and could cost you dearly. Second, the vast majority of Pantone colors can't be reproduced accurately from the four process colors (cyan, magenta, yellow, and black), even if your software forces a PMS spot color into a CMYK split. The problem lies in the fact that a Pantone book is often the only resource designers have at their disposal when choosing colors, so they make color choices that, in reality, can't be achieved within the constraints of four-color printing. If you know your project must print only in four colors, put your Pantone book in a drawer and resist the temptation to take a peek at all costs. **TS**

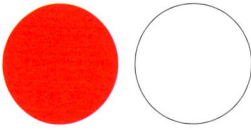

# DON'T use more than two Pantone colors with a CMYK print job

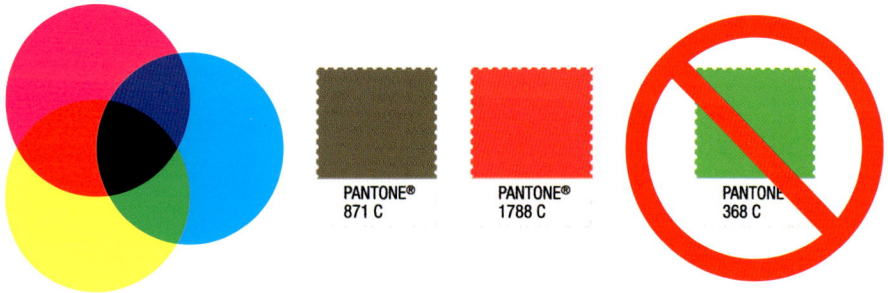

PANTONE®
871 C

PANTONE®
1788 C

PANTONE
368 C

There's an obvious benefit to using the CMYK printing process—you can create any color you want by mixing the four inks. To have more than two additional Pantone colors would be superfluous. Maybe you are adjusting ink channels and levels for a fluorescent or a metallic ink (or both) with the CMYK set, which is fine, although you should always make an effort to show restraint to avoid a potentially vulgar and "showy" design when printed. Another reason is the cost. There are five-, six-, seven-, and even eight-color presses, although most commonly found is six. So that's six plates: CMYK and two others or, more commonly, one special ink and a varnish, allowing the print job to be done in a single pass. Adding other special colors would require running the sheets through the press again, which would be expensive and wasteful. You also should ask yourself: will your design really be any better? **PD**

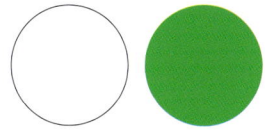

# DO use process color-built reds with no Pantone selected

**C0 M100 Y100 K20**

**Pantone Red 032**

In the village of Pantonia, behind the rainbow-swirled gates, lies a magical factory of Wonkaesque wizardry. It is here that the Oompa Loompas manage to create forty new colors each year, seemingly out of thin air. Plucking a toucan feather yields a decade's worth of hip and inspirational shades. The village's dedication to pairing a code number with every blip of intensity that our eye registers is admirable, to say the least. As would be expected in the closet of the average ad agency, there are multiple versions of simple black. So why is it that they have never been able to create a decent red? It's a sad fact that, no matter how many batches those Oompa Loompas swirl back at the plant, they just can't get it right. It's a shame, as red is often called into service in our world. Thank goodness, we can start at 0/100/100/20 and go from there. **JF**

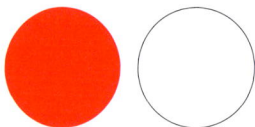

# DON'T specify print colors with RGB values

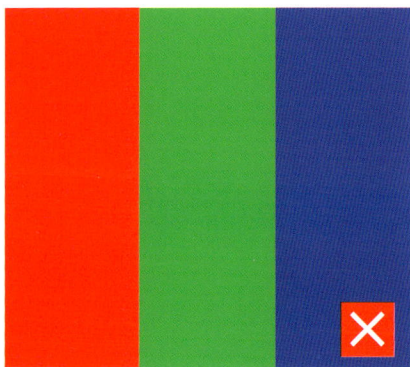

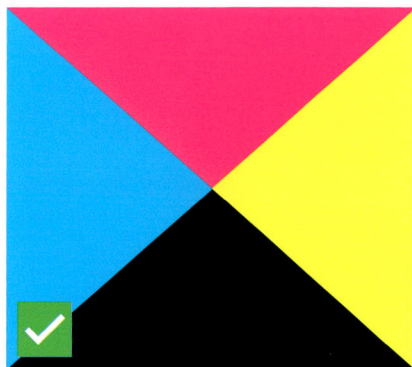

I know it's a real blow whenever we have to face this sad fact, but you can't print RGB colors. RGB colors are made from projected light; CMYK and Pantone colors are made from pigments that generate reflected light. RGB colors are generally brighter and more saturated because the RGB color gamut is much larger than the CMYK counterpart. It's tempting to look at a bright red RGB color on your computer screen and think how great it would look flooding the front cover of the brochure you're working on, but I'm afraid it isn't going to happen. It's simply not possible to achieve with the four-color process, although some Pantones can get close because white pigment can be mixed in. So if the budget allows for extra spot colors, that's the way to go. It's even more important to bear this in mind now that work is increasingly presented on a laptop or a tablet, so please explain to your client why the finished job won't look quite the same as it did on-screen. **TS**

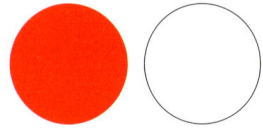

# DON'T create tints from tints

# 100%
# 45%

You have a layout all set to go, and a colleague wanders over to ask you what CMYK percentages you've used to create that really cool blue-green background tint. You happily take a look while congratulating your colleague on his excellent appraisal of your color choices, only to find that it's a 45 percent tint of 75 percent cyan and 30 percent yellow, which is, um—hang on while I get a calculator. You see, really annoying, isn't it? It's not a disaster as such because the color will still look good in the final job, but it's not great not knowing what the color actually is. The point I'm making is, by all means, create percentage tints from spot colors but not from colors that are already percentage tints. There is a quick, calculator-free fix. Select the color and delete it from the Swatches panel, replacing it with an unnamed swatch, then add unnamed swatches back in. Your actual color will reveal itself to be 34 percent cyan and 14 percent yellow. Nice! **TS**

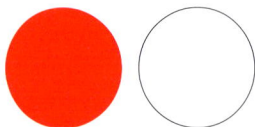

# DON'T screen a color to less than 7 percent and expect to be visible on the printed page

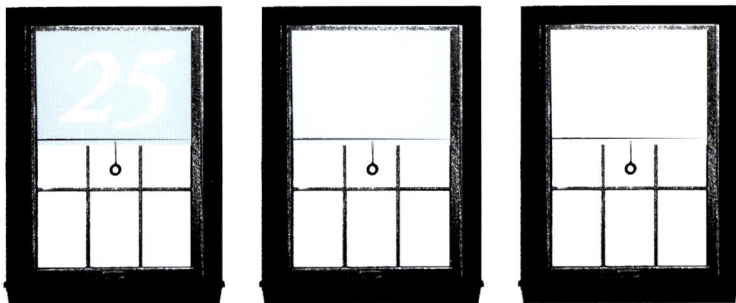

You know what looks dazzling in its subtlety on your computer screen? A 5 percent screen of your spot color. You know what has nary a chance of showing up on the printed page? A 5 percent screen of your spot color. The thing about commercial printing is that there can often be variation in how heavy the ink is running on the press. Combined with the gain of ink, or lack thereof, on varying sheets of paper, it is wise to keep a 10 percent minimum variation at the back of your mind. That is a worst-case scenario, but using newsprint or similar sheets can easily see unexpected results come to fruition. The reason? Using a small number of dots to produce a light tint makes it harder to produce an accurate result in the final print. If you really desire a light color, select a light Pantone and use it at 100 percent. **JF**

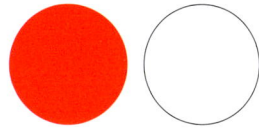

# DON'T use process color for small body text

Nihictur, ut quod unditas quibust doluptam doluptur aut ut od quis enimost autet as sam sum id explia quis in cor am dolut ut aria vollupt ionest, vendest, occat es quatur sum res incti ut volleni magnistio. Ut pa peritae comnimus enet quiaspe ditaque prorecum velecte ndanisi qui rercienda in rempor aut que nam fugiam quo ma cusa dolut laborepta inctescid quam doluptae. Onsequiae nam volorro ribusam qui odit qui aut poreic te dolupta doluptas molo od ullupta sit re nos re, nonsedipsum ent et vendam sitio. Nam, quist maior auditis sitiatquia quis eum esto est a velectur rehendi blabo. Itatius sim eturem. Volecti oriatur? Quis veribus ditaspelecae prat.

Nes eum ratibus, officto riorios ide porem acest, sum enderi recum ut post quam quo quibus in nobis estis mod mi, temporest, officip idictus sim idessit atibust es reprepero cusaperum aut untur, optas poreper iorposseque late nobist aut estium aut volora dolupta tiunto bearum quam que in et untiaerro doluptam quodit asimpedi aut autasim que inctur remos volorep erferum as venita ni comnis

Process colors, cyan, magenta, yellow, and black, combine to create four-color images. Black is a good choice for small body text, as it is legible and prints clearly. Cyan, yellow, and magenta do not work for small body text. Think about how we read: we look at individual letters and combine them to make words, which make sentences, and paragraphs. Differentiating the characters is the basis of the process. A section printed in magenta, cyan, or yellow only is too bright to read quickly and strains the eye. It's as if you're asking the viewer to look at the sun. It looks nice, but you will go blind if you stare at it too long. Make sure text is legible. Body text should be set in darker tones or black. **SA**

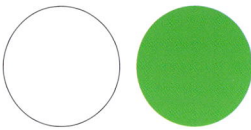

# DO learn how colors can share tonal qualities

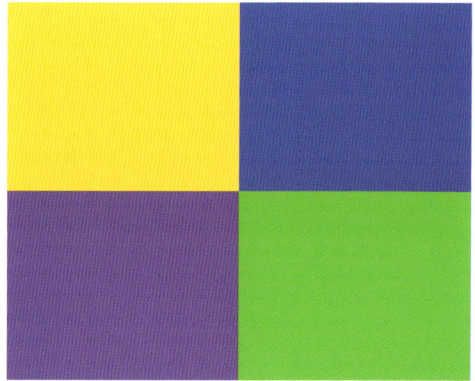

In its simplest terms, color tone is created by adding gray to a pure hue. Knowing this, you can see that adding the same amount of gray to different colors would create the same tonal qualities. Pantone books can be helpful in selecting colors in varying tones, as they can present a tonal range in sequential colors. More importantly, they provide color chips so that you can match up options and also train your eye to identify and register colors that share tonal qualities. Why is this important? At a base level, the eye requires contrast to process information: if you place a green next to an orange, if they are the same tone, they will ultimately blend together into one shape. This can be a desired effect, but one that can be properly achieved only by understanding how it occurs. **JF**

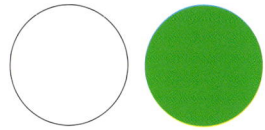

# DO learn how to group colors into hot and cold groups

When starting a project, I try to think about the colors in the most basic sense possible: are they hot or cold? There are numerous reasons for choosing a specific palette, and many projects will require a combination of hot and cold colors, while others benefit immensely from being cohesive. Many people will make the mistake of quickly lumping basic colors into hot or cold, with no leeway. The proliferation of color options has allowed for a greater breadth. Blues, in the cool category, can absorb doses of magenta until they find themselves in the hot group, where most purples will reside. Blazing hot yellows can give way to become cooler light greens. Even grays are lumped into cool and warm sections by Pantone. It is a distinction that can give your color selections a sense of community and also create compelling decisions when only one hot or cold color is applied to the solution. **JF**

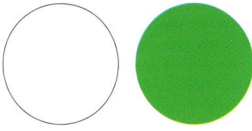

# DO use value contrast to divert or draw the viewer's attention

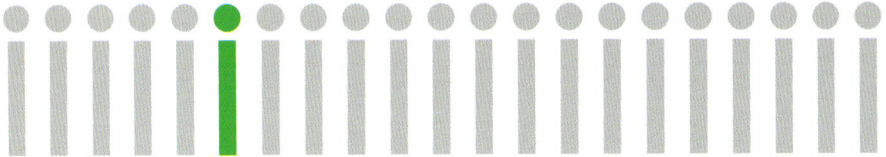

Fear can be quite useful at times. When encountering an oncoming train, a lion on safari, or an angry ruffian, fear can be a wonderful tool. Fear is not good in design. When the designer is frightened that the solution is too aggressive, bold, or exciting, he or she may fall into the trap of mildness. Perhaps the colors seem too strong and are dampened. Then all the shapes become a similar scale. And finally, the black tones are changed to midrange gray. The result is mild, pointless, and bland. Contrast is your friend. Strong value changes in contrast attract attention. They stand out in a crowded visual environment. At the extreme of value contrasts are 100 percent black and pure white. And they work. The world is saturated with multiple midtone colors, creating an over-all low-contrast impression. Strong black and white tones may seem old-fashioned, but this combination is rarely used. In the midst of a plethora of four-color images advertising products on billboards, imagine the impression of a simple black-and-white, high-contrast solution. **SA**

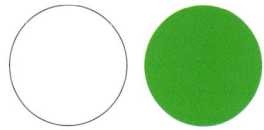

# DO learn to love the Eyedropper tool

I've been using Adobe InDesign since version 2, but it took me a long time to realize how useful the Eyedropper tool is. I thought it simply stored the color of any object you clicked on, enabling you to fill another object with the same color or apply it the to text, like it does in Adobe Photoshop. How wrong I was—you can copy type attributes too. Click on an item of text, even some text in another document, then drag over another item of text with the Eyedropper, and—bingo!—it copies not just the color of the text but many additional stored attributes. While it's true that good practice dictates the use of style sheets for all text formatting, especially in long documents, there's always a use for this functionality when you're working on a one-off job, like a poster or flyer, or when you're experimenting with type styles prior to committing to the application of style sheets. Time to stop ignoring the Eyedropper tool, I think. **TS**

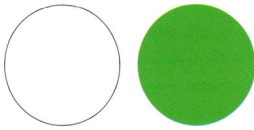

# DO use color to create movement

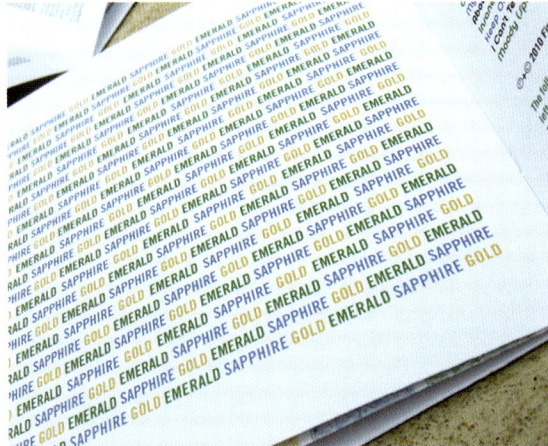

The ability to create movement using color is actually fairly easy, producing the illusion of action. When an image, or sequence of colors, has a wide variation in value running throughout it (note that this is very different from a layout that pans across to build to a different value), it allows for a kinetic reaction in the viewer's eye. Once you have this knowledge, you can harness it to create busy color combinations that dance in front of the viewer or pull back on it to create a soothing effect with colors of the same value. If you are feeling particularly bold, you can make color sequences of the same color repeating in a pattern, generating a rhythmic quality. This also provides you with greater appreciation for painting, in which this can be seen at its fullest effect—from the high-contrast rhythm of a Mondrian to the energetic skies of a Van Gogh. **JF**

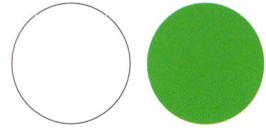

# DO use color to create tension

Explaining visual tension is similar to describing a color. It is an aspect of composition that uses unexpected color, shape, or scale to create energy. Often, designers create tension in their work, not to evoke anxiety but to offer the viewer a more dynamic experience. Using dissimilar, or jarring, color combinations is one way to do this. Taking advantage of spatial properties of color is another way. For example, warm tones appear to advance in three-dimensional space, and cool tones recede. If a large object appears closer to the viewer and smaller objects are more distant, then it would be logical for the large object to use a warm color such as red. If you reverse the expected and use a cool color on the closer, larger object and a warm red on the distant/smaller object, tension is created. The viewer is being told two opposing stories. Color can be used to create tension by combining tones that vibrate, such as blue and red, or by using color in unexpected ways, like coloring a chicken blue or the Brooklyn Bridge pink, which can also create tension. **SA**

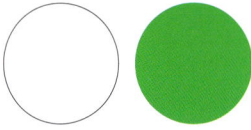

# DO use color
# to create calm

While recessive and banal should never be the goal of a project, a calm tone can be desirable. The anxiety produced by representation of unnerving subjects, such as surgery, dental work, and airplane safety, could be mitigated by the use of colors that are calming and reassuring. The first step is to understand the audience and its concerns. Does the audience need to be comforted, to feel safe, or to be put at ease? If so, calm colors can achieve this. Calm colors do not need to be light pastels. The context of each assignment dictates the color choices. Blood red is a bad choice for surgical brochures and websites. While there are exceptions, calming colors are less vibrant. They contain a higher percentage of white or black than a pure primary tone. Yellow can be made calming by adding white. A soft butter-yellow isn't as jarring and aggressive as primary yellow and still communicates optimism. **SA**

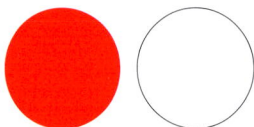

# DON'T place analogous colors next to each other

Well, we were bound to end up in color theory class at some point, huh? Analogous colors are those that appear next to each other on the color wheel. Included within a larger palette, they can create a sense of harmony. If you place them next to each other, however, they bask in their similarity and blend together in the worst possible way. We learned earlier to play tricks with tonal quality, but with this, you could end up with a violet next to a red with little to distinguish them but a muddy mess. In dressing yourself, the only thing worse than not matching is wearing two colors that are almost the same. Picture yourself in a red and orange outfit. You will quickly realize that you would be better off going full on with either color, but would be in big trouble if you try to wedge them together. **JF**

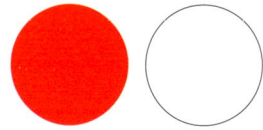

# DON'T place high-intensity complementary colors next to each other

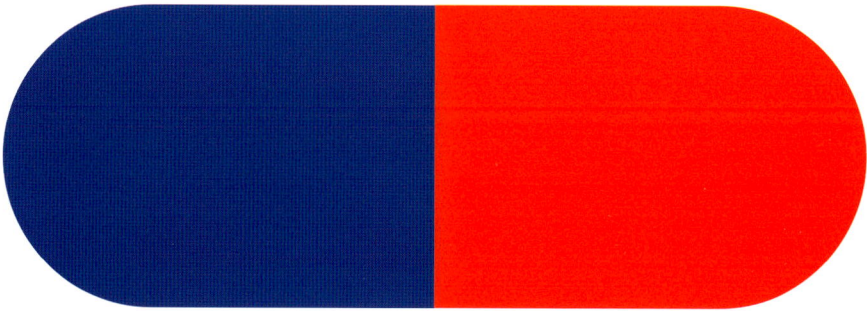

Unless the goal of a project is to annoy the viewer, it is a good rule of thumb to not recklessly slam vibrant primary colors together. Blue and red will create a visual vibration. Blue and yellow are good for nautical applications when visual clarity may be challenged but may be overwhelming on personal stationery. Red and yellow are perfect for McDonald's but lack the sophistication that may be necessary for a refined high-end Japanese restaurant. As in all decisions, being aware of the context, intended communication, and desired psychological reaction will dictate the choice of colors. Yes, there are instances when using all three primary colors together works. A preschool's identity may seem to be a good place to use primary colors—and a square, circle, and triangle. But then it will match every other preschool logo from Toledo to Taipei. **SA**

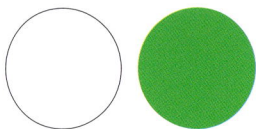

# DO use fluorescent inks with a purpose

Fluorescent inks can add a shine, similar to an enormous glittering gold necklace swinging from your neck or a crisp shine on your patent leather shoes. They always make an impact. Using them in the proper manner can be the tougher part. Not every occasion is suited to flashy neckwear, though a snappy pair of loafers goes well with most everything. Using fluorescent inks brings an intense brilliance, and a spot color of neon orange or green or yellow will instantly attract all of the available eyes, but the use has to be appropriate. You should know that those stylings are generally reserved for youthful entertainment and fashion-based applications. The more versatile option is adding it to your process inks to increase their intensity and shine. Another specialized use is employing a clear version on a project as a security measure, a version only visible when exposed to UV light. **JF**

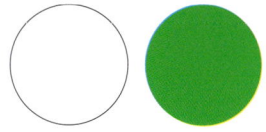

# DO utilize color profiles in your workflow

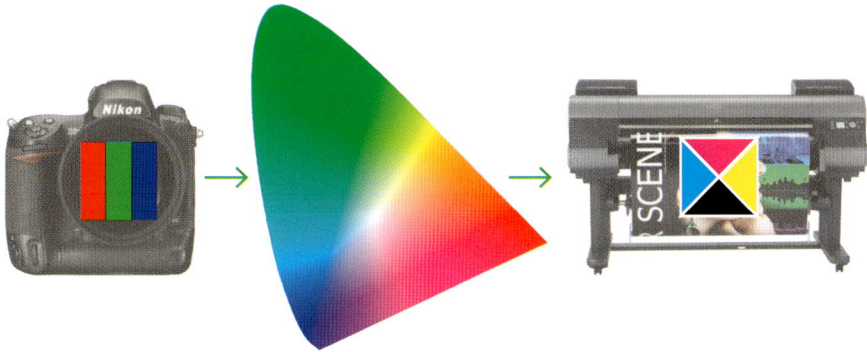

In order to manage and maintain the color of your artwork files, linked RGB images, and graphics, it's important to use color profiles and embed them into your work as you carry out any project. These profiles will then link to your color management system, which will maintain color consistency as the project moves from the RGB environment of the computer display to the final CMYK print. At the beginning of any job, I always ask myself a number of questions: How are we printing this? What stock are we using? What is the color composition of the images? All these factors may have an impact on your choice of profile, which in turn plays an important part in maintaining the project's integrity and appearance. I often speak to the relevant printer and discuss the available options and ask if they have profiles matched to their own presses that I could use. In doing this, I can then be sure that images embedded with the correct profile will display accurately on-screen and that the final print will be consistent with visuals. **PD**

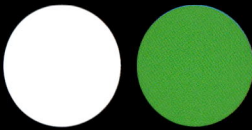

# DO use "rich black" for large black backgrounds

30C 30M 100K

100K

Printing black over a small area, for example, an uppercase *X* in 36pt Gill Sans Bold, will produce a strong impression with hard contrast between the black of the character and the white of the paper. However, if you print solid black over a large area, like an entire magazine spread, it won't look quite so solid. To make the black look richer, hence the term *rich black*, you can underprint various percentages of the CMY colors to create "blacker blacks." A typical rich black uses a 50 percent tint of all three colors plus 100 percent black; but use a combination of 100 percent black with 70 percent cyan, 30 percent magenta, and 40 percent yellow for a "cool" black. If you need a warmer black, try 100 percent black with 30 percent cyan, 60 percent magenta, and 60 percent yellow. Take care not to go too high with the percentages, however, as too much ink will produce too much wetness during printing (see page 217). Always check with your printer to see what they recommend for their presses. **TS**

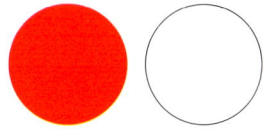

# DON'T allow rich black tints to exceed 300% ink coverage

Printing what is called rich blacks—the black printing with the three other inks (CMY)—can be troublesome when the percentage combination of all four colors adds up to more than 300 percent. All printers have a limit on their total area coverage, which refers to the maximum amount of ink allowed in the darkest areas of an image. The percentages vary from a maximum of around 300–340 percent for coated papers to 240–280 percent for uncoated papers. To be safe, I always check the values of any darker images (a night shot, for example) to ensure that the blacks of the sky and shadows don't exceed 300 percent. Not doing this makes the printing difficult to control when on press because of the huge amount of ink being laid down. It's also quite wasteful, and too much ink will lead to "set-off" when drying, which means the image will be pressed onto the following sheet—a disastrous and very expensive issue to resolve. Set-off pages can only be fixed by going back and amending the guilty files—so always check them first! **PD**

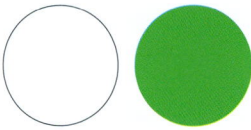

# DO take into account paper brightness and whiteness

Paper brightness has always been considered an important feature for any "white" printing stock and shouldn't be confused with whiteness. Brightness is the percentage reflectance of blue light at a specific wavelength (457nm in fact) and is more quantifiable than whiteness, which is the percentage of light reflected at all wavelengths. The brightness of the pulps and pigments used in paper manufacturing indicate how much whiteness can be achieved. Anyway—enough science. High paper whiteness boosts the contrast of any printed area and, in turn, can effectively increase the number of reproducible colors printed on the paper stock. It's not quite that simple, as colors will look different depending on viewing conditions. Broadly speaking though, the color gamut of the color model used for printing will increase with the greater whiteness of the paper stock. Paper with a slightly blue shade is considered whiter than stock that has a more neutral white shade and will make your colors really pop off the page. **TS**

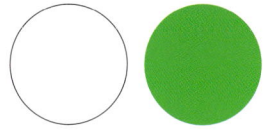

# DO specify colors for packaging a little lighter than you want them to print

The very wise Robynne Raye of Modern Dog Design once bestowed upon me an invaluable piece of advice. "Have you ever seen a piece of packaging printed too light?" she asked me. She then revealed that she often sets the final files up a uniform 5 percent lighter than the versions proposed and approved, knowing that the gain on press will still likely leave them with a darker final product than expected. Decades into packaging assignments, I wish that her observation weren't true, but all you need to do is ask yourself if you have ever seen a package on a shelf and thought that they held back a little on the ink for this one. The packaging for consumer items is often produced at various stages of the overall production cycle with the printer—sometimes printed with several other jobs, sometimes with jobs for other clients, or in insanely long print runs that use rubber plates. This means that the compromises that need to be made will vary. Trust me when I say that the press person will always add more ink. **JF**

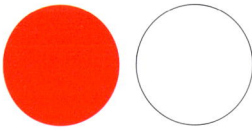

# DON'T ever specify a color for print based on its on-screen appearance

This is an age-old problem that is still relevant today. When you look at colors on the screen, you see an RGB representation of the color, which is never entirely accurate. An electronic representation of a CMYK or Pantone color will not be the same as ink on paper. Although the two can get close on occasion, there will never be a perfect match. This has always caused difficulties for designers and for clients, as what they see on their screen they believe will carry across and be printed. In addition, what they see on their screens will look different than when viewed on your screen. To guarantee the correct color is printed, I always use the color breakdowns or references supplied in the appropriate Pantone book and make sure the client sees them. Obtaining a proof will also ensure that they understand how the colors will reproduce in the final product. Be safe, never sorry. **PD**

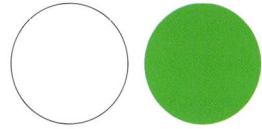

# DO learn about underpainting

Some people understand underpainting. Everyone else doesn't know how to paint. I was a terrible student in my college painting class. I just didn't know it. My instructor tried to explain what was lacking in my work by insisting that I take a painting I had completed and paint an entirely new piece on top of it. This stopped me from being precious about my work and also sent me on the most important color exploration of my life. Every single thing that I know about how colors interact with one another was informed by the experience. Midway through the course, she took time to fully flesh out how underpainting works. Using only one paint color, I learned to make a monochromatic sketch on my canvas that added a uniform base and visual style for my final piece. Later, I also learned how important layers of color could be— how yellow under the green grass was different from brown. It changed everything. **JF**

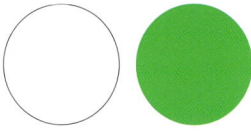

# DO ask your client color questions

After agonizing for weeks over a presentation to a huge nonprofit organization about their fund-raising gala materials, I was stunned to hear, five minutes into the meeting, that none of my options would work. My side of the room was still pulling their jaws back in place when I noticed the telltale look in the eyes of my main contacts sitting across from me. They could have told me this would happen. The reason was that the executive director's wife hated a certain color, one that made conceptual sense and was strewn throughout all of the options. It is an extreme example, but I knew that I had forgotten a vital step in my usual process: asking if there is anything I need to know about my client and colors. Always ask in advance, but also be sure to ask following feedback. Can I never use green again? Or should I just shy away from that particular green? It will save you a lot of trouble. Trust me. **JF**

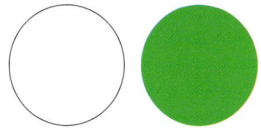

# DO respect an emotional response to a color from a client

One of the most frustrating things about working in design is when a client makes a subjective comment on color. Some of us, myself included, have set up presentation processes to circumvent this as much as possible. However, it would be terribly naive, and detrimental to your professional progress, to think that this will never occur. When your client says that they can't fathom using orange in their branding, because it was the color of their rival high school growing up, what do you do? If you think you are going to have any success forcing them to see the reasoning behind using that color, even if you are branding an orange juice company, you won't. When that emotional/irrational response happens, adjust, adapt, and, most of all, respect it. You don't have to agree with it. But you are in your client's shoes, burdened by their color history. **JF**

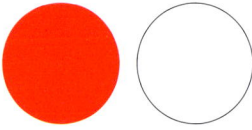

# DON'T get caught up in trendy colors for projects that need to stand the test of time

If you were dressing a person and knew that they had to wear the same clothes for ten, twenty, thirty years or more, would you dress them in bell-bottom jeans? Give them feathered Farrah Fawcett hair, or better yet, a Mohawk? Pierce their nose, or cover them in tattoos? Or would you research clothes until you determined what was built to last and what was trendy and sure to fall out of fashion soon? I hope that you would put in the time to do the research. When you are doing the same on your design projects, creating a final product or brand that holds its look far past today, you should take even greater care. Ignore those lists of what colors are hot and seem to be filled with made-up names for nonexistent fruits, and make solid decisions based on research and strategic thinking. **JF**

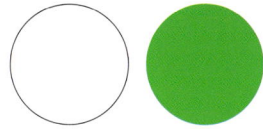

# DO remember that the popularity of certain colors shifts rapidly

Each year, many organizations publish lists of colors that will be in fashion the subsequent year. One year, we are told that silver is the color to use to be relevant. The next year, brown is the new black. A designer must stay current with popular culture, taste, and attitudes. But the designer should lead, not follow. When someone says, "That color is so dated," they are seeing it in a specific context. Avocado green will look dated on a 1970s refrigerator. Avocado green could appear fresh and current on an iPhone cover. Coral will be dated on a 1955 Cadillac. It could be perfect for an identity for a forward-thinking nonprofit institution. The lesson is to create your own rules. If color is used with confidence in purposeful and bold ways, it will be appropriate and original. **SA**

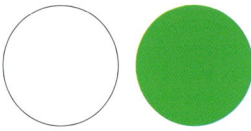

# DO recognize that color palettes change depending on an audience's age

One of the most valued abilities in design and advertising is the ability to create for an audience outside your age group. The rabid pursuit of young consumers has made this talent, especially considering that kids can't enter the workplace to do this for themselves, a golden commodity. With the graying of our populations, an entirely new marketplace has opened up, and marketing to it has become a clear specialty. While many factors go into reaching these different groups, one interesting factor, often forgotten, is that age directly affects how the viewer reacts to color. Children recognize only a smaller range of colors and respond to a widened palette as they grow older. Children also make early associations with specific colors (apples are red) and embrace bold and bright colors. As we become more savvy, or jaded, we also accept a wider range of colors and their applications. **JF**

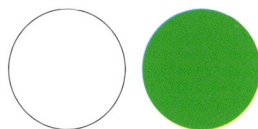

# DO research the color palettes of your client's competitors

Strange things can be revealed when a designer compiles a visual grouping of a client's competition. Typically, a clear language is visible, and a part of this language is color. For example, a search for financial institutions will disclose vast swaths of navy blues and forest greens. The designer then has the choice to either follow suit or go another way. A designer with little courage will look at the competitive research and determine that the client should look the same. The client may even say, "But everyone else uses blue." Conformity is valuable in the armed services; it is damaging in a competitive marketplace. The designer's job is to identify a client's strengths, weaknesses, competitors, and values, and then to create a visual solution that sets the client apart or above the competition. **SA**

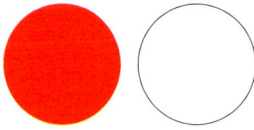

# DON'T let your personal color preferences hurt a project

Consider the design of a book cover for a noted writer's new romantic novel. She has used carnation pink on each of her twelve other novels. Her bedroom is carnation pink, and her nickname is Pinky. Pink, however, makes you recoil. You consider it weak and a sign of women's oppression. What should you do? Clearly, using carnation pink is the correct choice. Trying to convince the author that your favorite colors, ochre and black, are better choices will have two effects. It will make the client angry, and you will be fired. More important, however, is that the ochre and black would damage Pinky's brand. The money and time spent to reinforce the identification of pink with Pinky will be annulled. Bluntly, pursuing your own personal color choice over the needs of the project will ruin lives. **SA**

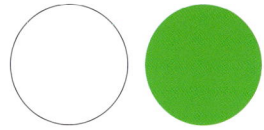

# DO design logos in black and white before applying color

Already established is the fact that clients may react emotionally to the colors that we present to them. Also, logos need to fit equally well applied on any item, from letterhead and signage to embroidery and everything in between. Now that we have talked through all of the pitfalls, it is the perfect time to give you a little secret into how to circumvent them. Working with your logo designs in black and white will help guarantee that the vector applications work well. Using only black and white while talking about the process with your client will also create solid acceptance of your design, without eliminating something because it was presented in a disliked color. Only the best designs will survive. Those conversations will also provide the base for your final color decisions. Often, both sides will find that they already know the colors they want in the final solution. And never forget, if it works in black and white, it will work in most any color. **JF**

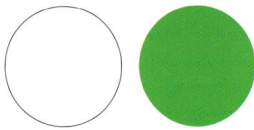

# DO remember that color + time can = brand

 = UPS

 = Coca-Cola

 = IBM

One of the most incredible marketing efforts, tied directly to color, took place over the last few years. The shipping giant UPS has had the brown color as part of its identity since its earliest days, chosen for its dignified and professional appearance. Now, eighty years later, its entire campaign is based around simply calling the company itself "brown." It is a stunning acknowledgment of how important the color is to the way consumers identify and interact with the company. Built through constant reinforcement, from its delivery vehicles to its employee uniforms, UPS has owned brown in the marketplace to such an extent that they can simply refer to themselves as such. This campaign stands as a vital reminder of how important color can be as a brand asset. It brings to mind companies with incredibly strong brands that lack in the logo department and the decades built on instantly recognizing the Coca-Cola red that sits on the supermarket shelf. **JF**

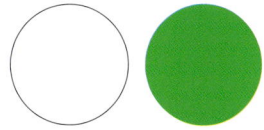

# DO accept that there is no such thing as a bad color combination

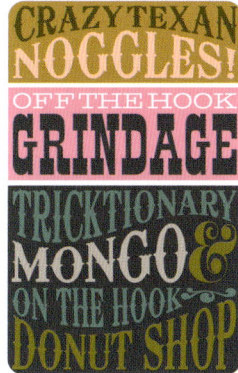

Rules are meant to be broken. There are valuable and appropriate rules for color. But once a designer reaches a level of proficiency and confidence with color, all rules are thrown out the window. Bad color combinations are timid color combinations. The viewer will sense when a designer is unsure and inhibited. A small patch of violet on the page against an equally wispy patch of lime green will look like an error. Slamming violet and lime green together in a large and bold way will make them look exactly right. Van Gogh combined yellow with rust. In the hands of a lesser artist, timidly applying a small amount here and there, the solution would have been regrettable. Van Gogh's *Twelve Sunflowers* is perfect. Doing something bravely and with self-confidence will always convince others that you are correct. **SA**

# Imagery
# & Graphics

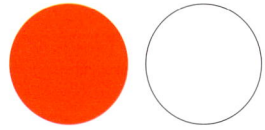

# DON'T use stock images just to save money

Don't get me wrong—I love the fact that we can go online nowadays and find 87,000 different shots of two business-men shaking hands while grinning inanely at each other. This is ultimately a good thing because, if that's the kind of image you need for a project, the bulk availability and lower overheads of online picture libraries mean stock images are now a relatively inexpensive option. However, you should always think carefully about whether a com-pletely unique image would serve your client better. Remember that other designers can download the same photos or illustrations you've selected for their own clients, and the better (and therefore more popular) images are pushed to the top of the list when you search by subject. If you think your client can afford original photography or illustration, always try to persuade them to consider that option first. It helps to keep the freelance community in work too. **TS**

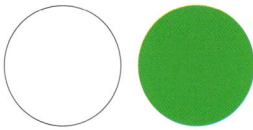

# DO always check to see if a perfect stock photo might be available

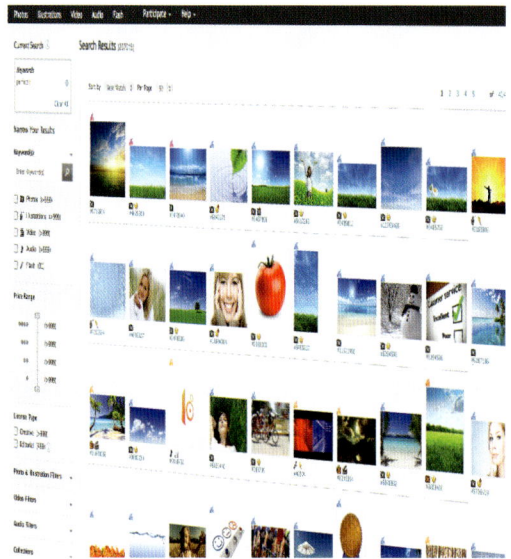

A very famous designer once told me a story about how one of his most iconic posters almost didn't happen. The client wanted a figure interacting with a specific, immediately recognizable cityscape. He was limited in his options and joked to the client that if they rented a helicopter, he could easily get the image. They begged him to at least give it a try. He scoffed and thought about just telling them that he researched without luck, so hopeless seemed the task. He did a quick stock search, only to discover a photographer who specialized in that region, leaving him with a number of options and an incredibly happy client, amazed that he so diligently succeeded in finding such a seemingly rare image. **JF**

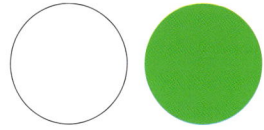

# DO do your best to use client-supplied images

I see you staring at me, that slightly out-of-focus shot of the executive director and four other people who seem mildly important. One of them displays his expensive watch, and they're all drinking glasses of wine. I can feel you edging your way toward my precious magazine spread. The one I have been filling up with pull quotes and about which I've been informing the client that there was no room for you. Besides the many image edits you would require, I take offense that you have been forced on me. You can feel my disdain, but you move forward undeterred. When my back is turned, you inch directly on top of my monitor, and whisper, "I pay your salary." A bead of sweat forms on my forehead, as I realize that I have been approaching this all wrong. As I turn to the monitor, resigned to make you the best image you can possibly be, you smile and add, "Plus, I come preapproved." **JF**

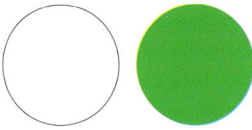

# DO also show a client better alternatives to their own imagery if necessary

Most clients have not been educated as designers. They haven't studied the history of photography. They don't understand complex rules of composition. And they don't need to. Clients understand the rules of their respective fields. This may lead to a client supplying really awful imagery. It may be blurry photographs taken by a friend who is interested in photography. It may be simplistic drawings of a client's pets, drawn by a relative. Or it may be a photograph that sends the wrong message. When the project is finished, there will be no note on the bad images that reads, "This was chosen by the client." The failure of the project will be on the designer. When faced with bad photography, art, or information graphics, the designer should find a better solution and present it as an alternative. Forcing this down the client's throat rarely works. Tactful and logical explanation, showing both alternatives, is the best approach. **SA**

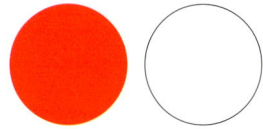

# DON'T assume that an image is good simply because it's been published online

There are many websites devoted to photography sharing. These allow people around the globe to upload their own images and share them with anyone or everyone else. They are remarkable tools to gaze into the lives of everyday people everywhere. But just because an image has been published online or on a photo sharing site does not make it good. There is no seasoned photography curator accepting the good images and rejecting the bad ones. Of course, some images may be remarkable; other images may be awful. The majority of the images are created not by professional photographers but by everyone else. Would I ask my four-year-old nephew to photograph an urban streetscape for an architecture client's website? Is my mother's photograph of her dog in a funny coat a good choice for a corporate capabilities booklet? No. When you're facing budgetary issues, stock image websites are the best source for stock images. However, hiring a photographer to shoot an original image is typically the best approach. **SA**

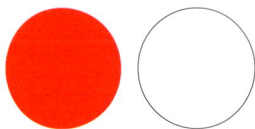

# DON'T repulse your audience with imagery unless briefed to do so

Shocking images are a valuable tool for the designer. An image that challenges viewers, or forces them to acknowledge an issue, is one of the strongest forms of communication. Repulsive and aggressive images are part of this canon. In the right context, this type of imagery can create a result that is spectacular. Repulsive images used for shock value alone are pandering. The solution may receive the desired attention, but the lasting effect will be one of anger and negativity. If the client is the Sex Pistols, this response may be appropriate. Most clients, however, would prefer to create a positive reaction. No communication is ever neutral. The response will always be clear or confused, positive or negative. The designer's role is to help guide that perception toward positive and clear. **SA**

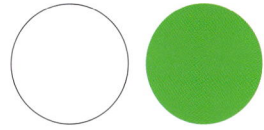

# DO carefully consider the political content of all image choices

In the 1930s, the Nazi Party began to censor art it considered politically degenerate. Obviously, anti-Nazi art was the first censored. As time passed, the political content of 95 percent of art produced was deemed degenerate, and the state only allowed benign landscape paintings to be exhibited. Every image has political content. A photograph of a group of people can immediately be deconstructed by race, gender, age, and culture. Even an inoffensive landscape painting can be seen as propaganda. Understanding the political implications of images, icons, and messages is a necessity for designers. Is the woman in a bikini holding a beer simply a picture of someone at the beach? Or is the image, according to feminist theory, an example of the objectification and oppression of women by a patriarchal culture? Each designer will need to determine this for himself or herself. Purposefully using an image and recognizing its political subtext is a basic skill. **SA**

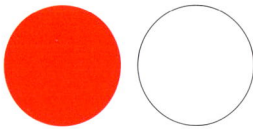

# DON'T run detailed images across the gutter

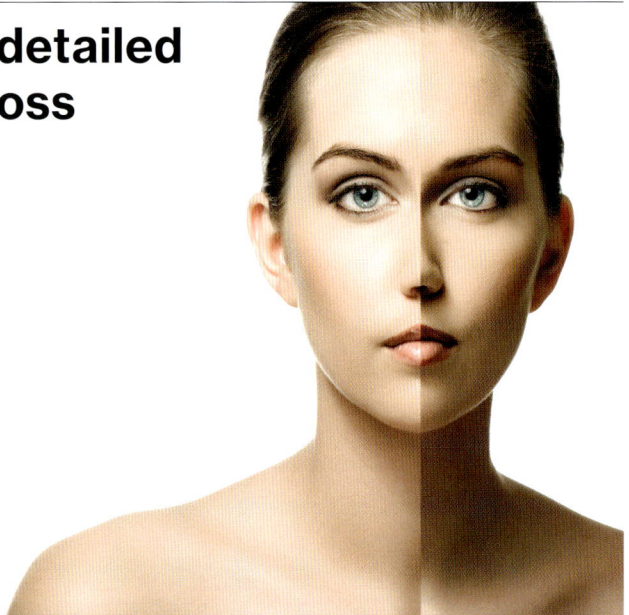

A full-bleed image run across a spread in a book or magazine creates great visual impact, and some pictures cry out to be used as large as possible. Magnificent landscapes or architectural shots can work really well, especially when they're overlaid with a strong typographic headline to open an article or chapter. Take care though, as it's easy to forget one vital detail—the gutter. When we design spreads, we normally work "spread to view" so we can see left and right pages side by side. On a flat computer screen, we tend to overlook the importance of the gutter because it's represented only by a fine rule, but in a bound magazine or book, much of the viewable page immediately adjacent to the gutter can disappear into the spine. Images like impressive landscapes can usually absorb this, but others, like portraits, won't. The cardinal sin is to slice through someone's face with the gutter. Don't cut off someone's nose to show the face. Take care to ensure that gutters only pass through neutral image spaces. **TS**

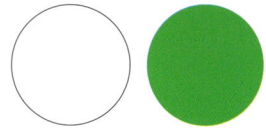

# DO check that all images have an effective 300ppi resolution

300ppi

72ppi

The industry standard resolution for printing four-color halftones is 300ppi. I say ppi (pixels per inch) rather than dpi (dots per inch) nowadays, as the vast majority of image reproduction involves a digital workflow, and pixels are more representative of image resolution. It's generally accepted that the average human eye can't differentiate pixel densities beyond 300ppi, which explains why this is the recommended resolution for high-quality image reproduction. Other factors such as halftone screens (see page 247) also influence this choice. Say you have

your 300ppi image at 4 × 6 inches. As long as you import the image to your layout at the same size (or smaller), you'll maintain a resolution of at least 300ppi, and the print will theoretically look great. However, if you enlarge the image on the page, you'll lose resolution. For example, enlarging the image to 8 × 12 inches halves the resolution to 150ppi, which will degrade the quality of the final print. The trick is, unless you have no alternative, never enlarge a 300ppi image beyond 100 percent within your layout. **TS**

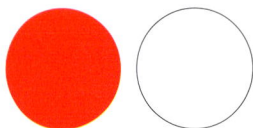

# DON'T import images with too high a resolution

We know that 300ppi is the industry standard resolution for quality printing, but what happens if we scan a halftone image at 600ppi? You might think it'll look twice as good when printed, but sadly you'd be wrong. In some cases, slight improvements can be detected in images printed at a higher resolution than 300ppi, but it's more of a fluke than anything else. The truth is that the extra resolution is wasted, serving only to make the document size larger than it needs to be and slowing down all prepress processing. In addition to this, banding (an uneven gradation of tone) can occur with images above 300ppi because the resolution doesn't correspond favorably with the commonly used 150lpi (lines per inch) halftone (see page 247). If you send PDFs to print rather than original layout files, there's a good chance that any imported images over 300ppi will be resampled down to 300ppi anyway. **TS**

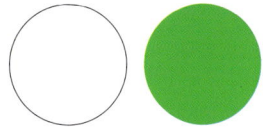

# DO resample all images to 300ppi before importing them to a print document

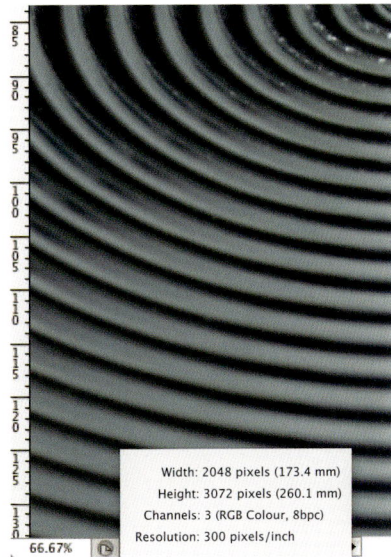

Width: 2048 pixels (173.4 mm)
Height: 3072 pixels (260.1 mm)
Channels: 3 (RGB Colour, 8bpc)
Resolution: 300 pixels/inch

66.67%

When working on any book design project, I receive hundreds of images to choose from. Invariably, these images will be a mix of resolutions—some high resolution (300ppi) and others that have been shot digitally, which, although large in dimension, are only 72ppi in resolution. If I were to place these latter images at 100 percent in my layout, I would in effect be including low-resolution artwork, which is never of high enough quality to print with. It is essential, therefore, that you consolidate resolutions to ensure that all images you use are hi-res. To locate the lo-res images before you import them into a layout, use software such as Adobe Bridge and adjust the resolution using Photoshop. If there are a lot of inconsistencies, run an automated action in Photoshop for the adjustments, but make sure that you constrain the proportions with the resolution so the images scale down correctly. Following this process means you can guarantee that every image will reproduce at least 300ppi as long as you do not scale them above 100 percent in the layout. **PD**

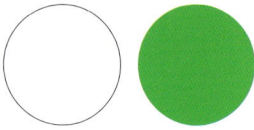

# DO learn about digital file formats

| PSD | EPS | JPG | PNG | TIFF |

We're really talking about the various image file formats here, all of which differ slightly and provide their own unique advantages. TIFFs (Tagged Image File Format) remain a top choice for print workflows, as they can accommodate embedded information such as alpha channels, which allow masks to be imported directly into a layout. Native Photoshop files are also a popular choice for the same reasons. JPEGs (Joint Photographic Experts Group) are great if you need to keep file sizes down, but be careful how much compression you apply when saving, as quality can suffer. A JPEG is also a bad choice if you think you'll need to edit the image farther down the line, as quality is lost every time you save a JPEG. Forget about EPS files (Encapsulated PostScript), as they're rarely used now—go with native Illustrator files for vectors. PNGs (Portable Network Graphic) are popular formats for online use, offering the advantage of transparency support. I recommend some further reading, as you may find you've not been using the best formats in your own image workflows. **TS**

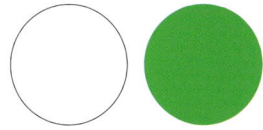

# DO learn about bit depth

Bit depth is the number of bits, or binary digits, assigned to each pixel in an image. Bit depth isn't about resolution, it's about color quality—the higher the bit depth, the more tones you can achieve—subtle color gradations improve as bit depth increases. Pure black-and-white images in which each pixel is either on (black) or off (white) are termed 1-bit. Black-and-white halftones with gradations from black to white are 8-bit, with 8 bits of color information per pixel. Color RGB images are 24-bit because there are 8 bits of color information per channel, so 8 × 3 = 24. Photoshop can handle up to 32 bits per channel, or 96-bit images, but you'll find that many adjustments and filters won't work at this bit depth, and any extra quality provided may be lost during print. When working with 48- or 96-bit originals, it might pay to create a 24-bit copy for use in your layout. Check with your print supplier to see what they can achieve with their equipment. **TS**

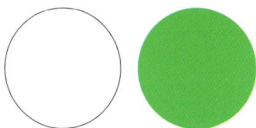

# DO understand the relationship between resolution and image size

**100%**

**600%**

This is a pretty straightforward relationship, but it's important to understand how resolution and image size affect each other. Any original image recorded by a camera or scanner has its resolution set by the device. However, if you then resize it in InDesign to make it either more or less than 100 percent its original size, the resolution will change. A 300ppi image won't create more pixels when you enlarge it; the pixels will simply get bigger and more visible, thus reducing the quality of the reproduction. For example, enlarging a 300ppi image to 600 percent within your layout will reduce the resolution to 50ppi. If you're interested in how the math works, it's $100 \div 600 \times 300$. Alternatively, set your Links panel to list the effective ppi for imported images, and you'll easily spot any image with a resolution that has transgressed acceptable boundaries. You can get away with less than 300ppi if you have to, but don't make a habit of it. **TS**

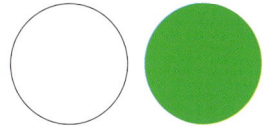

# DO understand the relationship between image resolution and halftone screens

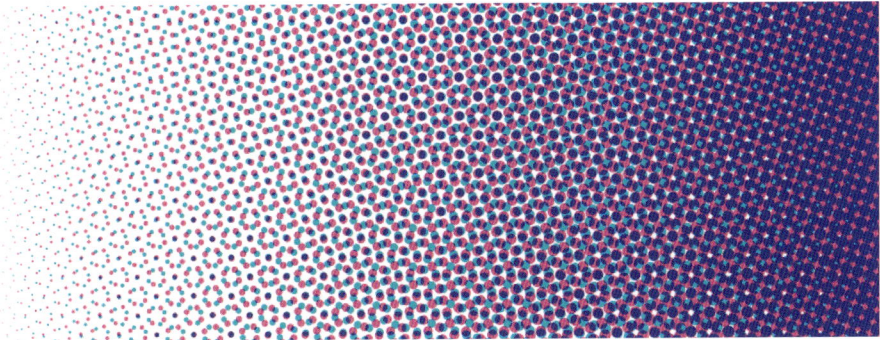

All four-color process images are made from dots and are alternatively referred to as *halftones*. A photographic print isn't made from dots and is known as a *continuous-tone* (*contone*) print. *Screening* is the term used to describe how a contone is converted to a halftone. The chosen print method and paper stock must be taken into account when selecting which halftone screen to use, with a higher value providing better print quality. A screen resolution of 150lpi is standard for quality printing, while a newspaper will use a screen as low as 70–80lpi. The coarser screen will actually help prevent individual dots from merging when inking the more absorbent newsprint. The relationship between image resolution and screen resolution is simple enough in that image resolution should be about twice that of the screen used, hence the industry standard of 300ppi and 150lpi. There's some leeway in the equation. Softer images without many straight lines or angles will stand up to coarser screening than anything containing much in the way of fine detail. **TS**

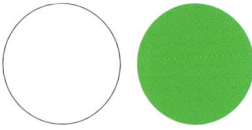

# DO choose images based on their appropriateness as well as their quality

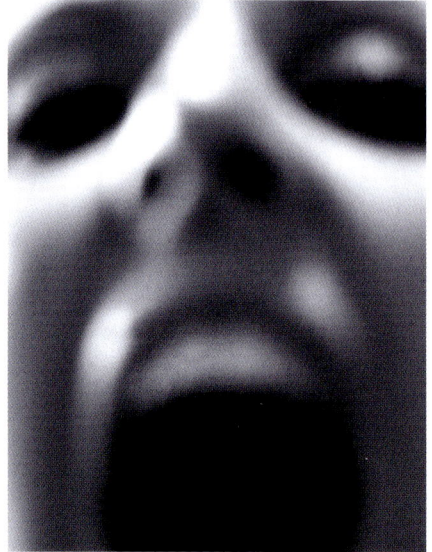

Is it better to use a great shot that's not a perfect exposure or a perfect exposure that's not quite the best shot? Ultimately, the decision might not be yours, as your client may value slick presentation over content quality, but for me, choosing the shot that's the most appropriate is always the better decision. Think about all the wonderful images that have come out of the journalism field, which does not prioritize getting a perfect exposure. How about those lucky accidental shots when you were doing the right thing by looking down the lens rather than at the settings on the back of the camera. When you look at the very best images, a pattern emerges—content is king. Beautifully exposed images that are exactly right for a cover or spread are, of course, the ideal option, but it's wrong to choose an image purely because of its technical quality. The reaction and the emotion a shot creates in the viewer must always take precedence. **TS**

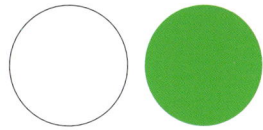

# DO devise a system for the consistent naming of digital image files

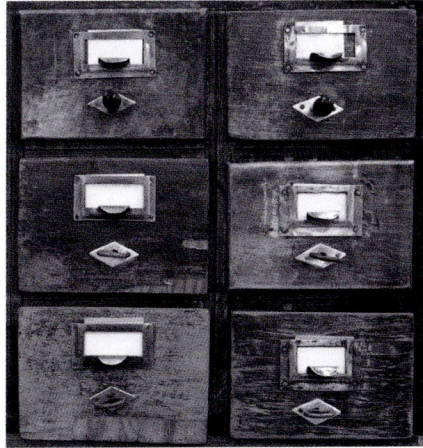

0249_ComS.tif

It can be difficult when you are working on a large-scale project to manage and identify the many files that have been supplied. In some instances, a client or a publisher may have supplied the image files with logical and consistent names and in an organized manner. Often, though, you may not be so lucky, in which case it's worthwhile to organize and rename the files yourself before importing them. This will enable you to find and compare images more easily and to maintain the correct links if the files are ever moved between workstations or servers. For book and brochure projects, you may choose to use the chapter and folio numbers as a prefix for the image, so they appear in running order when listed alphabetically. However, if the pagination changes, this method may cause confusion—a simple system of unique numbering and/or coding that doesn't follow a page order may prove to be more dependable in the long run. By taking stock of what you have and how the design is structured, a system of organization will likely become evident. **PD**

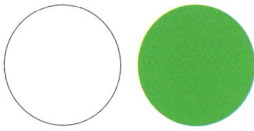

# DO work with Camera Raw image files

Adobe Camera Raw is, in a word, brilliant. If you shoot (or receive a shot) as a JPEG or TIFF, it is what it is. You can adjust it, color correct it, resize it within reason, but that's basically it. Camera Raw is like having an old-style film negative because you can go back to the original to create new versions from scratch. A Camera Raw file contains all the raw data recorded by the camera at the point the picture was shot. Camera Raw files aren't compressed or subjected to any in-camera processing, so you can do a whole lot more with them when you open them up in Photoshop's Camera Raw plug-in. You can reset temperature (or white balance), tint, exposure, brightness and contrast, clarity and vibrancy, and a whole host of other adjustments. You can even open images at a size larger than the original, which can be very handy indeed. Ask your photographer for or shoot in Camera Raw whenever possible. **TS**

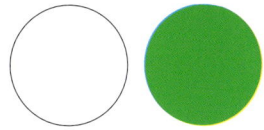

# DO utilize Adobe's DNG format when archiving images

We just mentioned how good Adobe Camera Raw is, but it does have its limitations. The format is governed by the make and model of supported cameras, and the Camera Raw plug-in can't guarantee that it'll support every camera forever. This means that there may come a time when you won't be able to open an archived image. Enter the solution—Adobe's DNG (digital negative) format. Saving your images as DNG files removes the compatibility issue.

They become "time proof," making them a much better option for archiving, and you can still open them with the Camera Raw plug-in. The file sizes are slightly smaller too, which isn't a bad thing, and there are cataloging advantages to boot. This is a huge advantage if you choose to follow the advice on page 252 and create a Digital Asset Management (DAM) system. DNG is the way to go. **TS**

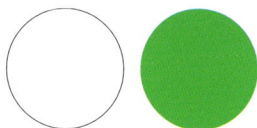

# DO use DAM to catalog image files

What's more boring, cataloging all your photographic images and illustrations or spending all day searching for that great shot that you may or may not still have on file somewhere? Personally, I would say the latter is more dull and definitely more frustrating. DAM sounds like the dull option, but it's actually really easy to do once you've got your system in place. You can buy specialist software like Extensis Portfolio, which creates standalone catalogs of all your images, or digital assets, as they all have potential commercial value. If you don't want to fork out for extra software, you can use something like Photos, which comes standard with every Mac, or perhaps the Google Photos online photo album service. Alternatively, you can just file images carefully in named folders and use Adobe Bridge for your image searches. Whatever system you go for, get a grip on metadata, which is defined as "data about data." Use *metadata* to embed key words into your image files, and tracking them down in the future will be a breeze. **TS**

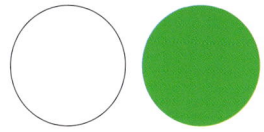

# DO always apply some sharpening to digital images

On close inspection, many images shot with a digital camera will appear to be slightly blurred. This happens because, just like the grain produced in shots from old-style film cameras, digital sensors produce a random speckling of tiny electronic dots across the shot, known as noise. Digital cameras attempt to suppress noise by setting sharpness to the lowest acceptable level, which means that postproduction sharpening will be necessary. Your photographer may do this for you as part of his or her contract along with any required color adjustments, but if not, the odds are that you'll be using Photoshop to do this yourself. Use Unsharp Mask or Smart Sharpen; don't use the basic Sharpen filter, as it's an all-or-nothing option and offers no real control over the end result. A word of warning—don't overdo it. Oversharpened images look worse than the "straight from camera" shot, so easy does it. Oh, one more thing, complete any and all image adjustments before you apply any sharpening. It should always be the last thing you do before importing the image to your layout. **TS**

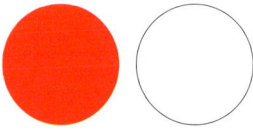

# DON'T crop well-composed images excessively

When an artist sits down at their easel to sketch out the composition of a painting, they're thinking carefully about what's happening at the edges of the work as well as what's happening at the center. Imagine how horrified they would be if they were to walk into a gallery, only to find that a picture framer had decided to chop six inches off the top of their work so it lined up nicely with the other paintings on the adjacent wall. Photographers do the same thing when they look through a camera viewfinder and compose the shot, and photographic images should be treated the same way as paintings. Sure, not all photographs need to be treated with the same reverence, and some are shot with the intention that they be cropped at will, but something like a fine landscape image or an immaculately composed portrait should be treated with respect and cropped as the photographer intended. It's kind of rude to crop heavily without good cause. **TS**

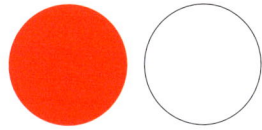

# DON'T crop landscape to portrait and vice versa

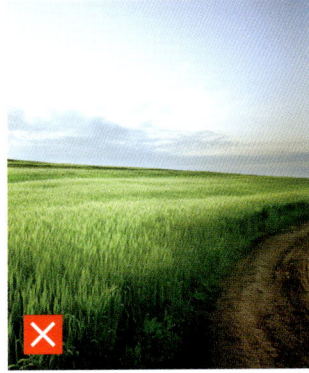

Another professional's work should always be treated with respect. This is no less true when working with a photographer; their experience and creative "eye" for a good shot contribute to the careful composition and formatting of each photograph they produce. By taking their picture and cropping to a different format, you are likely degrading the overall quality of the image and negatively affecting its composition—as well as being disrespectful of the photographer! Most photographers I know often take a landscape and a portrait of the same subject matter, with the orientation dictating their choice of composition. Check if there is an alternative before you start laying out your design. This rule goes for any type of image, art reproduction, or illustrated work too. Meet the challenge and work with what you are given. **PD**

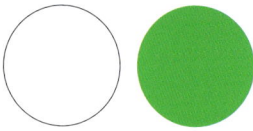

# DO use the right Photoshop tools for color adjustment

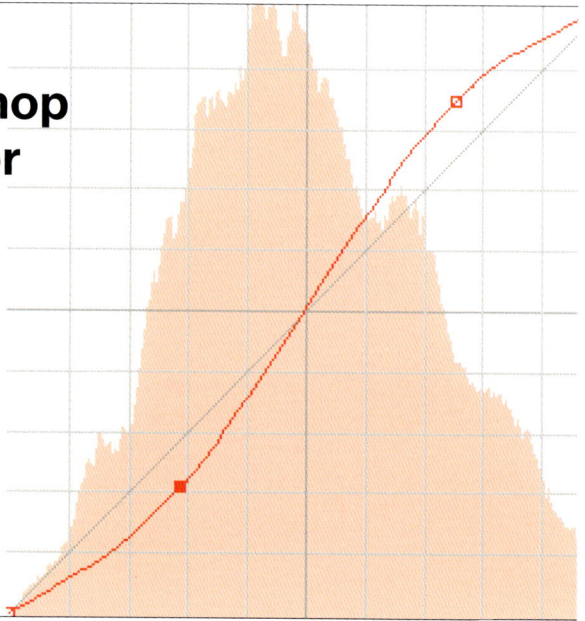

If you feel that an image needs color adjustment, it may well need a bit of tonal adjustment first. Color is directly affected by tonal adjustments because saturation will increase or decrease when darkening or lightening an image, so check Levels first. Don't bother with Brightness and Contrast, as the adjustment isn't sophisticated enough. Drag the black and white point sliders of the Layers dialogue in to meet the ends of the histogram to achieve good tonal balance. A Color Balance adjustment can solve simple color problems, but for better results you need to study the workings of the Curves adjustment. It's not that complicated and is arguably the most powerful adjustment tool in the whole kit. Read up about the popular S-Curve approach to color adjustment, and you'll be well on the way to becoming a real pro. Knowledge of the color wheel will help you here too. Here's a little side tip for any adjustment procedure: decide what the worst issue is and deal with that first. It may be all that's needed. **TS**

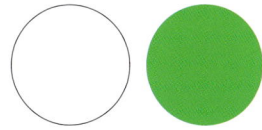

# DO always edit images nondestructively

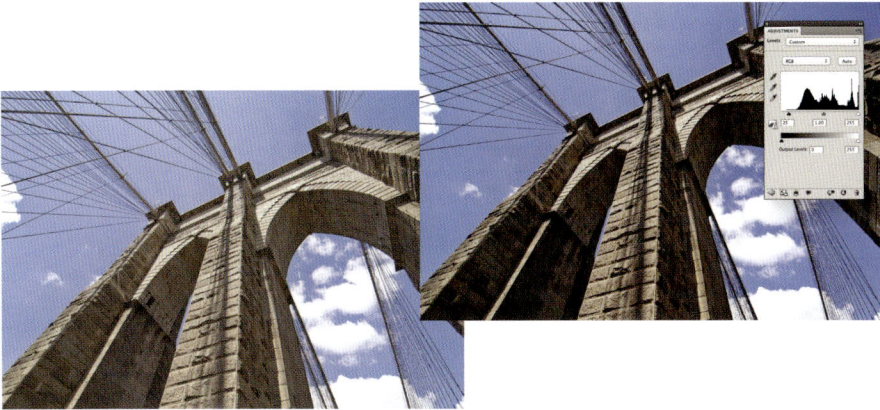

Since they were first introduced way back in 1994, Layers have always been one of the best things about Adobe Photoshop. In 1996, the functionality of the Layers panel took another leap forward with the addition of Adjustment Layers. Now, can you think of any reason you wouldn't want to take advantage of what's termed nondestructive editing by using those wonderful Adjustment Layers? It's nondestructive because if you change your mind about any of the edits you apply, you can readjust them or take them out completely, so this is a bit of a no-brainer, to be honest. However, some folks still manage to forget all about them and either apply adjustments directly to an original image or make endless saved-as versions of files in case they want to go back to an earlier version. This is completely crazy and pretty much inexcusable! As you can see, I feel quite strongly about this one, so check out those Adjustment Layers and use them well, even for basic Levels or Curves adjustments. **TS**

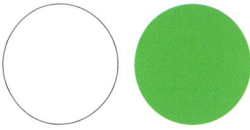

# DO worship Smart Filters

We know that nondestructive adjustments are the way to go, as discussed on page 257, but what happens when we want to apply other effects without permanently changing the original image? When Photoshop CS3 was released in 2007, it was the end of a long wait (after the arrival of Adjustment Layers) for the brilliant Smart Filters. Smart Filters are possible because of Smart Objects, introduced in CS2 to allow more flexible ways of working with scalable vector graphics and are basically Adjustment Layers for filters.

All you have to do is open your original as a Smart Object and apply whichever filters you care to choose. Each applied Smart Filter is linked in a stack to the selected layer and can be edited with Blending Options or reordered as many times as you like or deleted completely if you decide you don't need it after all. They're applied as a Layer Mask, so you can also paint areas out to reveal the original image beneath without the applied filters. What's not to like about that? Smart Filters deserve the attention. **TS**

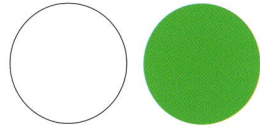

# DO eschew deletion in favor of masking

Returning to the theme of nondestructive editing, creating cutouts can also be given the same treatment through the use of Layer Masks. I prefer to keep as many previous workings of an image as is practical because I may, for whatever reason, need to return to an earlier version. On the flip side, I don't really like keeping dozens of files labeled version 1, version 2, etc., so a mask carries the advantage of not deleting any data from an image. You can always revert to the original if need be. In addition, tiny adjustments can easily be made to a Layer Mask with a small brush, and Photoshop's excellent Select and Mask tool provides options for detecting, adjusting, smoothing, and feathering any selection. The one thing you always have to remember if you create a cutout with a mask is to check the Save Transparency box when you save the image. You also have to save as either a TIFF or a PSD, since JPEGs can't contain multiple layers. **TS**

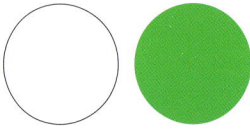

# DO create clipping paths in Photoshop— not in InDesign

It's easy to create a quick clipping path in InDesign using the built-in functionality, and it's equally easy to create a frame directly from the resulting clipping path. This is fine for a one-off job that needs to be turned around quickly or for something you're unlikely to come back to or edit. However, it's not really the best way to create a proper clipping path, as it only affects the picture box used in your layout. Additionally, it's unlikely that the InDesign clipping path will be quite so accurate as the one you first created in Photoshop as part of the original image. Photoshop provides so many more options for creating all kinds of paths and allows you to refine and feather edges in ways that InDesign doesn't. Remember, too, that if you use the image again elsewhere, your cutout work is already done. Never try to create a clipping path from a polygonal picture box drawn directly in InDesign. It's a really shoddy way of working, and your print supplier will hate you forever, so best not to, I reckon. **TS**

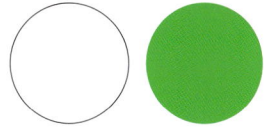

# DO always include a photography or illustration credit when it's due

Image © Tony Seddon 2011

A good editorial layout depends very highly on skillful use of space, good typography, and an eye for structure and navigation. However, if the piece is also illustrated, the images are more than likely the element that first elicits a response from the reader. The best layout in the world will never fully succeed if the images are only okay, and will fail miserably if the images are just plain bad. Given this, it's really only proper (and polite) to make sure that the person who created the great photographs or illustrations for a piece gets credited. It doesn't have to be in 16pt text underneath every image, but if someone wants to know who shot the images for the fashion article or who created the cool vintage-look illustrations for the music feature, they should be able to find that information. The majority of photographers and illustrators are freelancers and need to publicize themselves constantly with the work they do for others. It's important to try to provide that platform for anyone you work with. **TS**

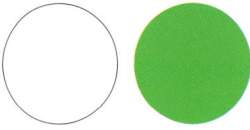

# DO allow a photographer or illustrator to input creatively whenever possible

Image courtesy of Nikon

I've been fortunate to work with some incredibly gifted professionals during my career. These individuals are specialists in their fields and are extremely creative, knowledgeable, and experienced. I've found it's always worthwhile to listen to what they have to say, whether it is a suggestion or an observation. Invariably, their comments will add value and improve your project. Of course, you don't have to take on every suggestion they make, but it pays to listen, since you never know what may come out of the discussion. There have been a number of occasions when I've been on a photo shoot, and the photographer and I have struggled to get an image of a product to work. Despite our efforts, the shot wouldn't come together, even though the initial idea was great! It's at times like these that open communication and a willingness to listen will benefit all parties and result in solutions that lead to successful work. **PD**

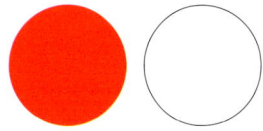

# DON'T edit an illustrator's original work without permission

As with a photographer's work, it is important to be respectful of an illustrator's output. I've worked with many; if you brief them correctly and thoroughly, the work they produce will fulfill all the requirements and often exceed expectations. However, there will be the odd occasion when changes need to be made to the illustration, whether it's adding or removing elements, altering colors, or adjusting the size. In these situations, go back to the illustrator and ask for the changes to be done. It is more professional, and the commissioning contract will often include a clause prohibiting modifications to their work without permission. The last thing you want to do is break the terms of a contract for what will likely appear to be a simple change. Explain the situation, and they will most likely accommodate any alteration requests. **PD**

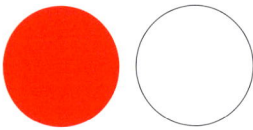

# DON'T do it yourself if you have a budget to commission

If there's a good argument supporting why you should personally create illustrations or shoot photographs for a layout you're working on, then fair enough. Perhaps you're genuinely the best choice for that particular task— no reason why you shouldn't be—but there's more to it than illustration and photography skills. Time is also a major factor, and the more you decide to do yourself, the more time you'll need. I have a confession to make—in the past I've made bad decisions about how much I personally took on for projects when I could easily have delegated work to others while staying within budget. These decisions are sometimes driven by a desire to increase your personal stamp on a project or simply that you really enjoy the tasks. Take a step back and answer the following question: Am I truly the best choice for the work? Do I want to be in the office until 2 a.m.? If the answer is "maybe" to the first question and "no" to the second, pick up the phone. **TS**

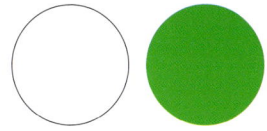

# DO learn to use an SLR camera in case you have no budget for photography

Part of my education required that I take a color and black-and-white photography class. In retrospect, it was probably one of the three most important classes I have ever taken. Not only did it teach me some visual framing techniques but also, more importantly, it made me comfortable with holding a decent camera in my hands and expecting decent results to come from using it. Little did I know that I would need those skills in tight-budget assignments, shooting band portraits for album packaging, menu photos for small restaurants, and anything else that was financially out of reach. I always use top people when I can, but that isn't always possible. Now, with everything digital, I shoot my portfolio as well, and not a day goes by when I don't shoot something for reference or for use as a base to manipulate for an image or a texture in an illustration. I love my camera, and it loves me back. **JF**

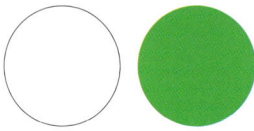

# DO accept that your phone is not necessarily your best camera

Today, we all walk around with a powerful camera packed with features in our back pockets. This wasn't always the case; not so long ago, a phone's built-in camera was not capable of capturing an image of publishable quality. The capabilities of camera phones today are quite astonishing, but is your phone really the best option at your disposal? It is typical for images taken with a phone to be viewed on the phone itself, on a tablet, or perhaps on an online space such as Instagram or Flickr. Images viewed at this size on-screen will often look great, but what about printed at a larger size? You may be surprised how they look, with lots of pixelation and color "fringing," when edges look indistinct and discolored. A phone will never replicate the quality of even a midrange SLR camera (not yet anyway). If you need an image for a project, think carefully about which type of device to use. If you are fortunate and have a budget for professional photography, you will likely be quite alarmed if the photographer turns up at the shoot with only an iPhone. **TS**

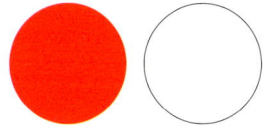

# DON'T use Photoshop filters to disguise a low-quality image

At school, a common, clichéd excuse for missing homework is "the dog ate it." In graphic design, a common excuse for using a Photoshop filter is that "the project needed it." Both excuses are obvious and pathetic. Nobody is fooled by the dog and homework story. Nobody believes the image was wonderful, but the designer still decided to poster-ize it. Bad images are bad images. Low-resolution photographs are low-resolution photographs. There is no hiding from low quality. This is an instance when you need to request a better image. Alternatively, you can photograph a new image. You may also set the low-quality photograph aside and create an original image in a differ-ent media. And if all else fails and the poor-quality image is the only option, use it large. Print it out and photograph it as a physical snapshot. Make the poor quality highly visible and a part of the solution. **SA**

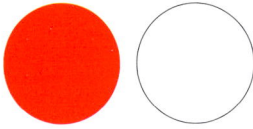

# DON'T try to repair a bad image by desaturating

authentic

artificial

Desaturating an image is criminal. It is not legally criminal, but it is wrong. One of the tenets of modernism is to let materials be what they are. This means wood should look like wood, metal should be metal, and stone should be actual stone. There is no faux-painted marble in a Mies van der Rohe house. Bad images are bad images. Attempting to disguise one by desaturating it has one effect. It makes a bad image look desaturated. Sepia-toned photographs from the late nineteenth century look good because they are actual sepia-toned photographs. Taking an image photographed in the twenty-first century and making it sepia results in an image that has clearly been manipulated. If the imagery is artificial and attempting to deceive me, how can I believe any of the text? The entire solution is compromised and has lost integrity. **SA**

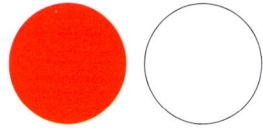

# DON'T scan a commercially printed image that has been screened

When a piece is commercially printed, the collection of CMYK dots that make up the base of the image forms the visual you see. The dots can also create a moiré pattern when scanned. Although a photo or a slide might be smooth and continuous, the printing process fragments this. It works perfectly on the original presentation, but if you try to drop that magazine cover into your layout straight from the scanner, be prepared for a bizarre visual pattern to emerge. The trick is to create a photograph of the image. Light that printed piece and be sure that it is squared up and as flat as possible, with no flares or shadows. Take several photos, select the best, sharpen it digitally, and then you have a perfect file to work from. The extra steps are more than worth it. **JF**

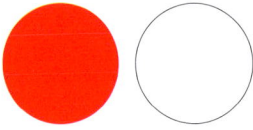

# DON'T enlarge images excessively in layout

When you're placing hi-res images in a layout, it's essential that you don't overscale them. Your hi-res files should have an image resolution of at least 300ppi, the correct resolution for screen rulings used in the litho printing process (see page 247). Increasing the scale of the image will reduce the image's effective resolution when printed. By way of an example, enlarging the image to 200 percent will reduce the resolution by half to 150ppi. If you need a higher resolution file to achieve the best layout, it's worth asking the client or the image source if one is available. If a replacement is not possible, then work with what you have. However, there is usually a small amount of leeway available. If the image is of a high quality, you should be able to increase the scale to around 105 percent, maybe slightly more if in a pinch. You will find that most of the detail, as long as it is not too faint, will be retained when printed. **PD**

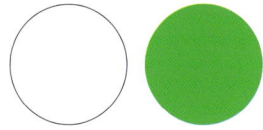

# DO enlarge images incrementally in Photoshop

Take a look at the Image Size dialogue in Photoshop, and you'll see that there are different options (with helpful labels) to select when resampling an image. Photoshop has to create or delete pixels using clever things called algorithms when you resize an image, and it recommends either the Preserve Details or Bicubic Smoother feature for enlargements. These settings will give surprisingly good results for enlargements of a fairly high percentage but is limited. Some say as much as 200 percent is acceptable, but I would say the practical limit is actually lower.

If you're ever forced to enlarge a digital image beyond 50 percent, it's a good idea to consider using the incremental enlargement technique. It's a simple process involving gradual increases in size of between 1 and 5 percent. Using small increments means Photoshop doesn't have to create as many new pixels for each enlargement, so color accuracy and clarity are maintained to a slightly higher degree. For the best results, always enlarge images in Photoshop first—never enlarge them in the layout. **TS**

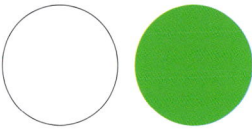

# DO choose images that support the text without repeating it

Many of us have attended a lecture where the speaker shows slides of his or her work. The worst speakers tell us what we see on the screen. A poster with a red headline and image of a hat appears on-screen. The speaker says, "Then I made the headline red and used a hat." If the audience is sight-impaired, this is acceptable. The best speakers show the work and expand on it with a story, context, or hidden meaning. Text used as captions or headlines should give the viewer additional information. They should not repeat the obvious content of the image. As an example, a portrait of a man might have a headline such as "Wesley Thornton, Hero of the French and Indian Wars." A headline that reads "Portrait of a Man with a Black Shirt" only tells us what we already know. Images support the text, and the text supports the image. Each adds strength and information to the other. **SA**

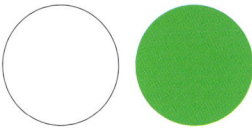

# DO keep icons simple and expect them to convey only a single idea

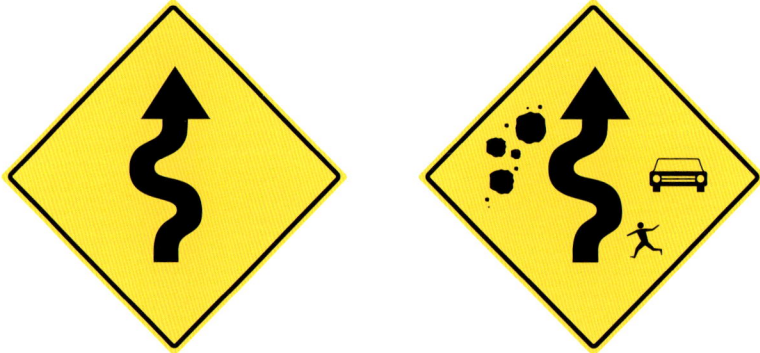

The *Concise Oxford English Dictionary* defines an icon as follows: a sign that has a characteristic in common with the thing it signifies. Successful icons communicate a singular and typically simple idea. A car on a winding road conveys the message, "winding road ahead." Poor icons attempt to communicate too many ideas. In addition to the car and winding road, boulders appear to be falling, and children are running across the road. This is no longer an icon. This is now a painting. Many clients will want to say multiple things at once. The designer filters this information and suggests a clarified and more legible solution. **SA**

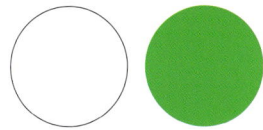

# DO know the difference between similar, example, symbolic, and arbitrary icons

We adore icons. As designers, we help place them all around us. It is important to know that icons fall into four specific categories and to understand the difference. *Similar* icons are usually very literal and use simple objects, actions, or concepts. Many road signs fall into this category. *Example* icons usually convey a complex action in a single image. They usually use an image that we readily associate with a larger range of activity than the image itself, like a plane for an airport. *Symbolic* icons are used when an action or concept can be conveyed with a recognizable shape and are more conceptual, like a padlock for security. *Arbitrary* icons use imagery that bears little immediate connection to the concept and must be learned to make the connection with the meaning. An obvious example is the icon for radioactive materials. **JF**

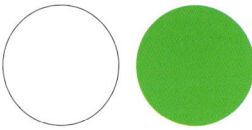

# DO create logos that identify rather than describe

Each of us has a name. That name identifies us to the rest of society. Our first name may indicate our gender and origin. Our surname may indicate our cultural background. When introduced to Comte de Meux et Chalon Robert de Vermandois, I might presume this person is a man from a French family. Queen Alfgifu of England will likely be female and British. Beyond these facts, however, I know nothing else. The names do not tell me if Comte de Vermandois is kind or mean, if Alfgifu is generous or thrifty. Good logos do the same job. Good logos identify an organization. They do not tell the viewer everything there is to know about the organization. The logo is the foundation of the visual system. It must exist in a variety of contexts. It should be able to fit in an advertisement selling a product as well as a letterhead expressing condolences. Logos that describe are rarely legible, memorable, or accurate. **SA**

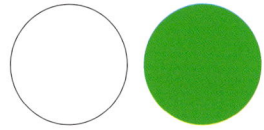

# DO create logos that work in print and online

Thirty years ago, designers made logos for print, and occasional wayfinding needs. The visual system required a full-color, one-color, and reversed version. Today, logos are applied to print, signage, broadcast, and online applications. The good news is that designers are now able to animate a logo, use a broader color palette, and think three-dimensionally. The bad news is that every logo needs to be legible on a printed piece and reduced to a small number of pixels online. A logo previously spent most of its life in a static two-dimensional world. Four-color logos were difficult and expensive to reproduce. A simple black-and-white logo with a two-color variation was preferred. Now, multicolored and three-dimensional logos are possible online. But, as in traditional print design, small hairline rules, delicate and tiny typography, and complex colors will not reproduce in print and will fall apart on-screen. **SA**

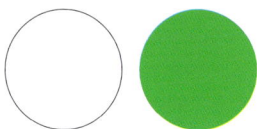

# DON'T ever use pixels when you can use vectors instead

Vector graphics have one massive advantage over pixel-based images—they're not resolution dependent, meaning you can enlarge them as much as you like with no loss in quality. Vectors are made using geometric primitives, which are points, lines, curves, and polygons, and mathematical equations calculate how everything intersects. It sounds complicated, but don't worry, the software does all the tricky stuff—all you have to do is draw the lines. They're not so good for the fine tonal gradations and subtle color shifts that bitmaps can handle, but for diagrams or logos, they're perfect, and you can avoid the troublesome EPS file format, since native Adobe Illustrator files can be imported directly into page layout programs. If it's possible to use vectors for an illustration or graphic (i.e., one that doesn't require the typical properties displayed by a photographic halftone), choose a vector approach every time, and you'll never have to worry about any of the issues associated with resolution and image size. **TS**

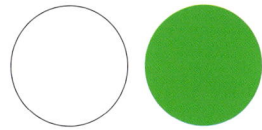

# DO avoid Live Trace—
# it makes you lazy

Some designers are remarkable at drawing. These people were the students the art teacher asked, "Did you trace that?" This was not intended as a compliment. This question points to laziness, deceit, and trickery. While Live Trace is an incredible tool technologically, it raises the question "Did you trace that?" It is the tool of the weak and lazy. And it will always look like Live Trace. Especially disturbing are examples of handwritten letterforms that have been subjected to the rigid abuse of Live Trace.

Recalling modernist tenets, allow something to be what it is. If handwritten text is necessary, write it, scan it, and use it. Using Live Trace will create forms that appear inauthentic. This deletes any spirit of spontaneity or life. If an object needs to be drawn as a vector form, the designer should use the pen tool and draw the form. This controls any odd curves and stray points. It is the difference between a sloppy, careless approach and a meticulous, energetic solution. **SA**

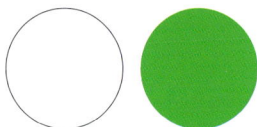

# DO know that things that are noticeably different tend to be remembered

*Dinner*

When we solve a problem, we are forced to engage with the issue at hand. Elements that are unexpected or out of place create a problem that we must resolve. Using an image of a baby with the word *Baby* below it asks us to do little. Using an image of a baby with the word *Dinner* below it creates an emotional response, and we are left to question its meaning. This example will be remembered. Speaking to the audience with a remedial tone is condescending. Good design should not function like reading flash cards with simple icons and simple words to describe them. Good design asks questions, poses a point of view, and encourages the viewer to complete the thought. **SA**

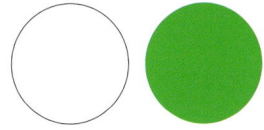

# DO understand the face-ism ratio

Quite simply, the face-ism ratio is the ratio of face to body in an image, which influences how the viewer perceives the person depicted. The more face one can see in an image, the higher the face-ism ratio. There is specific math involved, if you are so inclined to pursue it, but we are going to talk specifically about the significance. This equation is hotly debated in terms of how it is used in regard to gender. Historically, images of men tended to be dominated by the face, emphasizing their personality and intellectual qualities and focusing squarely on character. Images of women, however, tended to show significantly more body, often the entire figure, focusing on their physical attributes and often with a sensual undertone. This is consistent in almost every culture. The point, as a designer, is to pay attention to how much face is shown in a cropped image and to be careful about what that conveys to the viewer. **JF**

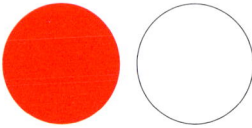

# DON'T allow any images above 105% to go to print

# 105%

On page 243 we discussed why you should ensure that images are 300ppi before you import them to a layout. In addition, be sure that the scale of the image does not increase beyond an acceptable amount once it has been placed. The rule is never bigger than 105 percent. As you increase the scale of the placed image, you are in effect decreasing its resolution and therefore its quality. For example, if I place a 300ppi image at 150 percent, the image has increased by 50 percent in size over the original—or the original takes up two-thirds the width of the scaled image. This now means that the resolution of the scaled image has decreased to two-thirds the original resolution, or 200ppi. This is a significant decrease, and, when printed, the image quality will likely show the degradation. If absolutely necessary and if the image is of very good quality, then 110 percent might be acceptable, but stick with 105 percent and you'll be safe. **PD**

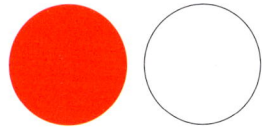

# DON'T print images that are less than 300ppi

# –300ppi

When sending a project to print, it's imperative to check that all images have a minimum 300ppi resolution. When publications and books are litho-printed, the printer will employ a screen ruling of 150–175 lpi to create the printing plates for the various colors. In order to calculate the required image resolution for the printer's screen ruling, simply double the lpi figure. Resolutions lower than 300ppi can sometimes be acceptable, depending on the project and paper stock, but it is generally accepted that 300ppi will work for most screen rulings, including finer screens of 200lpi, which would be considered for use on art books and monographs. The above, when coupled with the previous rule of not overscaling images when placing into layout, will help to ensure that everything prints well. A quick and easy way to check your images is to use Adobe Bridge to collate and identify any files with stray resolutions. **PD**

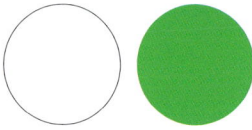

# DO consider converting all images to CMYK before sending to the printer

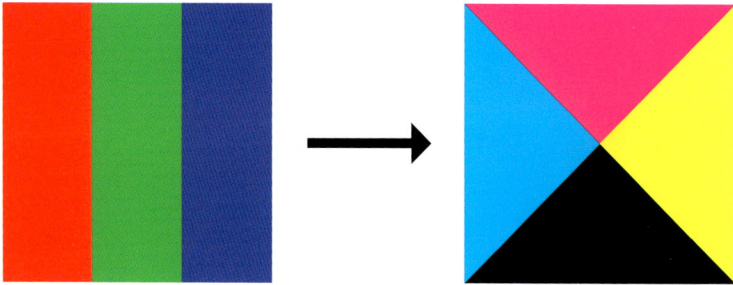

As has been discussed elsewhere in this book, the color printing process uses four colors, cyan, magenta, yellow, and black (CMYK), to reproduce color images and graphics. Many of the image files supplied to you, such as digital photographs, will have been created in red, green, and blue (RGB) mode, which is incompatible with the printing process (RGB-formatted images are used for screen-based graphics, such as on websites). Before you embark on converting them all, it is a good idea to talk to your printer. Not only is it possible to convert the images to CMYK, but also you will be able to add the correct CMYK profile to the images, which will be a great help to the printer, particularly if there are a lot of images. Simply find out which CMYK profile the printer intends to use and then carry out the conversion in Photoshop, killing two birds with one stone. If there are a large number of images, you can run a batch of them through an automated action, saving you a lot of work and affording you the time to go and have a cup of coffee. **PD**

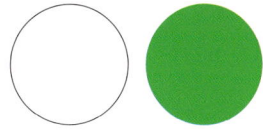

# DO use a mixed RGB and CMYK image workflow

There's a rumor kicking around that all images must be converted to CMYK (see page 284) before they're sent for reproduction. This isn't a bad idea—but it's also fine to implement a mixed RGB and CMYK workflow as long as you use color profiles. Color profiles (for example, Adobe RGB 1998 or FOGRA39) contain data that describes how any one device, which could be a screen or a printer, will deal with the color information contained in an image. They use LAB, a device-independent color model (see page 180), to closely preserve colors that move from one color space to another. As most of us now send a majority of our artwork to printers as PDFs, we can set Color Conversion to Convert to Destination (Preserve Numbers) when we export a PDF, making sure that any RGB images in a layout convert automatically to CMYK while maintaining color consistency with the RGB original. This cuts out the need to convert all your images beforehand and makes it possible to keep RGB originals that are better suited to color correcting and manipulation in Photoshop. **TS**

# Production & Print

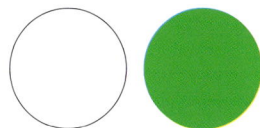

# DO include at least 3mm of bleed on all artwork

If you elect to have full-page images that run to the edges of a page, they are referred to as "bleeding" off the page. When the page is trimmed, you must ensure that additional image content is provided past the page edge to avoid the potential for any white edges showing, due to the inevitable slight variations that occur during trimming. This extra element of the artwork is called the bleed and should appear only on the trimmed edges of the book—

it isn't necessary at the spine. I have been asked on occasion by a printer to provide 5mm bleed, but the minimum is 3mm, allowing for small degrees of movement with the cutters as the collated sections are passed through the trimming machine. When you place your image and you're viewing it on-screen, remember that what you are seeing includes the bleed, so make sure that no important element of the picture is too close to the trimmed edge. **PD**

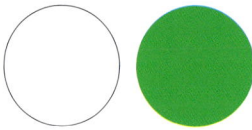

# DO always insist on obtaining a hard proof, even for 1C print projects

**Proof has been checked and is:**
☒ OKAY AS IS
☐ CORRECT AND SHOW NEW PROOF

**Folding is correct as shown on proof:**
☒ YES   ☐ NO

**Check**

**REMARKS:**

I know you think it is silly. A waste of time, or even worse, a waste of money— but when you stop and think about it, even the smallest job has had time and money invested into and worth the cost of ensuring that it prints correctly. How many times has someone been told that a low-resolution PDF proof will be fine in the final printing, only to see one little photo or logo at 72dpi included? Catalogs and shopping flyers are full of these mistakes. Even the very best printers sometimes have technology foil their efforts, or they rush a PDF proof out, only to have everyone be sorry in the end. It is always the right choice to review even the simplest job properly. Always. **JF**

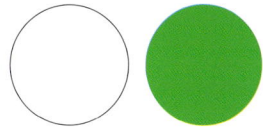

# DO run color proofs on the correct paper stock

Every designer has faced a situation when a client insists that the color of the printed piece is wrong. The client is convinced they saw a proof that was perfect, but what they have been given is different. There are several reasons why this could occur: First, clients remember what they want to remember. Save the proof and show it to them. Second, the printer made an error. If possible, go on press for each job to verify the correct color. And third, the color proofs were on the wrong paper stock. The client saw proofs on a white-coated stock, and the job printed on an uncoated cream stock. The solution is simple: always show the client proofs on the correct stock. Explain the differences between digital proofs and offset printing. They are entirely different technologies and will never match exactly. If the printer provides an ink drawdown, make sure the ink is printed on the exact paper to be used when printing. **SA**

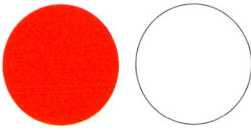

# DON'T use laser printers to produce color proofs

As described earlier, in much the same way you wouldn't specify a color for print based on its on-screen appearance, the use of color lasers should not be relied on at all to provide an accurate color representation. I've found that color lasers are great for checking that all the elements are in place. I am always happy if a printer supplies them to me for signing off on content and editorial changes, but they should never be used to check color. The first reason for this is that the process is entirely different from litho printing and is much cruder. Litho is an ink-based process using a combination and arrangement of ink dots that, when blended, creates a high-quality output. Lasers are toner based and overlay the colors in a more "instant" and opaque way, resulting in a lack of refinement and accuracy in color and images. The second problem with lasers is the machine itself. It is in constant need of calibration, and I have found that factors such as temperature and toner levels greatly affect the color output. **PD**

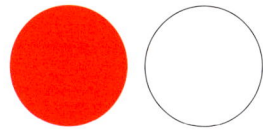

# DON'T accept a PDF unless time saving is more important than quality

Business is about balancing compromises. Design is about trying to keep those compromises from dampening the integrity of our projects. It is with great pain, since we have extolled the necessity of seeing a hard proof on even the simplest business card, that we offer one up to the compromise gods. We make most of our decisions in regard to how wonderful a final project could be but based on the available time. Will we have time to do things the right way, to truly give them thought and exploration? Even when the answer is yes, we can have our legs cut out from under us by an accelerated production schedule. Few things in this day and age are not weighed down by the expectation that it be delivered yesterday. We look compromise hard in the eye, and we weigh time versus quality. We fight for quality, but we know that a project that delivers after an event has occurred is of no use to anyone. **JF**

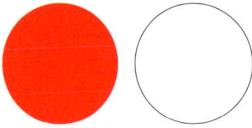

# DON'T ever assume the printer will understand exactly what you require

✓ **Quantity**

✓ **Proofs**

✓ **Due Date**

✓ **Delivery**

✓ **Press Checks**

✓ **Samples**

There are many extraordinary printers. They are committed to meeting deadlines and providing honest and quick answers, and are immaculate in their craft. Then there are printers who might as well be rhesus monkeys. Some people may walk through life trusting others, believing that most others have the best intentions and want to do good. This is a great, albeit naive, attitude in day-to-day life. To believe this to be the case with all printers is foolish.

Designers may be good at offering the client clear design solutions but can be less than clear with printers. Making any assumption with the printer is risky. Itemize every aspect of the project: quantity, proofs, schedule, delivery, press checks, and processes. Do not assume anything, ever. In the end, the printer will appreciate the clear direction, and there will be fewer surprises. **SA**

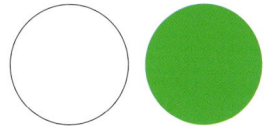

# DO get your printer involved as early as possible in your project

You seem like a pretty smart cookie. Are you able to keep up on every innovation in design and advertising, from software to philosophical trends? Of course you can't. No one can fully keep abreast of one's own vocation, much less another field altogether, no matter how related it might seem on the surface. Printing and design, though they often hold hands, are wildly different industries. Recognizing that you should know enough to have an intelligent conversation with your printer but could never fully understand the ins and outs of the business is a good start. The sooner you engage your printer in your project, the quicker they can enhance it, adding special techniques and innovations in the industry. Better yet, the printer can update you about cost savings while still delivering an amazing product, or let you know of delays or complications in specifying certain materials. It makes all the difference. **JF**

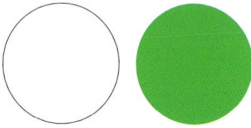

# DO confirm that all materials from the client fit specifications immediately upon receipt

Is there anything more frustrating than being in the middle of cooking a huge meal, only to find that your spouse picked up regular sugar rather than the brown sugar specified on the shopping list? Building an extension on your home and putting the new window into the frame, only to find that it is 90 percent of the necessary size? There actually is something more frustrating—hiring a catering company to cook that meal or a contractor to complete your extension, only to be told that the job can't be done with the materials on hand, even though they confirmed the receipt of the list of materials days, weeks, even months beforehand. This is the way your client feels when you ask for a bit more copy or an image in a higher resolution right before the deadline of a project. Not only have you announced that you didn't start on the job until the last minute, but you have also come across as disorganized and far from detail-oriented, a vital trait in this business. **JF**

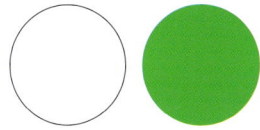

# DO build contingency
# into all printing schedules

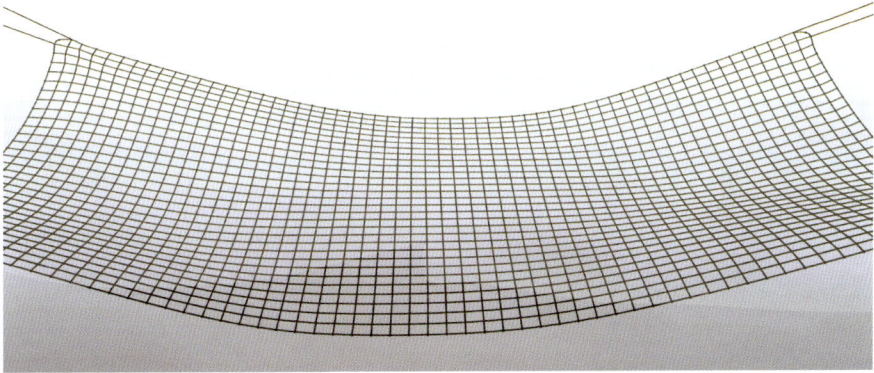

In printing, things happen that can delay a project. A client may have last-minute alterations. The press may break. The ink color might be flawed. The paper shipment may be delayed, or incorrect. Printing is a physical process that involves people, trucks, machines, ink, and paper. It is not instantaneous like printing on a desktop digital printer. There are too many components and people involved in any job for it to be completely issue-free. The proj-ect might be delayed because the client decided to correct a word in a paragraph after the job began

printing. This means that the job had to be pulled off the press, new files created, the files proofed and approved, additional paper ordered, new printing plates created (for offset lithography print runs), and then rescheduled on press. This one small change could delay a job by twenty-four hours or more. Unfor-tunately, the client will not recall making the change; they will only remember that the designer didn't deliver on time. Add time into the printing schedule to create a buffer for the unexpected. **SA**

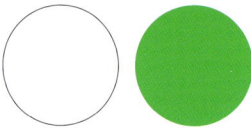

# DO communicate scheduling issues to your printer as soon as they occur

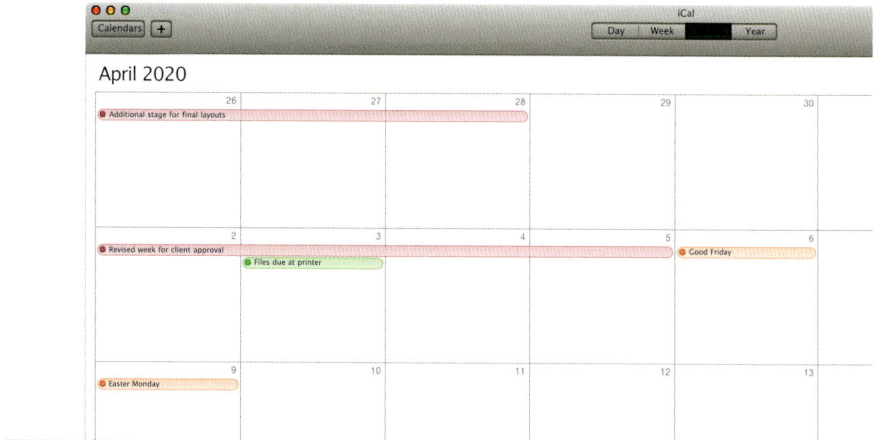

As much as we love our work creating cool and sexy designs, a big part of our role (and I emphasize BIG here) is managing the production process. One of *the* most important parts of this is liaison and communication with the printer. It's imperative that if the schedule shifts, the information is passed on to the printer immediately, to prevent any disastrous impacts on the production schedule. A client may ask if a delivery schedule can be brought forward or pushed back slightly—never say yes until you have checked with the printer. Don't make a commitment that cannot be kept, breaching the trust of the client and putting yourself in a very difficult position. Keep open and honest communication going at all times, and, if things change, get on the phone immediately, ask the right questions, and update the client responsibly. **PD**

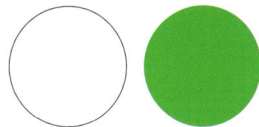

# DO keep an off-site archive of all completed projects

When disaster strikes, you never know what will happen to your work space or assets, so make sure you have an off-site archive of your work. If your studio gets flooded, say au revoir to any computers, and if your studio archives get damaged, then you are in serious trouble! The same goes for a fire. If a thief should walk away with your equipment, you won't have an opportunity to recover any data. Providing yourself with an off-site archive guarantees that you will recover most, if not all, of your lost data.

Every piece of work you create is an asset as well as a potential asset: a fair share of design work can return in the form of updated editions of brochures or newsletters. Many years ago, I learned the hard way when my studio was burgled and all of our Apple computers stolen. Fortunately, we had just backed up our server and work-stations, but it was a lesson I'll never forget! Data is your livelihood; protect it at all costs. **PD**

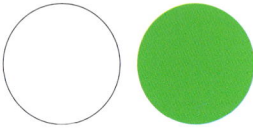

# DO back up and archive constantly

If you spent six months building a perfect scale model of the Titanic, you would make sure it was put in a solid case to protect it and hope that it will last longer than the original ship. You should feel the same about the design work that you spend weeks or months creating for your clients. If you leave this material lying around on your computer desktop without creating a proper backup on a constant basis (Apple's Time Machine application, for example, is excellent), you'll have no option but to start from scratch if the files are lost or damaged—not good. Invest in good-quality external hard drives or a dedicated server for in-house backups and archived material, or, better still, maintain an off-site backup using additional large-capacity hard drives or an online cloud-based solution. **TS**

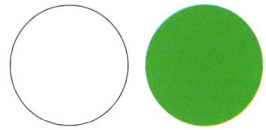

# DO obtain a printer's template before beginning a packaging design assignment

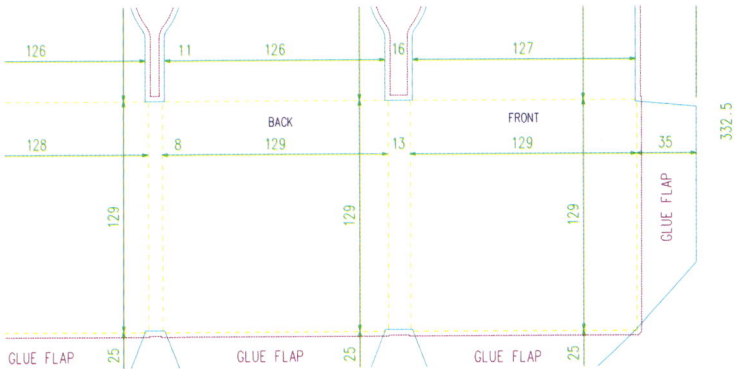

Every manufacturer has its own guidelines to consider. No matter how many music-packaging projects you have completed, every vendor will have requirements that differ slightly, such as variation in size or where the folds and scores occur. It may not be noticeable in the marketplace, but it could mean a vastly different placement of design elements: a formerly left panel now becomes an upside-down top panel, with bleeds and glue panels organized in radically different positions. You can't guarantee that every element of your design will line up or correspond with the extra bits and pieces that get added to a pack during production. I could go on for days, the point being: save yourself the huge nightmare of reconfiguring your designs to wedge onto a template; get the full template from the printer before beginning design, so you can accurately predict how it'll end up. Then, you can embrace it and design something special around its little quirks. **JF**

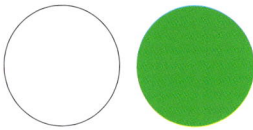

# DO assemble a full-scale mock-up of any packaging / dimensional project

Building a house on your computer screen is a far remove from using a shovel and moving earth. On a smaller scale, the same is true about designing anything dimensional, especially packaging. What looks like it might work structurally may not bend as planned, lock together, or even stand up straight. Even after you have made adjustments and tested out the very core structure, you may discover even more nuanced aspects of designing in three dimensions. How does a small piece of type read now that you know it will sit back a little on the shelf? Should the name of the product bend around to the point that you can't see all of the letters unless standing in a specific spot? How does the design work at the folds and seams? Where does the legal copy sit? After all that, does it fit in the shipping containers and the commercial display cases and shelves? Test, test, test. **JF**

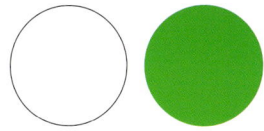

# DO request a paper dummy from your printer

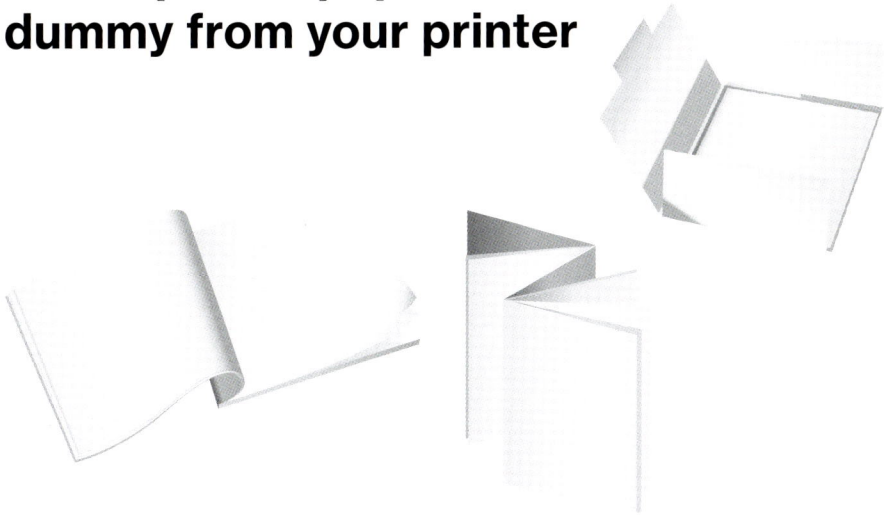

I love paper samples, and it's always great thumbing through them and deciding which materials are appropriate and how they can be employed in a project. It is always worthwhile to get a dummy, whether for a brochure or a book, to better judge how production factors may affect the design. I also think it is important to show dummies to clients so that they know what to expect with the final product. If they have something else in mind or would prefer a different material for the cover or interior pages—it is much better to know this at an early stage. Otherwise, you risk receiving negative comments ("Oh…I think the text pages are too light") after the final product has been delivered. **PD**

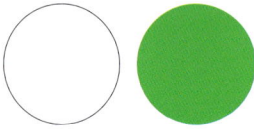

# DO learn about dot gain for different paper stocks

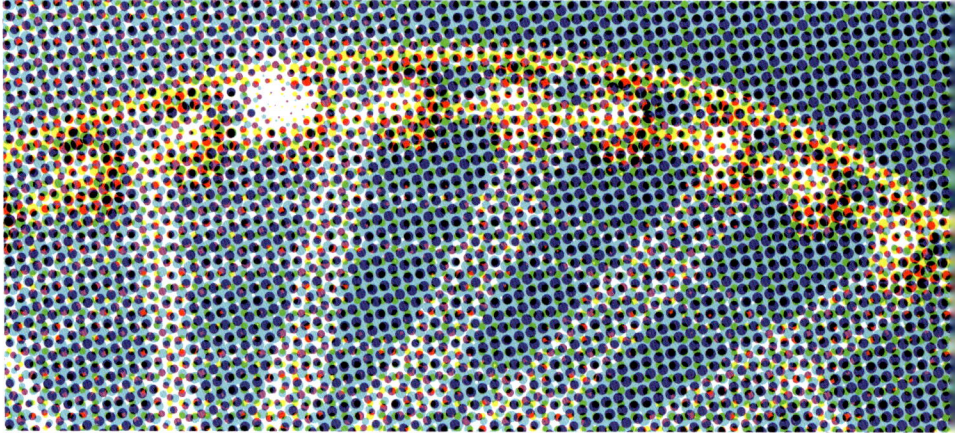

As far as a digital image file is concerned, dot gain doesn't exist. Every dot making up a digital halftone image will stay exactly the same size no matter how many times you duplicate it. However, when you physically transfer the image to paper, it's a different story—they get bigger, and the image or color tint darkens. There are various reasons why dot gain will almost always occur regardless of the paper stock used, but the main culprit is ink absorption during the drying process. Printing on coated stock will diminish the effect caused by dot gain because it is less absorbent than uncoated paper and the ink spreads less. This doesn't mean that high-quality print should always be paired with coated stock, as dot gain can be offset using press profiles matched to your printer's machines. Screen ruling plays an important role in the process: coated stock can cope with values from 150lpi to as much as 300lpi; standard matt-art paper, 150–175lpi; and lightly textured stock, 120–135lpi. For newsprint, a screen ruling as low as 85lpi is about right. **TS**

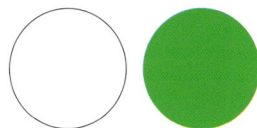

# DO select printers who already know what dot gain means

When you work with low-price-point printers, one of the most common issues is that your job returns darker than expected, especially when you specify uncoated paper. This is a sure sign that your printer has either not accounted for or doesn't understand dot gain. When this happens across all four plates in process printing, it can account for as much as a 20–30 percent shift in how dark the final color can be. As we learned on page 302, dot gain can shift between paper stocks, and vendors take great care to provide information to help printers, by working with their prepress departments, to make sure that the sheets perform the best they can. This information needs to be factored into how the individual presses run and sometimes how the operators run them. Working with a printer who understands dot gain and how to control it is absolutely essential in getting optimum results. Never assume that a printer will take the necessary care this issue demands. **JF**

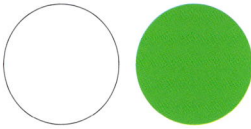

# DO investigate whether to overprint or knock out additional spot colors and metallics

Adding a fifth color can be a defining point in a project. Whether it is a spot color to keep color consistent to corporate branding or a shiny metallic or fluorescent to provide maximum bang for the visual buck, once you have made that move, the most important decision is whether to overprint the additional color or to knock it out and trap it. Be sure to talk to your printer and get their advice, factoring in the sheet you are printing on as well as the desired results. Distinct colors may involve different considerations. Metallic silver ink can have an issue with trapping against dark colors and images; overprinting can require laying on the ink thicker to hold opacity, compromising small or fine type, whereas knocking out can allow for tight control in those areas. Big impact. Important decisions. **JF**

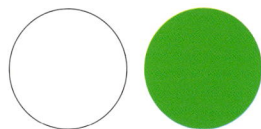

# DO run advance test proofs when utilizing unusual printing techniques

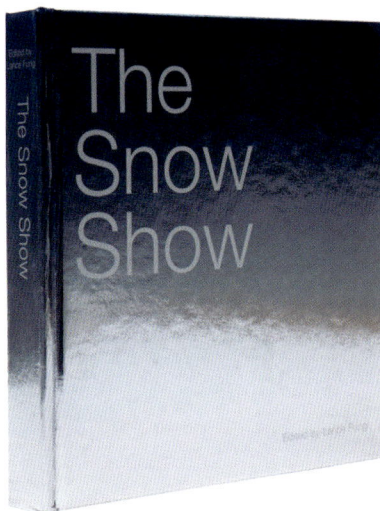

I always like to err on the side of caution if the design incorporates any unusual printing techniques or methods that require a lot of advance preparation to ensure correct printing. A process that I always test proof in advance is foil blocking (or any other type of blocking for that matter), to confirm that the block has been correctly made and that there are no faults in the etching. In addition, you see the actual color of the foil and have an opportunity to make changes if needed. The same goes for color palettes. Requesting test proofs is not unusual during the printing process, and I try to get them done when possible. I test the colors and their tints, with a number of type treatments employing the colors to see how they work when applied to typographic elements. It's a far safer way to do it, and the client has a chance to comment well in advance of the project going to press. **PD**

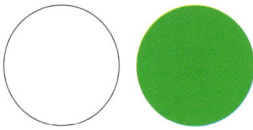

# DO consult a publication's specifications prior to designing an advertisement

Magazines, newspapers, and publications that use advertising have strict policies regarding the artwork for ads. They may seem sensible, arbitrary, or ludicrous, but it's their magazine, their art department, and their prerogative. Before designing an advertisement, request an artwork specification sheet and the exact ad order placed from the publication. Regardless of who purchased the ad space, the designer must verify the size and requirements.

Unfortunately, people sometimes make mistakes. They think they purchased a full-page ad, but actually ordered a half-page version. The artwork specifications will clearly state trim size, bleed, ink requirements, screen size, and any other pertinent issues to the production of the magazine. Turning over an ad that is RGB, the improper size, and the incorrect resolution will likely be troublesome and is wrong. **SA**

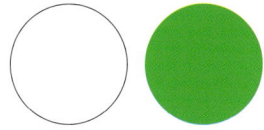

# DO ensure that all text in black is set to overprint background colors

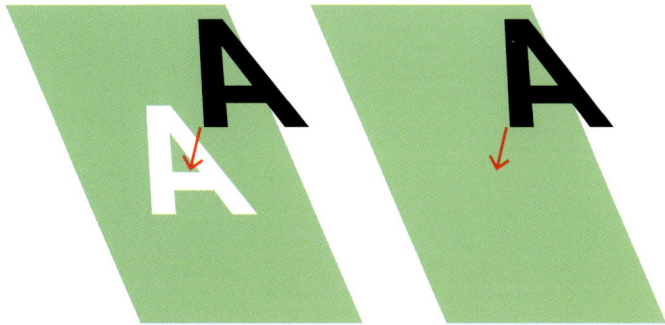

When I am designing books that are to be coeditioned (translated into foreign-language editions), the English text is set on an additional black text layer that overprints on top of the other elements on the page. That way, the black text plate can simply be removed, and a foreign-language text can be overprinted in its place. Even if your work isn't going to be translated, it is still important that all black text sitting on a colored background be set to overprint. If you don't overprint the black text, it will "knock out" of the background (i.e., the color will show the paper behind the characters). This can cause registration issues, especially if the text elements are small, such as the folios, captions, and even some of the body text. To make the text overprint in InDesign, select from the palette menu: Window > Output > Attributes. Highlight the text and check Overprint Fill. You can preview the effect via View > Overprint Preview. Of course, this treatment works with any color, so have fun experimenting. **PD**

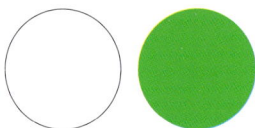

# DO always include crop and registration marks with artwork for press

In order for a printer to trim the page correctly and match up the printing plates so they are true, the inclusion of crop and registration marks is essential. With most current desktop publishing software, the inclusion and output of these marks are easy—a few clicks of a button at the print-output stage, and they will be incorporated. Usually, a printer will do this if you are supplying the source files and related hi-res images. However, many printers now require you to supply artwork as repro-ready PDF files. When creating PDFs, it's important that you remember to incorporate crop and registration marks. Items that are to be die-cut, such as a folder, not only need crop marks and registration marks but also need a "cutter guide" (an outline of the element to be cut out) for the printer to follow. **PD**

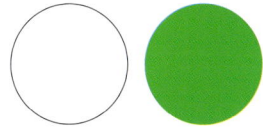

# DO own
# a copy of,
# or subscribe
# online to,
# a style manual

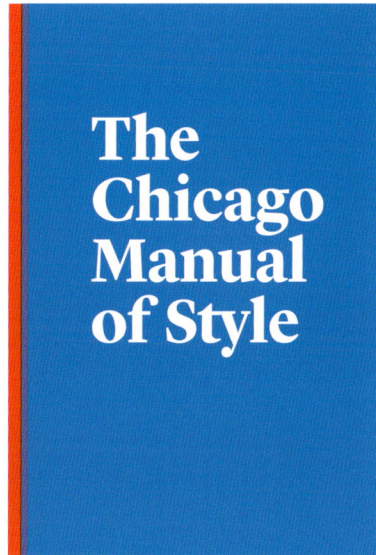

**The Chicago Manual of Style**

What if there was a book on your shelf or a website you could go to that could answer nearly every single question you could ever have about correct usage? Something to cut short all those emails, texts, and forum postings, asking friends, relatives, coworkers, and strangers what a certain proofreader mark means or when to use a certain form of punctuation. Surely, you would own such a book or get access to such a site. If only someone would put such a thing together and update it regularly to keep pace with the evolution of language and grammar. A guide for editors and writers alike, and those of us who deal with copy every day. Wait a minute. You say such a thing already exists? It's called *The Chicago Manual of Style*. **JF**

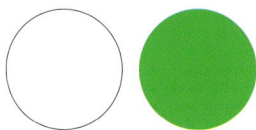

# DO set up folios
# on master pages

**E**    PRODUCTION AND PRINT

Earlier we talked about the benefits of employing master pages in long documents, particularly with respect to how they can save time and guarantee consistency for common and repeated items on the page. Another key feature of master pages is the ability to set up automatic folios. The folios can be styled how you wish them to be, with font, size, and color all adjustable. The insertion of a special character (in InDesign this is referred to as Current Page Number under Markers) then allows for the page folios to be automatically numbered. These folios can still be adjusted on the page or deleted by unlinking them from the master, but adjustments made on the master pages will still affect them. If you need to move pages around, fear not—by moving spreads around and repositioning them, the folios will renumber instantly, giving you one less thing to worry about or attend to! **PD**

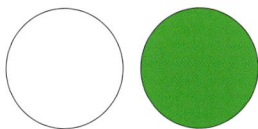

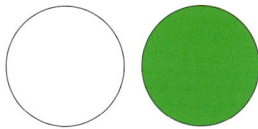

## DO press check every project possible, even business cards

Once, while visiting a massive mansion, I was startled by a bathroom sink with faucet handles installed backward, making it awkward to reach to turn them on and off. I was certain that, despite the gorgeous and extravagant structure all around it, I could never live with a sink tormenting me so. It reminded me that no part of a job is too small for proper attention to detail, and an oversight can ruin everything around it. Press inspecting a job allows for the designer to make adjustments, as well as ensure that all the elements are in place, every *t* crossed. At a minimum, you can make certain that the job prints as expected. At best, you can improve the final product, with a color popping or matching to another piece, and make it all that it can be. **JF**

## DO match paper stock to the appropriate printing technique

Ideally, you should be able to choose from a wide range of paper stocks when planning the print side of a project, but sometimes the printing process will narrow down your choices for you. For example, sheet-fed offset lithography requires paper with good surface strength, which provides good dimensional stability. Paper stock that stretches during full-color printing is a recipe for disaster, as misregistration will occur between each color as it is laid down. Other factors to take into account are smoothness, absorbency, opacity, and compressibility. Standard stock sizes for sheet-fed processes are also important; will they fit your supplier's press, and how much will be wasted during trimming? The paper is, more often than not, the most expensive component of any print project, so do your research early and always choose your paper stock with care. **TS**

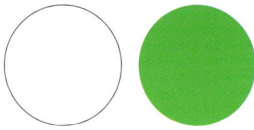

# DO be aware of paper show-through

A hotshot architect was recently commissioned to design a Japanese-style apartment for a client and decided to incorporate some cool-looking screens to divide up the guest bedrooms. During a visit to the manufacturer's factory, the architect was advised to take a look at them outside in daylight, but he arrogantly refused to do so, thinking that his judgment is always the best, no matter what. The screens were installed in the light and airy guest rooms at considerable expense, but the next site visit did not go well. "These are no good," reported the client. "I can see straight through this screen into the next room." Paper show-through works in much the same manner. Exposure to light affects the opacity, and thin sheets, in particular, can allow for the image or text on the subsequent spread to "show through" to the one you are viewing. **JF**

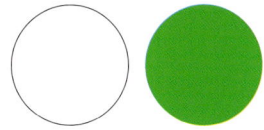

# DO ask your printer for the panel sizes of a folded leaflet

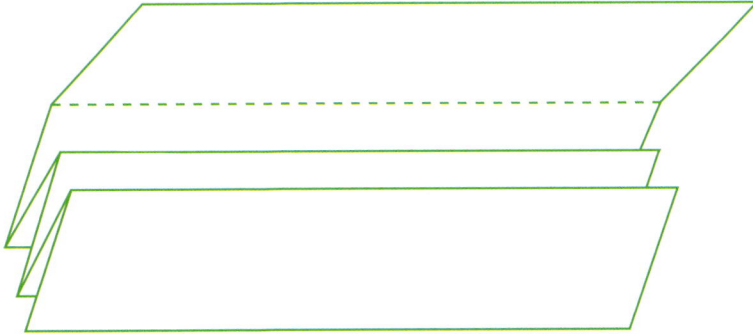

There are dozens of different ways to fold leaflets and brochures, the only restriction being the sheet sizes of paper stock and the available folding machinery your printer can access. Folding sequences become more complicated as the number of panels increases, which may seem obvious, but it's not just because of the panel count. The panels that fold in on themselves need to be sized differently to allow a leaflet to lie flat when completely folded. Take, for example, the wrapped accordion fold, a standard accordion bookended by integrated front and back covers that are the full width of the folded leaflet, let's say 4 inches. The accordion panels folding within the two covers need to be slightly narrower, allowing them to fold inward comfortably within the cover dimensions. The recommended reduction in width varies between sources, but something in the region of .083 inches should do the trick. The weight of the paper stock also has a bearing on the amount of adjustment. The bottom line is, always request a template from your printer. **TS**

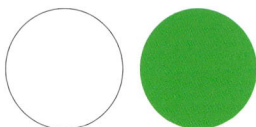

# DO work in halftones and vectors when silk screening

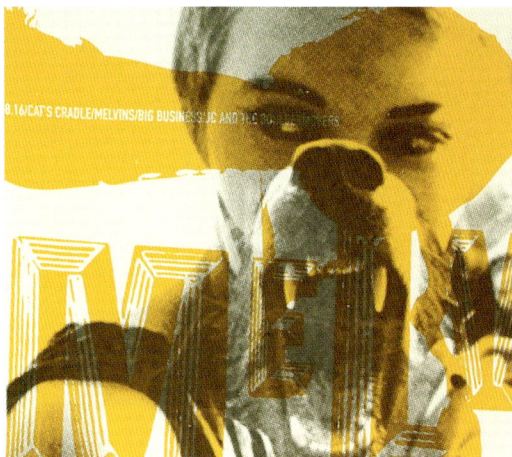

For ages, silk screening was thought of as one of the roughest forms of printing. As new generations of designers have come to embrace those very qualities, along with the attractive economics when making short-run projects—from posters and T-shirts to most anything you can imagine pressing up against a screen and dragging ink along it—it has emerged as a powerful niche. Currently, it is so popular that I am working on something being produced via screen print every day. I love the thick ink and the way no two pieces are quite the same. It is the polar opposite of process commercial printing. But I have to be mindful that it also differs at the production end. The way screens are created/burned requires that all art be either vector- or dot-based and exist at 100 percent of the color. The open areas of the screen are the portions of the screen that lets the ink through, and shades are not an option. It requires a complete rethinking of how you approach design and production. **JF**

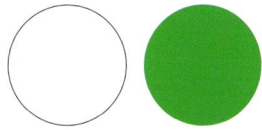

# DO always have up-to-date paper swatch books

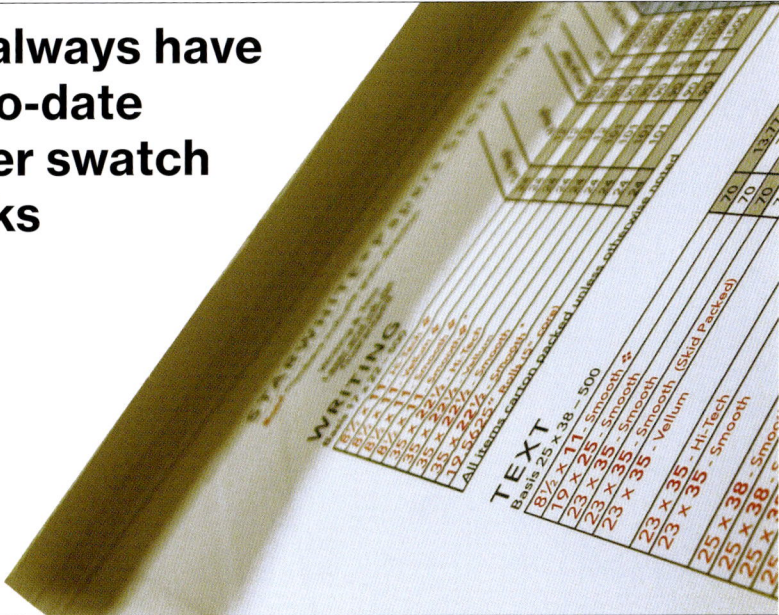

Paper companies have long used the swatch book to show off the capabilities of their sheets, combining current design trends with flashy techniques, in the hope that you will choose their line and put it into use on a stunning final product. Most studios, firms, or in-house departments will eventually have a visit from a printer, whose representative will make sure that you have all of the current swatch books. Making sure that swatch references are up to date is vitally important. One day in the future, you may go to spec a sheet and find that a swatch doesn't exist any longer, or that that finish is gone, or the weight of paper is no longer available. Paper companies are all too happy to send these to you. Take advantage. **JF**

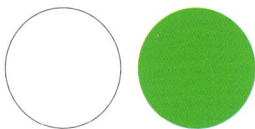

# DO look beyond a printer's in-house paper stock for a wider choice

There are many paper and materials manufacturers out there, and it's beneficial for the graphic designer to be aware of the range of print companies and products available. There are times when a concept may be driven by, or nearly always enhanced by, the materials the designer chooses; often, with an unusual print process thrown into the mix, a really successful and powerful end result can emerge. Familiarizing yourself with what's available is fun, and all paper makers have swatch books and printed examples available to send out. They usually offer a samples service to help you make decisions on specifications or for use on mockups and presentations. Don't limit yourself to companies that exist in your home country. There are truly fabulous papers available from around the world, and most can usually be shipped in bulk to your printer. **PD**

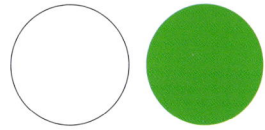

# DO familiarize yourself with international paper sizes

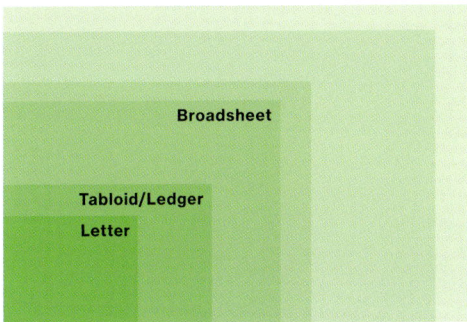

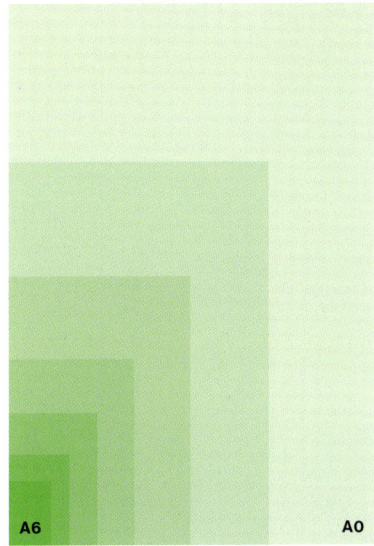

**Broadsheet**

**Tabloid/Ledger**

**Letter**

**A6**

**A0**

To enable designers, clients, and printers to discuss matters of specification and pricing on a level playing field, it is advantageous to establish an understanding of available paper sizes. Standard US and European paper sizes do differ, so it's worth getting an overview of how the respective systems work. Paper sizes in the United States are based on multiples of 8.5 × 11 inches (or Letter), but some sheets will be a little larger to allow for images that bleed and to allow for grip when on press. In Europe, the system most widely employed is ISO 216 and is based around the A formats. The A sizes are ordered downward in size, being approximately half the area of the next size in the range, with A0 at $1\,m^2$ and A6 at just $155.4cm^2$. In addition, the C series provides formats for envelopes and postcards, where a C4 envelope is slightly larger than an A4 sheet. Finally, the RA and SRA ranges provide untrimmed format options for commercial printers that are slightly larger than the A sizes and allow for grip when on press. **PD**

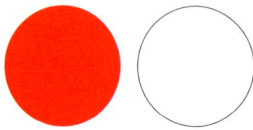

# DON'T specify cheap paper stock

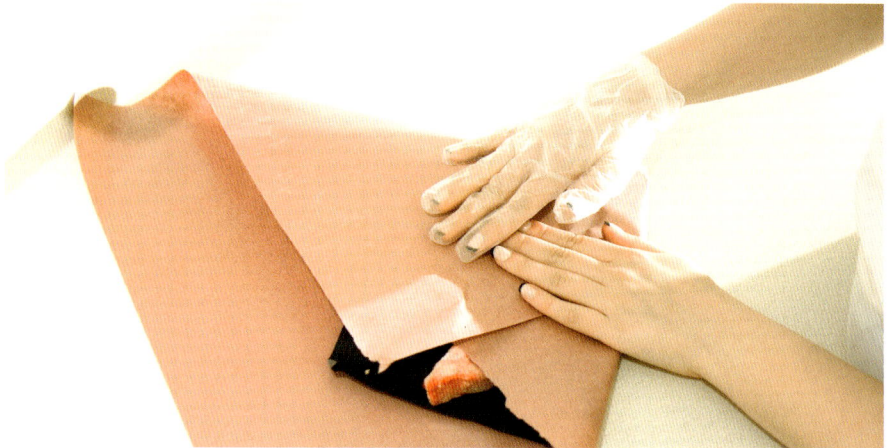

It is said that salt is salt. But if you are a chef, you will explain that salt from the supermarket is different from refined salt from New Zealand. Paper is similar. The layperson will say, "Paper is paper. Isn't it all the same?" Designers, like a gourmet chef, know the difference. Paper stocks vary in tone and surface. They range from sheets made of 100 percent postconsumer waste to very little recycled material. Cheap paper will be, yes, less expensive, but the resulting product will never match a higher-quality paper. A cheap paper will not accept ink as well and may cause scoring and folding issues. There will also be deviations in brightness and whiteness from one sheet to another. Unless the job has an incredibly small budget or paper costs are a large fraction of the budget, never scrimp on paper. The end product may be slightly more expensive but will be infinitely more successful, and the client will be pleased. Alternatively, the client might save some money, hate the final product, and fire the designer. **SA**

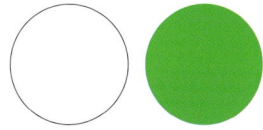

# DO know where the glue sections are and make sure that they are ink-free

Do you know what glue likes to stick to? Paper. Do you know what glue doesn't like to stick to? Ink. Simple enough, right? However, the glue area on most pieces and products falls inside a fold, which, at the same time, requires that there be bleeds so that the package sports a finished look rather than have paper stock awkwardly peeking out at the seams. Folded mail items need to be closed and glued, possibly with complicated folds, but need to be easy to open for the end user. That means that the areas where glue will go down during production, as well as anywhere the user may place it, need to be well thought out and marked early on. Once that happens, be sure to take extra care to keep them clear. **JF**

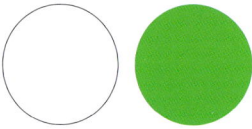

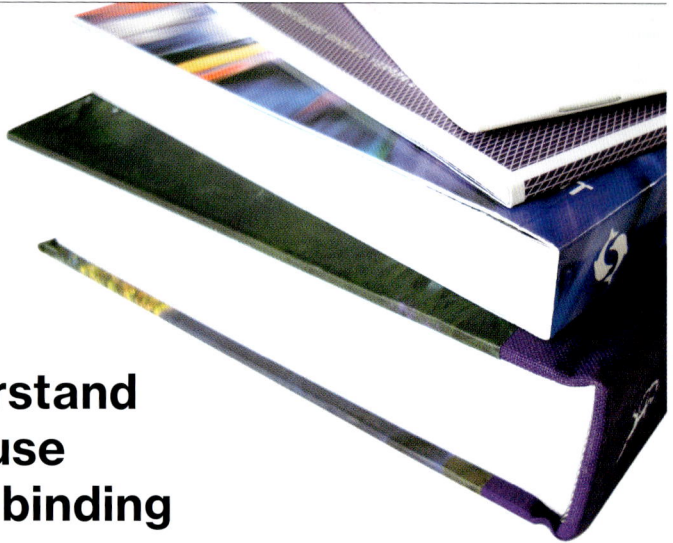

# DO understand when to use different binding techniques

There are a number of different commercial binding techniques that offer varying aesthetic qualities and practical applications. Which technique is best for your project depends on specifications such as page extent and format. For example, a 6 × 9 inch forty-page concert program can be either wire stitching or perfect bound (glued pages into the cover). The application of case binding, which is used for hardcover books that have pages that are collated in sections and held in place by use of an endpaper, would be wholly inappropriate for a brochure. First, you don't have enough pages for the cover to physically work (the thickness of the pages when collated is too thin to allow the binding to be "built"). Second, even if it were possible, the cost would be prohibitive; case binding is a much more expensive process. Consider not only the suitability of the binding to the project but also the cost implications. **PD**

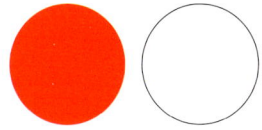

# DON'T saddle stitch an extent more than ninety-six pages

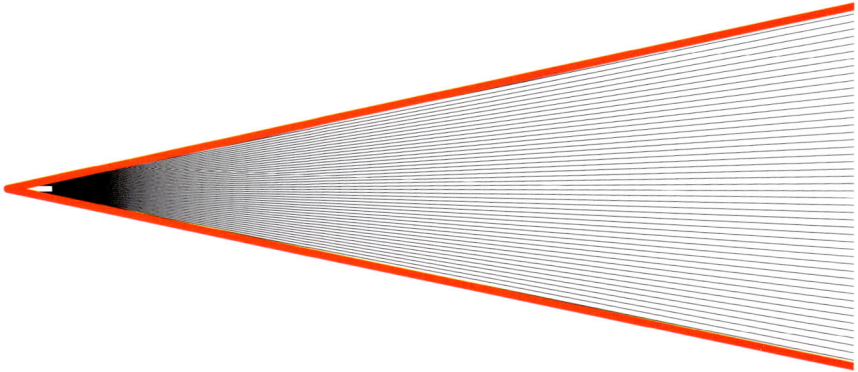

*Saddle stitching* is an alternative term for wire stitching or, simply, stapling. The staples used for saddle stitching are different from those in an office stapler. They're longer and made from a rounder profile wire, usually in stainless steel to prevent rusting, which is fed from a roll rather than a clip. It's called saddle stitching because printed sections are placed over an inverted V, like a sharp saddle, prior to being stitched together on the bindery production line. It's the most popular way to bind magazines or brochures because it's the cheapest and is also much quicker than other binding procedures. However, there is one important restriction—it can handle only a limited number of pages. If a publication's extent goes beyond the ninety-six-page mark, you'll need an alternative method. The weight of the paper stock must also be taken into account, not only because of page extent but also to account for the unavoidable "creep" (see page 322) that will occur. **TS**

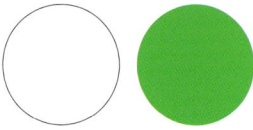

# DO ensure layout allows for "creep" at trim and spine when binding

*Creep*? No, we're not talking Radiohead here. When a book's or a brochure's pages are folded together or collated into sections prior to being bound and as the pages are stacked together and increase in number, the gauge of the paper forces the inner sheets to protrude until they are misaligned with the outer sheets. The result when trimmed: the inner's outer margins will be thinner than those of the outer pages. Not only will this be unpleasant on the eye, but also any items dangerously close to the trim edge could be cut off. Similarly, one must be aware of the binding mechanism being used, as some techniques appropriate more of the page gutter than others. An example is perfect binding, where up to .25 inches of the gutter margin on the page can be lost. When deciding on your layout and working out the margins, consider the page extent and the binding so that you can counteract that dreaded creep! **PD**

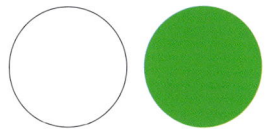

# DO use matte and gloss lamination appropriately

Lamination is the most popular technique used for finishing the covers of books, brochures, and magazines. It provides additional stiffness to the selected paper stock, and it helps to protect the printed cover from dirt and marks. Lamination can be applied in the form of a film, which is glued to the stock by passing it through a heated roller, or by the application of a polymer resin, which solidifies when exposed to UV light. It's broadly categorized as either matte or gloss, but which one should you use and what criteria should be applied to the decision? Gloss lamination doesn't mark easily and makes printed colors really pop off the page, so if you've got a gardening magazine or a book about color photography, gloss lamination would work really well. Alternatively, matte lamination feels contemporary and would work well for a cool fashion magazine—and it's a very popular choice for quality fiction. The one thing to make clear is gloss shouldn't automatically equate to high style and wealth, as in a "glossy magazine." That concept is outmoded. **TS**

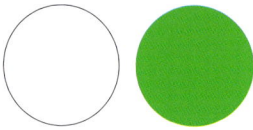

# DO learn the difference between embossing and debossing

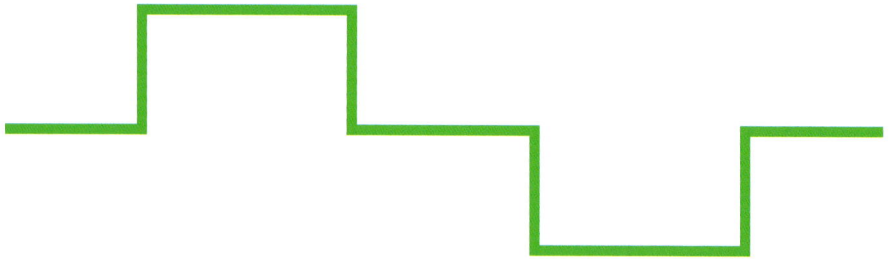

This is always a fun question to ask any designer because there's a good chance the answer will be something along the lines of: "Yeah, embossing is when the surface is pushed up and—no, hang on a minute—it's when the design is pushed into the surface and…um…err…bear with me while I look that up." I usually forget which is which because debossing is also occasionally referred to as embossing, not to mention blind stamping, so I always have to check before specifying one finish or the other. The correct definition is that *embossing* is where an area of paper or board is raised above the surface so it stands out from the background, and *debossing* is where an area is pressed into the surface to create an indentation. Both techniques require the use of a precast die, effectively an ink-free printing block, which is applied to the surface under pressure to create the required shape. So there you have it—at least I think that's it. I'd better check. **TS**

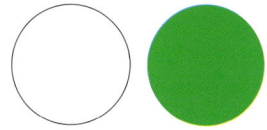

# DO press for H&T bands
# when a hardcover is specified

H&T (head and tail) bands are the decorative addition at the top and bottom of the spine when a book is hardcover bound. A small strip of cloth with either a solid color or pattern, they offer a small detail but one with a big impact. In the past, they were an intrinsic part of the binding process, as the pages to be held together were sewn to this cloth strip. These days, H&T bands do not contribute to the integrity of the binding but are retained as an attractive feature. What I love about them is they really finish a book off, and it's these little details that provide beauty and longevity to a book's lifespan. They remind me of the traditions of bookbinding's past and add a colorful finishing touch to the end design. It may be that the budget doesn't allow for them, but if you don't ask you don't get, so always ask! **PD**

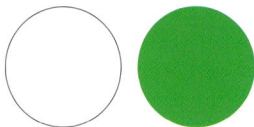

# DO always think about small details that create a big impact

One of the drawbacks of the computer is its inability to simulate special details. Gold foil, embossing, engraving, and die-cuts exist in the three-dimensional world. As most work is done on a computer screen, it is easy to forget these small details. But it is these details that create impact. A book cover embossed with a gold foil sparks an emotional response and transforms the ordinary into something treasured. Engraved business cards may seem old-fashioned and unnecessary. But in a world where most communication is digital, a physical object can be more significant. The extra consideration of the feel of engraved typography begs the holder to caress the business card. These small details may be more expensive to produce than traditional offset printing, but their impact cannot be overstated. Creating an artifact that will be kept because it has that little extra is true sustainable design. **SA**

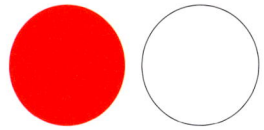

# DON'T specify predictable white endpapers

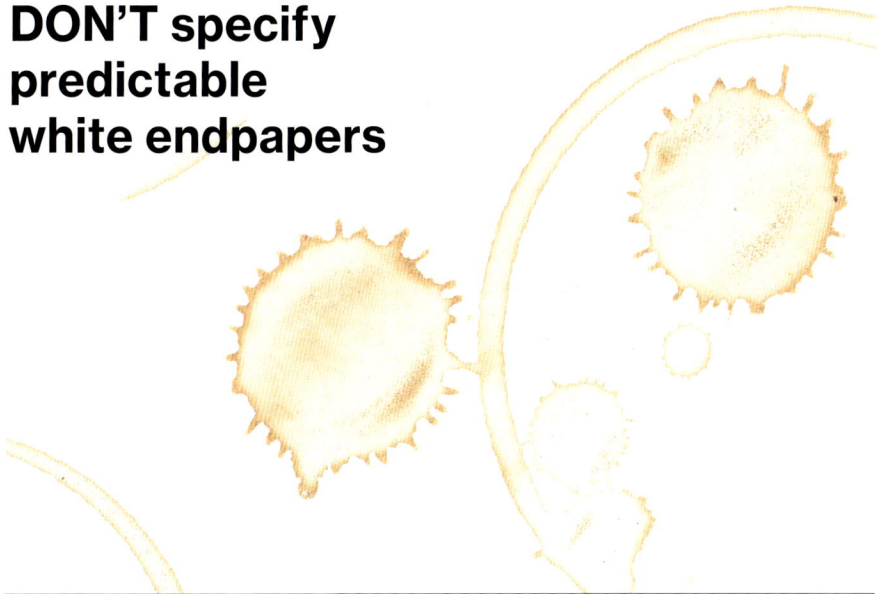

Being predictable is good in long-term relationships. Marriage with one partner who is loonier than a March Hare with wildly shifting emotions would be hard to maintain. Predictability is good for cars. It is nice to know that it won't break down in the middle of an intersection. Predictability in endpapers, however, is sad. An expected white endpaper in a book is dull and a loss of an opportunity. Endpapers can be a variety of colors and textures. Endpapers can be printed. As long as the paper stock has the correct content and will remain glued to the book board, anything is game. The endpaper serves in the construction of a book. The endpaper, though, is like a theater curtain: Blank white curtains are dull and send a message that the play will not be particularly exceptional. Or the theater is incredibly cheap and doesn't care about the viewer's experience. White endpapers are exactly the same. **SA**

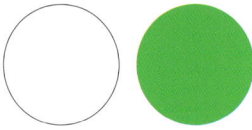

# DO clean up the pasteboard before sending a job to the printer

This isn't a case of being overly fastidious with one's artwork. (Although one can never be too tidy!) It is a way of ensuring that the artwork handed over to your printer is precise and cleaned, and contains no additional elements that could cause errors or faults. Examples could be a lone text box that has a text wrap applied to it. This could cause issues if accidentally moved onto the layout from the pasteboard.

Another could be a linked text box that, if moved or deleted, could cause issues with the flow of narrative or content. Also, unused images that are still sitting on the pasteboard will get packaged up with the final artwork and possibly create additional work for the printer when working on image files. The artwork is your responsibility, so keep it clean and precise. **PD**

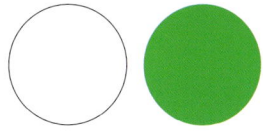

# DO check that CMYK colors are not set to print as spot colors

I've been in situations when artwork set up by a third party has contained many color-coded sections, not all the colors CMYK (when they should have been). Some were also spot colors. A CMYK print job was set up to print with more than thirty spot colors—an impossible specification! The problem is easy to fix, and checking that colors are CMYK should always be added to your checklist as you finalize the artwork. In InDesign, it's a quick action to highlight the color and switch the

color to CMYK. Not doing this can cause confusion and possibly incur costs if a printer has to adjust your files. If you are supplying PDF artwork and the problem has not been spotted prior to the digital-proof stage, the proofs will provide an inaccurate presentation of your artwork. Although most printers will alert you to the fact that the artwork has not been set up correctly, save them the trouble and get it right yourself by checking first. **PD**

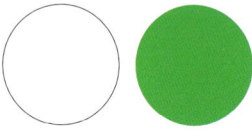

# DO learn about different finishing techniques

Loop-stitch binding: mostly used for brochures intended to be put in three-ring binders.

A printed object is a three-dimensional form. Just because Adobe InDesign displays standard double pages on a spread does not mean that this is the only format. Paper can be cut, perforated, folded in unique ways, and trimmed to unexpected shapes. A business card can be oval, die-cut, or folded. A publication might incorporate techniques such as a gatefold. A letterhead can be trimmed with rounded corners. When appropriate, add scratch and sniff. This might be more difficult to sell to the client if it's a pet company but perfect for a florist or candy shop. Remember, the page, book, or poster is a piece of sculpture. It can be flat or as intricate as origami. Unless you are aware of the possibilities, your work will remain flat—no pun intended. **SA**

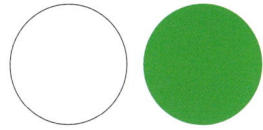

# DO consider effectiveness against cost for special finishing techniques

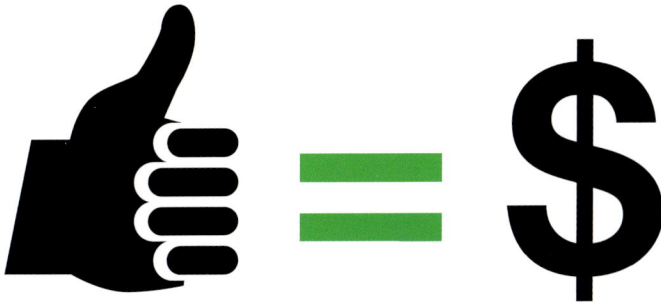

I mentioned earlier on that, with certain projects, production and print considerations often play an important part in the overall concept. For example, two colors may be selected for the way they work together to communicate a specific idea. Often the use of a foil block, a deboss, or a special color can add real value or impact to what you are trying to say—if it facilitates effective communication, then go for it. However, there is always a risk of creating a design with everything but the kitchen sink. The addition of needless print processes does little to increase the design's effectiveness or its tactile qualities. If anything, it can dilute or hinder the design and definitely cost more to produce. I would always balance the intent and ambition of the project against the target audience and the budget. You'll find that the specification will be refined through consideration, and a better end design will result. **PD**

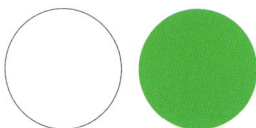

# DO learn about PDF/X standards for artwork delivery

You'll have noticed the various PDF/X options under the Adobe PDF Presets menu in InDesign, but what do they mean? The first thing to explain is that PDF/X isn't some kind of alternative file format but more a subset of the Adobe PDF specification. The idea behind PDF/X was to create a standard specification for PDF export that would help to eliminate common mistakes, like missing fonts or images, and encourage the implementation of a properly managed color workflow. Put simply, each PDF/X standard requires a PDF file to match certain criteria, such as compression, color conversion for output, transparency flattening. If you attempt to export a PDF/X file with incorrect settings, a warning triangle will alert you to any problems. The PDF/X-1a:2001 preset is older and quite basic, and it doesn't support a color-managed workflow. If you need to incorporate color profile information, PDF/X-3:2003 and PDF/X-4:2008 are preferable for offset printing and digital output. **TS**

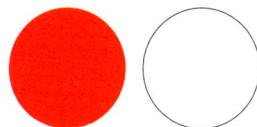

# DON'T pretend to know more about printing than your printer

Everyone knows someone who hovers over the plumber when he comes to fix a leak, questioning every turn of the wrench and boring the poor fellow, trapped under the sink, with tales of their own plumbing battles. That same person questions every detail of a car repair, wasting everyone's time debating each knock and ping and the cost of parts, until all of the mechanic's veins are bulging in frustration. Don't be that person. If you are a designer, you use plumbing and drive your car far more often than you send a project to the printer. It doesn't make you a plumber or a mechanic, and it does not make you a printer. Hire people knowledgeable in their field, and be informed enough to express your expectations for the job. Then, let them do what they do best just as you hope your clients will let you do what you do best. **JF**

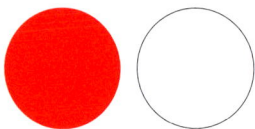

# DON'T accept what a printer tells you is possible without solid proof

I've been very fortunate to have worked with some brilliant printers whose expertise and diligence make them invaluable collaborators. However, there have been many occasions when the client has chosen the supplier for me. Usually, this relationship is professional and productive, but because you are not the one holding the purse strings, it can be a challenge to get the best results. Even though both parties are working toward the same objective—keeping the client happy—the designer and printer may not share the same priorities. This is where a little perseverance goes a long way. For example, you might want to make an adjustment to the artwork to improve its appearance but are told by the printer that it is not possible. Don't take no for an answer: ask them to explain why and request some kind of verification. Only when you are satisfied that it can't be done should you look at alternatives. Remember—if you are persistent, you may find that it can be done. **PD**

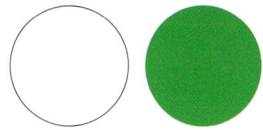

# DO understand the strengths and weaknesses of different printing processes

Every good team is an assembly of specialists (even if your specialty is being serviceable in several roles), whether it is in professional sports, a Broadway production, or your very own agency/studio. Some team members might provide the big glory moments, others might do the dirty work, and others still might provide microspecialties, the very best at a specific task. When selecting a printer, it is a good idea to think of your vendors in this way, to suit your needs. In order to do so, you need to understand the nuances of the printing processes they specialize in. For each project, think about what you want to accomplish and choose the process that works best. Do you need lithography, screen printing, embossing, etching, thermography? The answer is very different if you are printing a T-shirt versus an annual report, or a business card versus the side of a bus. **JF**

# The Practice
# of Design

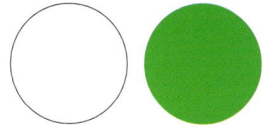

# DO think of the idea before the visual

What do you do when you first sit down with a fresh design brief and a blank piece of paper (or perhaps a blank screen—more on this later)? Do you get stuck on designing the grid and thinking about what typeface to use, or do you scribble away on a notepad for a while to get the ideas flowing? I would strongly urge you to opt for the latter every time. All too often, designers sit in front of a computer and start on the visual right out of the blocks without spending any time thinking about the idea. This isn't a great way to work. All your creative energy is going to be focused on designing a visual around an idea that might not end up being the best solution to that brief—and an idea isn't about typefaces and grids. The visual exists to present and support the idea, and if the idea isn't great, the visual won't be great either, despite all your efforts. Reclaim the humble pencil and get sketching. **TS**

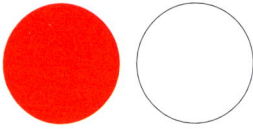

# DON'T turn to design annuals or portfolio websites for creative inspiration

I have to be careful here; I don't want anyone to think I'm out to dismiss design annuals or portfolio websites. I love them, and as I type this, I'm sitting with my back to a groaning shelf full of said design annuals and magazines. However, the last thing I do when I'm trying to come up with a new idea to answer a design brief is reach for one of them. The problem with design resources is that they're full of great ideas that other people have already had. Anything you look at will immediately discount any of your ideas that remotely resemble the annual's content. That's a pretty frustrating position to find yourself in because there's no shame in coming up with a good idea on your own, then finding something similar after the fact. A common adage is that there are no new ideas left, which I don't believe is totally true but the saying does have some merit. Try to look elsewhere first for your inspiration before checking out the ideas that have gone before. **TS**

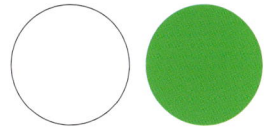

# DO read books that are not about design

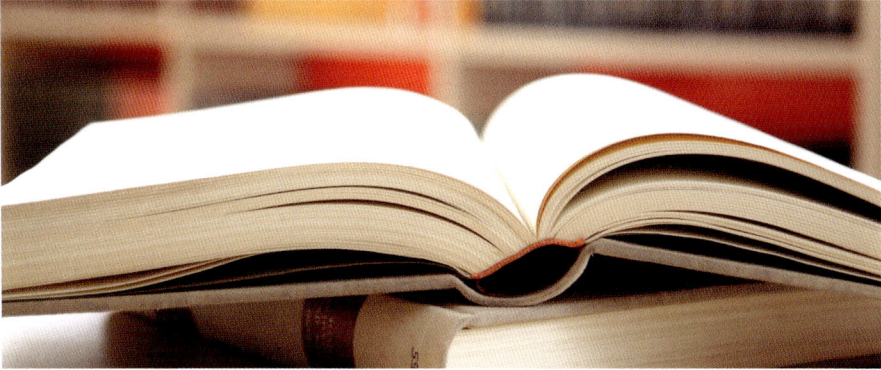

The dullest people are those who can discuss only one subject. I have been told that sitting next to me at a dinner party can be unpleasant, as I enjoy discussing American history for hours. Dull people tend to have limited life experience, or they are genetically predisposed to being boring. Designers who only read design books and publications may be well versed in multiple design ideas and noted designers but, like my American-history facts, are dull. Design is about ideas. Almost any subject outside design could be informative. A book on quantum physics may inspire a new way to envision information. Books about history can help us rethink proportional systems. A fiction book may be written in a minimal way and teach us to communicate more succinctly. Most importantly, books force us to question, be introspective, and reconsider our lives. If we are genuine creative people, this is not only a pleasant and straightforward addition to our process but also at the core of a successful method. **SA**

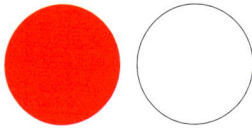

# DON'T rely solely on Google for research

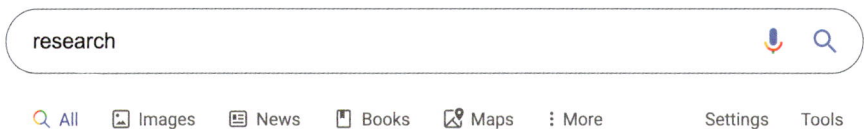

research

🔍 All    🖼 Images    📰 News    📖 Books    🗺 Maps    ⋮ More      Settings    Tools

Google is a wonderful tool to use to search for a good local Chinese restaurant or look up eighteenth-century Virginia history and software tips. Google is a poor substitute for actual scholarly research. Libraries are a better resource. A well-trained librarian is a human Google. He or she can help direct a designer to the correct area of interest. Searching for information on Google is like wearing blinkers. For example, a search for Cecil Beaton will lead to multiple sites about Beaton. Some of these may be well researched and accurate, others may be complete fiction. This search, furthermore, will lead only to Beaton. Scanning books on the shelf of the library could result in accidentally stumbling on Irving Penn, Ansel Adams, or a multitude of other photographers. Research is compiling verifiable data from multiple credible sources. A website about Beaton created by a fifteen year old for a school project is none of these things. **SA**

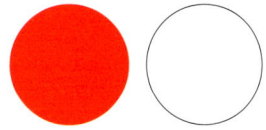

# DON'T *knowingly* plagiarize

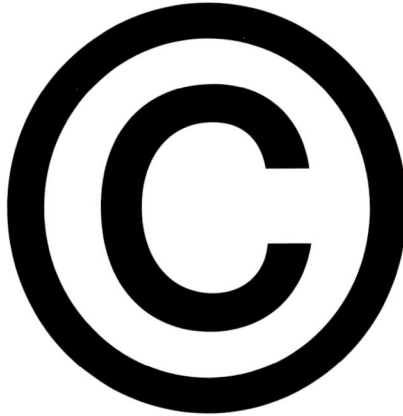

The phrase "what goes around comes around" can often be applied to our industry. Visual trends are created and followed, only to be replaced with a new theme a short time later. When trends arise and with more designers taking the same approach, there is often a greater chance that work of a similar concept or appearance will occur. On a few occasions, I've had my ideas and work copied. While flattering (briefly), it is also frustrating because all your efforts have been lifted in a moment. Design for the brief and create your own ideas—that's the challenge of what we do and where the enjoyment comes from. It's being original that counts, and this is what makes the successful designers stand out from the pack. Be honest, and you will take greater satisfaction in what you do—your work will be appreciated more because it is original! **PD**

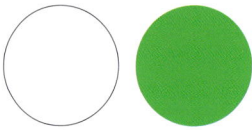

# DO insist on
# a written brief for
# every project

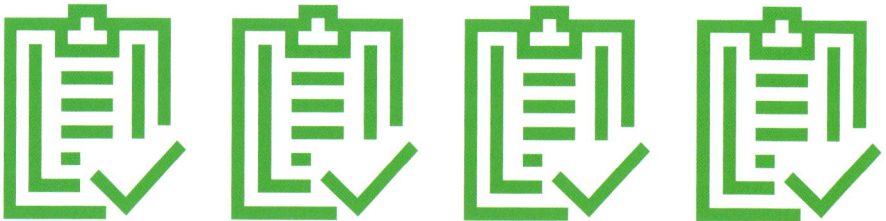

John, the designer, is looking forward to working with his new client and arrives in good time for the briefing. "Good to meet you," says Trevor, the client. "I've looked at your website and love your work—it's so our kind of thing." "What do you have in mind for your brochure?" asks John. "Oh, we want you to decide, as your work is so our kind of thing," says Trevor. "I'd really prefer some direction from you first so I know I'm on the right track," says John. "No need," says Trevor. "We love everything on your website." "Well—Okay," says John. Two weeks later, John arrives to present his concept for the brochure. Trevor looks over the visuals, turns to John, and says, "Oh dear, this approach really isn't what we had in mind. Sorry, John, but I'm afraid you'll have to start all over again and not get paid any extra money." "But…," says John. "No buts, John. It's that or we'll have to look elsewhere," says Trevor. The moral of this sad tale—always get a written brief. The end. **TS**

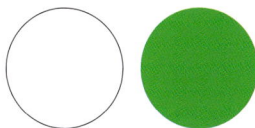

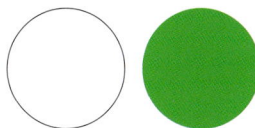

## DO ask clients questions in addition to the brief

That written brief is a real plus at the start of any project, but more often than not, it can bring up more questions. These can be many and varied, but don't be afraid to ask them—just don't ask questions that are answered in the written brief already! What you will achieve by asking questions is to tighten up the brief, which will invariably help focus the client's mind and allow them to make decisions about the design, management, and production of the product. I often receive briefs verbally and take notes, but there is always a need to ask additional questions. The obvious is usually stated, such as schedules and budgets (or sometimes not), but questions that arise may include assignment of responsibilities between client and designer, budget structure, and billing terms. **PD**

## DO confirm all deliverables in writing

If you are working for a client who has commissioned graphic designers before, the protocols and division of responsibilities are likely to be well understood. But when you receive a new brief, it is vital that you put in writing what you will deliver and by when. I've often gone into a briefing meeting with clients who discuss the project with me as if I have prior knowledge of what's needed. They have, of course, been discussing and planning the brief for weeks, maybe months; therefore, a key task would be to go back to the start and establish exactly what they require. Get the deliverables established and confirmed in writing. That way, the clients will know exactly what to expect, and everyone will avoid disappointment and any potential tension in the relationship. **PD**

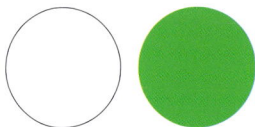

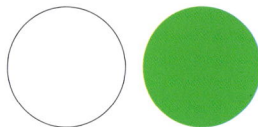

## DO agree on costs in writing before beginning each project

## DO question a budget if it is clearly not enough to answer the brief

If there is one subject that is going to cause disagreement between a client and a designer, it's money. Clients do not like surprises, especially those of the "project cost has gone up" kind! To avoid a dispute, confirm the crucial question of how much a project will cost. Whether working for a fixed fee or a daily rate, make sure you have it in writing and get the client's explicit acknowledgment of the sum. In addition, if you are preparing a quotation, make sure that all elements of the prospective job are included: correction costs, print management, meetings, commissioning of photography and illustrations, etc. If this isn't possible at the beginning of a project, state clearly on your quotation that certain aspects of the project are to be confirmed. If the client understands what they are paying for from the outset, then all will be well. **PD**

Despite the fact that designers possess a creative side, and we all enjoy our vocation, it is our job, and we have to make a living from it. There is no point in working on a project and not getting paid enough (or worse, taking a loss). There will be occasions when a client comes to you with what promises to be an exciting project but with little in the way of budget, and, as you read the brief or discuss with the client what needs to be done, it becomes clear that their expectations exceed their bank balance. Don't be afraid, be willing to raise the issue with them—you are entering into a business arrangement, and they are buying your skills and experience in order to achieve the desired results. I find discussing options and differing formats will often deliver a solution that works for both parties. **PD**

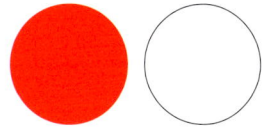

# DON'T try to do everything yourself at the expense of a project

If you're a freelancer working for your-self, this rule doesn't really apply to you, so please skip to the next page. If you work in a design management role or as any part of a team, then please read on. This rule shouldn't be confused with the rule on page 264, which concerns commissioning. This one is more about being prepared to relinquish control over aspects of a project that other people can handle as well as or better than you. Delegation of responsibility can be a lot harder than you might think, probably because in the back of your mind, there is a troublesome little thought that someone else's mistake might come back to bite you, compelling you to try to take responsibility for everything yourself. This attitude can do far more harm than good to a project and is unlikely to produce a better result. It's more likely to weaken the project, especially in the areas you couldn't give 100 percent to, and make you look like an idiot. If you learn to put your trust in others, they'll respond positively and generously. **TS**

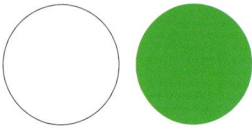

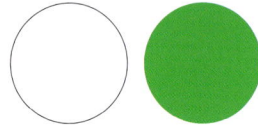

## DO accept that every project will probably be more difficult than you expected

## DO accept that every project will take longer than expected

Designers have a tendency to challenge themselves. We don't want to do the same project repeatedly, and once we become proficient in one area, we want to venture into new territories. Therefore, almost every project will be more demanding than expected. Even the simplest projects tempt us to rethink and reimagine possibilities. If a person wanted to repeat projects without challenges, a career in a canning factory might be preferable. The downside of the designer's need to challenge himself or herself is time. Rarely does a project offer too much time. A designer will work on something until it is dragged from his or her hands. A good rule of thumb is to honestly calculate how long a project will take, then triple that number. **SA**

I would really like to write more about why every project you ever work on will take longer than you think it will, but unfortunately my deadline for the submission of this text has passed, and I've run out of time. I was sure I had another week to go before I had to hand this in. Oh well—just goes to show, doesn't it! **TS**

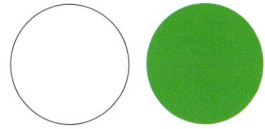

# DO dress for work according to your client's or your employer's expectations

It is a mistake to believe that you are dressing to express your creativity and that these choices only reflect on you. We dress to show respect to those around us. If we are meeting with a group of friends at the local bar, it is reasonable to dress for the occasion, to fit in with the group. Wearing a giant teddy bear suit will make most friends uncomfortable. The same is true when meeting clients or working at the studio. The clothes reflect the respect shown to the client or employer. This works in both directions. If a client is formal, and it is traditional in their office to wear something less casual, follow suit. Shorts and flip-flops are a not-so-subtle way of saying "F*%# you." But if a client is casual and takes pride in their relaxed atmosphere, it is a mistake to wear a suit. The questions to be asked when confused are these: What will make my client feel that I took the time to present myself in the best way? What will create a comfortable situation for myself and others? **SA**

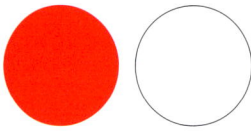

# DON'T present an option you don't want your client to choose because that's the one they'll choose

A. **Univers**

B. **Clarendon**

C. Bauer Bodoni

D. **Hobo**

It is an old maxim to never show a client a design you dislike. They will choose it, and you will be unhappy. It is a designer's job to solve the problem and create the best possible solution. Showing an unsuccessful solution is a disservice to the client and to you. Alternatively, if a client asks for a specific solution, do not ignore this. There is a reason for the request. Few people are simply mad and willy-nilly, throwing out wild ideas. Stop and ask not how to visually solve the problem but why he or she wants the specific solution. The answer may be extremely valid. You, as a designer, will be able to offer a better solution. Never ignore the client or refuse to explore their solution. Everyone wants to feel important and valued. Nobody wants to be ignored and treated as an idiot because they "don't understand design." Explore the suggested solution, and return with that and a better option. Explain why one solution is more successful, not in design terms, but with an eye on the desired result of the project. **SA**

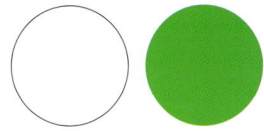

# DO be nice to colleagues working above and below you, as things can change

In Hollywood, there is an old saying: "The ass you kick on the way up is the one you kiss on the way down." If you are selfish, self-centered, and a sociopath, this saying alone should appeal to your sense of survival. If you are not a sociopath, you probably believe that most people should be treated with respect and kindness. It is easier to work with others when there is a feeling of mutual congeniality. Others are more likely to offer help and support if you haven't abused them or threatened to harm them in their sleep. This is especially true for well-known designers. If you find yourself courted by the design media and climbing the ladder of fame, never believe your own hype. You are not the best thing since sliced bread. The people you look down on and treat badly will remember these slights. They will tell their friends, who will tell their friends, and soon you will be a global pariah. **SA**

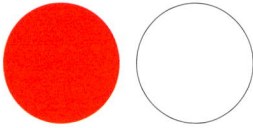

# DON'T present reams of written research with a proposal just to impress the client

The teenager paces the kitchen, telling her parents all about the new safety studies, referencing quotes from other neighborhood parents, citing peer considerations, and pulling out charts on mileage and fuel economy. Soon, reams of information seem to be flying at them as she piles high automotive magazines and consumer publications; it is getting to be a bit much to take in. The plot is firmly lost during the fifteen minutes of a bold discourse on how the color of an automobile reflects its owner. By the time the kid is going on about how "if this car were an animal, it would be…" the couple finally raise their hands and plead for mercy. "If you want us to buy you this car, just ask," they sputter. A solid idea only requires a little bit of explanation. You are not impressing your client, only boring them. **JF**

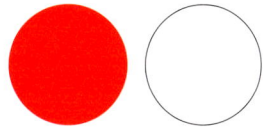

# DON'T present mood boards unless specifically asked —and even then

This industry has a lot of dirty little secrets, and one of them is that certain agencies charge a lot of money for the pleasure of cutting up magazines and printouts of web images onto collages as if they were decorating their high school lockers. Originally conceived to provide inspiration by assembling the types of images, patterns, colors, and various items that a project should aspire to, they have degenerated into messes that are meant to aid clients who can't "see" where the project should be headed. If you read that last line, you will realize where the issue is. These are meant to be internal tools based on researching competing brands and the tastes of potential users/viewers. They aren't as effective as a communication between creatives and the client, because your client should already know all of this information like the back of their hand. If they don't, and request these, you might have a bigger issue on your hands. **JF**

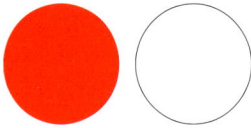

# DON'T work for free

As designers, we enjoy what we do. We mistakenly believe anyone could do our job. This is because we have a rare talent and cannot imagine that everyone else doesn't. It comes so easily that it seems ridiculous that the person next to you at a film couldn't tell the difference between Garamond and Bembo. Consequently, we give our skills away and devalue the profession and ourselves. There has never been a client with too much time and too much money. There are hundreds of important causes that need support. But often, when a nonprofit client approaches a designer and asks for free work, other vendors are being paid. The printer, caterer, staff, and delivery services may all be charging fees. As a designer, it is assumed that this is the easy job and can be done in five minutes. Compensation is necessary for the client to value the work and respect the designer. This compensation can be in the form of cash, goods, or recognition. But no job should ever be completed simply out of kindness, without payment. If you are moved to do this, stop and volunteer for the Red Cross. **SA**

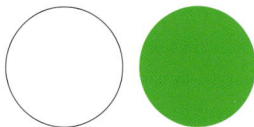

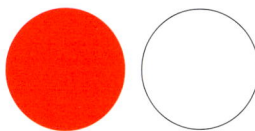

# DO invoice regularly and on time

One of the hardest aspects of running a design business is the business. Invoicing regularly and on time is more important than any other aspect of the business. It may be tempting to spend another hour refining the typography on a poster, but invoicing must come first. It is a basic in business to work with clients who pay their bills and to invoice on a regular basis to manage cash flow. Some design firms invoice regularly once a month, but the most successful invoice weekly or daily. If a project is lagging, invoice a progress billing. Always invoice at the completion of each phase. Invoice outside costs immediately, even if this is a bill for those alone. Maintaining cash flow is job one. Invoicing on an irregular basis or too late creates opportunities for mistakes, and the client will perceive the design firm as amateurish. **SA**

# DON'T accept assignments purely for the money

For some reason, it is inevitable that work created exclusively for financial reward will go horribly awry. There is no logical reason for this. Perhaps it is the distaste felt for the project reflected in its solution. Or this is simply God's way of saying, "Do what you love." In addition to the unbecoming outcome itself, it will lead to other similar projects. Good people with good projects know other good people with good projects. And bad people with bad projects know other bad people. If the issue is money alone, graphic design is a poor choice for a profession. If cash above all else is the goal, there are many other careers that accommodate this desire. You never know, you might be hit by a bus tomorrow. No designer should spend his or her final moments working on a project that produces only misery. **SA**

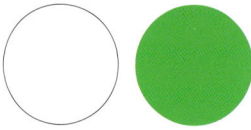

# DO take days off— especially if you're a freelancer

A wise older designer once gave some sage advice: "Never work on Sunday." The issue is not one of religion but of sanity. As a creative person, it is important to remember that downtime is as crucial and productive as working time. Taking time away from design provides an opportunity to clear the head and think of new ideas. Minimally, time away from design promotes a balanced life. Passion about design is important.

Exploration and refinement take time. But design will expand to fill all time available. If a project has a deadline in fifteen minutes, the project will take fourteen minutes. That same project, with a two-week deadline, will take two weeks. Unless you are doing brain surgery and the patient is moments from death, you can take one day off from your work. **SA**

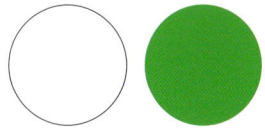

# DO learn the rules before you break them

Many people have looked at a vintage Picasso and scoffed, with thoughts that they, too, could paint figures with pinched heads and wildly extended arms emanating from boxy shoulders. None of them are familiar with his near-photographic early paintings, or else they would quickly realize that they might be able to make a rough approximation of the style he is best known for, but they would never have arrived at it on their own. Therein lies the difference. Picasso spent years plying his craft in the accepted ways, until he was able to replicate nearly any image with lifelike efficiency. He understood every nuance about how the human body was formed. He knew the rules, and he knew them well. It was this understanding that made it so groundbreaking when he discarded them, manipulating parts and pieces as they never had been before. His solid foundation allowed his creativity to unleash itself in the most influential areas, forever changing the world of art. **JF**

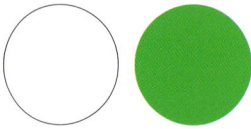

# DO acknowledge your mistakes rather than try to cover them up

It takes a very mature person to accomplish this. I know I struggled with this early in my career. Can I figure out a way to fix this without anyone noticing? Make it up to the client, or coworker, in some other way? I didn't want to disappoint anyone or admit to myself that I was failing in some way. I soon realized that the best thing to do when you make an error—and we all make mistakes, so don't pretend otherwise—was to be honest about it. The sooner you come clean with your boss/client/vendor, the sooner you can limit the impact or, better yet, rectify the issues. Everyone involved will respect that you came to them right away (as they recall their own mistakes in the past) and appreciate the opportunity to try to fix them as soon as possible. Grown-ups make mistakes. They also fix them. It's part of being a grown-up. **JF**

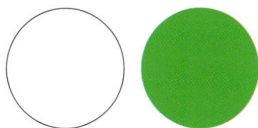

## DON'T ask someone else to do what you can do yourself

Smart people surround themselves with smarter people. Teamwork is important. Learning to delegate tasks to someone better is a key to success. There is a difference, however, between collaboration and servitude. Limited people find exceptionally dumb people and gracelessly force them to do menial tasks. If a task can be done well personally, then do it. If you are capable of pouring a cup of coffee, then don't ask the designer across from you to fetch it. If you have the time and ability to call a messenger, do it. It may seem fun and give you great satisfaction that you are the lord of the office, but this will only lead to dissatisfied and angry coworkers. Eventually, they will turn on you. **SA**

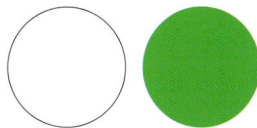

## DO find a design mentor (and be prepared to be one in the future)

If you haven't figured out by this point in the book that the world of design is filled with secrets, there is not much else we can do to help you. Well, I take that back. We can give you an important piece of advice, one that will lead to a lifetime of guidance: find someone who has been through the battlefield already, and form a trusted and cherished professional friendship. Finding a mentor can happen naturally—you encounter someone more experienced and begin to ask them questions, easily forming a close bond—or you can search out others whose work you respect via networking or professional organizations and begin a conversation. Ask as many questions as they can stand, but be prepared to fill the same role for a young designer in the future. **JF**

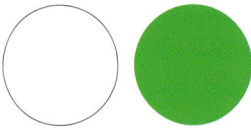

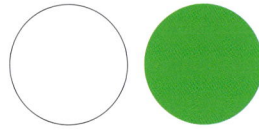

## DO remain humble in your work

## DO respect focus groups but NOT at the expense of gut feeling

There is nothing worse than being trapped with a mediocre and self-satisfied designer—the type of person who will talk endlessly about his or her vast success and experience. By the end of the conversation, you will know their entire CV, in detail, and that they are the most accomplished person on earth. The clear subtext in the conversation is that you are a loser in comparison. Every single person on the planet wants to feel important and valued. Charm is the ability to make the other person feel respected. Humility is a virtue. Humility is not self-hate. Understand that every person has value and is needed and loved by others. This does not make you lesser. Reinforcing the positive aspects in others makes you genuine. **SA**

Focus groups have found themselves with a bad reputation, in some ways justified, as they have been misused over the years. Having said that, there is a lot of value to be gleaned from direct feedback from potential users. If a focus group is selected properly, it can be vital to shaping how a product or brand is positioned. Creatives are quick to chafe at the feedback delivered from those exercises, but take the time and digest the comments. There can be important information in there, and, if nothing else, respect the time and money the client dedicated to the process. Now that we have gone through all of that, let's talk about the nagging feeling that lies deep inside us when we know we are on the right track. If your gut is screaming out to stay the course, don't let an unconvinced pool of people derail you. **JF**

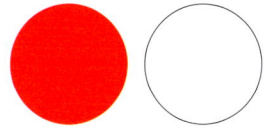

# DON'T quantify your creative abilities with software skills

Maybe it's an inevitable by-product of the digitalization of the design industry, but the average designer's CV looks quite different these days. I'm venturing into angry old man territory here, but when I first put a CV together, I didn't include a whole paragraph of stuff along the lines of…

- I can paste up artwork
- I can draw really straight lines with a mechanical pen
- I know how to blend Magic Markers with lighter fluid…

I assumed that potential employers would expect me to be able to do those things, and I hoped that they'd be more interested in my ideas anyway. Fast-forward to today, and many CVs include such long lists of software skills that they begin to resemble a catalog for a computer store. Knowing how to use InDesign doesn't indicate that you're a good designer. To be honest, that information isn't particularly relevant. Besides, people will take it for granted that you can use InDesign because you're a designer. It says so at the top of the CV you've just submitted. **TS**

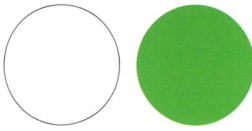

# DO rest your eyes periodically throughout the day

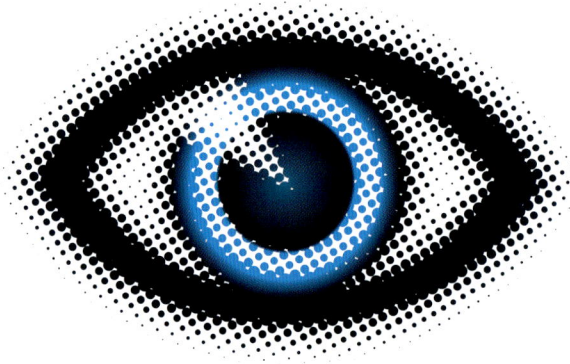

The great designer Alvin Lustig slowly lost his sight toward the end of his life. Nevertheless, he continued working, directing others to complete ideas. Alvin Lustig being who he is, I'm fairly certain that his assistants followed his direction, using red, or Clarendon, or whatever he suggested. Many of us don't have the same command of others. If you were to lose your sight, you may ask your assistant to use a yellow background and singular image of a beach ball. He or she may then choose to ignore you and create a chaotic mess with dark tones but still tell you that the poster is yellow with a beach ball. To combat this scenario, it is critical to rest your eyes. Stop, at least every twenty minutes, and focus on a distant spot, or take a walk around the office. When the computer screen begins to seem blurry and dark, you have exceeded your viewing allotment. **SA**

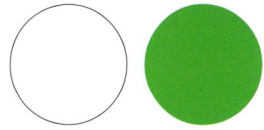

# DO work with talented illustrators, writers, and photographers

The single most important thing I have learned in my years doing this is to hire amazing people and let them do what they do best. I might be able to write, but I can't write on every subject and in every tone. I might be proficient with a camera, but others are so much sharper and creative behind the lens. I know my way around a pen, pencil, and paintbrush, but incredible illustrators inspire me at every turn. People in all of these areas have shown the ability to make my projects a thousand times better than they ever could have been in my hands alone. Fight (and plan) for the budget to bring on the best, remembering how they lighten your own load, and prepare to bask in the accolades that an incredible piece will bring you. **JF**

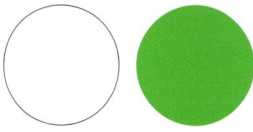

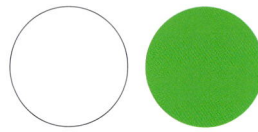

## DO hire a good accountant, and save more than you spend

It is not uncommon to hear a non-designer ask, "I designed my own logo and business card. What do you think?" What can you say? "It's hideous. You're a sap. Are you brain-dead?" Of course not, but it is rare that the result is anything more than sad. The designer who says, "I don't need an accountant. I know how to do this," is just as stupid. Designers enjoy breaking rules and playing loose with facts. These are not good traits in an accountant. Therefore, hiring a good accountant is a priority. And like hiring a designer, the accountant who charges a ludicrously small amount will probably not provide the best result. As a rule, always hire an accountant more expensive than you believe you should. You will appreciate the results, and you will save money. **SA**

## DO build a team that complements, not duplicates, your abilities

Not every member of a barbershop quartet needs to sing bass. Similarly, surrounding yourself with a bevy of people who think and act just like you can be more than counterproductive, it can be downright creepy, like a science fiction movie filled with clones moving silently in concert with one another. In practice, it limits the possibilities of how you could approach creative problem solving by curbing the diverse backgrounds and mindsets that could be contributing to your work. The chances that all of your clients are exactly like you is remote at best, and a team with some range will come in handy at every turn. Of course, we still need to be able to work together and bond quickly, so be careful to build your team with complementary skills, not divergent mentalities. **JF**

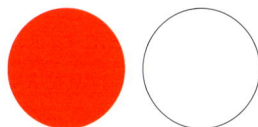

# DON'T be afraid to share ideas and collaborate

Keeping your ideas close to your chest is understandable if an original idea represents the difference between you winning or losing a lucrative contract. If you're pitching against other designers (and not for free, I hope), the last thing you're going to do is turn up at the meeting and say to your rivals, "Hey guys, do you want to see what I came up with?" However, there are times when sharing ideas will gain you contracts. For example, you've designed a brochure, and your client tells you it's great and that they'd now like to roll out the concept to their new website. Oh no—you're a print designer and don't do websites. It's time to go see the web designer who rents the office across the hall. The original concept is yours but what's to stop you from collaborating with another designer with different skills to ensure that you keep the contract? It's a good idea to have paperwork in place defining how a project is divided before you start, but collaborative working is nothing to be scared of. **TS**

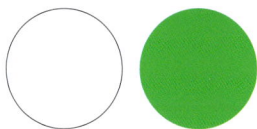

# DO get client approval on a visual before racing to finish a project

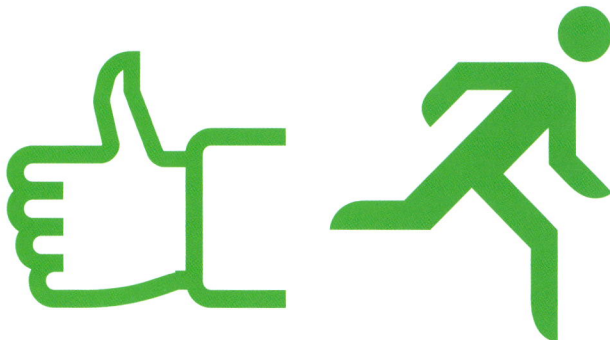

Deadline, deadline, deadline. I am haunted by the deadline. Balancing numerous projects is the hardest part of my job. The second hardest is figuring out the layout. Something just isn't working, and I have been putting in long hours trying to resolve it. With the minutes ticking away, I am quickly running out of time to fix what is bedeviling my project. What was that hitting my keyboard? A drop of sweat? This deadline is really stressing me out.

Wait, that's it! A photo of a water drop would be perfect. Inspiration just before the final cutoff. I just need to swap out this illustration of a hose, and package my files, send them off to the printer, wait for my client to be surprised, be on the hook for the fees to change it back, and possibly be fired. Oh, right, I should always get approval before finalizing a job, no matter how tight the deadline. **JF**

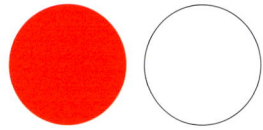

# DON'T demonize another designer because you don't happen to like his or her work

Put things in perspective. As important as we say design is to society, it is, after all, only graphic design. A weak solution will not kill someone. A bad poster will not bring about the ruin of Western civilization. An incomprehensible logo will not deprive your family of a home. Forming an opinion about work and viewing it with a critical eye is good. But demonizing a designer who created a piece you dislike is foolish. Hating an evil dictator is a good idea, but a designer who uses a typeface you don't like is not evil. The best designers are those who remain open to new ideas and new ways of working. The worst designers are close-minded and rigid. They are the designers who wander through their careers despising their peers and truly hating younger designers. The tragedy here is the loss of opportunity to learn, grow, and create friendships. **SA**

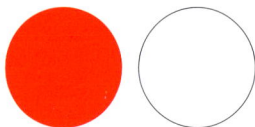

# DON'T discuss one client's business with another

One of the greatest joys in this business is working with people whom you truly like. Following a taxing project, you might find yourself bonding with a client over a shared childhood experience, or some travel mishap, or a pop culture reference. Sooner rather than later, our favorite clients become some of our favorite people and our friends, and we feel comfortable talking with them about almost anything, including what makes up the bulk of our waking hours—work. It makes sense that they would talk to us about their work at times. Surely, we should reciprocate.

Talking about someone in the office who annoys you can be precarious— they may be assigned to the client at some point. Complaining about your workload might make them think that you are overburdened, and they might consider sending some work elsewhere. Talking about the secrets you are privy to with your other clients is the ultimate sin, going against your unspoken (or perhaps written) agreement with said client and making your other client unsure about how loose you are with their information. **JF**

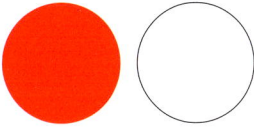

## DON'T criticize another designer in front of a client

Consider this scenario: you need an architect to design your house. The first architect tells you how awful all the other architects are. The second and third architects do the same. You are left with the sense that all architects must be untrustworthy and spiteful. When we criticize another designer to a client, we are doing the same. When trying to convince the client that another designer is bad, we denigrate the entire profession. The design profession is in a constant battle to be respected and understood by the business community. There are enough nondesigners who berate the profession; we do not need to attack one another from within. This only reinforces the idea that designers are temperamental and difficult and have questionable ethics. **SA**

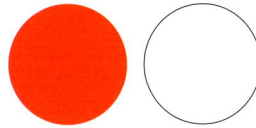

## DON'T criticize work previously commissioned from another designer

It is tempting to sit in a meeting and complain about previous work created for a client. It may be true that the solutions are inappropriate or weak. It may seem that pointing out these weaknesses will elevate you somehow. Unfortunately, you may not realize that the work was likely created in collaboration with the client. You are saying, without intending to, "You really don't know what you're doing." Never criticize previous work. Rather than castigating the work, point out some positive aspects. There is a good chance that the work may have good points, but they don't work cohesively as a group or support a new communication goal. **SA**

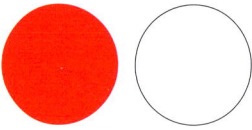

# DON'T pretend you know more about a client's business than they do

A common mistake a designer makes is to believe that he or she is omniscient. "What you need," he or she may say, "is a new identity and completely different inventory and accounting system." Designers, like all people, are not omniscient. A client will always know his or her business better than the designer. The client, for example, may be the director of a museum. While the designer has visited the museum and understands the audience and communication needs, he or she may be ignorant of other issues such as staffing, acquisition, and security. Listen to your client. Clients typically have valuable information that informs the project. Don't be quick to disregard the client's issues and concerns. There may be a critical reason that you are not aware of. **SA**

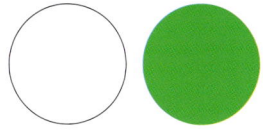

# DO be available to your clients at all times, but on your terms

As you sit outside the restaurant, with your meal cooling and your date freezing, you listen to your client telling you how they just are not sure about the orange and that maybe it needs a little more red, no, yellow, no, the orange is fine—you come to the realization that the line between work and the rest of your life has forever blurred, to your chagrin. There is no use in pretending that a creative vocation means straight nine-to-five shifts at the office. We are a service industry, often working for top decision makers, which means having to be available virtually at all times. Just accept this aspect and move on. But now, get your life back. Being accessible doesn't always mean being accessible immediately. Decide what is appropriate, and work directly with your clients to establish this. Let them know you coach your kids on Tuesday or that you will return the call in an hour when dinner ends, and they will do the same. **JF**

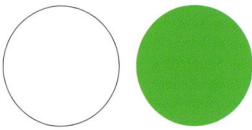

# DO actually talk to your clients—real conversations build strong relationships

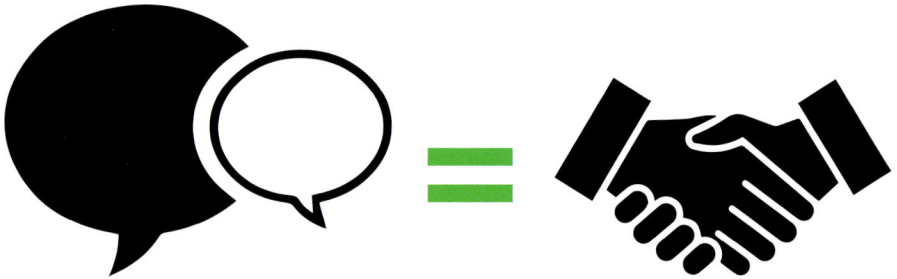

People hire people they like. It is more costly, time-wise and financially, to find a new client than continuing to work with an existing client. A client will work with a designer over time and build a relationship through good work and dialogue. Strong relationships built on mutual respect are likely to withstand problems. When a project delivers late, a typesetting error is not caught, or a check is lost in the mail, a strong relationship is vital. A longtime client is also more likely to refer you to another client. Building connections happens through honest communication. Take the time to have lunch with a client, play golf, invite her to a barbecue. These small touches build trust and make the difference between being a vendor and being a partner. **SA**

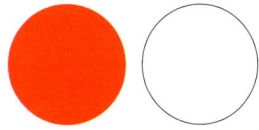

# DON'T discuss design with your client unless they express an interest

When your car is not working, you take it to the mechanic. You want to know briefly what is wrong, how it will be fixed, and how much it will cost. Unless you are an automobile aficionado, you do not care about the type of timing belt, spider gear, shift fork, or slave cylinder. When a designer discusses a solution with a client, the latter will want to know what the solution is and how much it will cost to implement.

Typically, clients do not care about complementary colors, the history of Baskerville, or letter-spacing issues. Talk to the client about communication issues, audience perception, and desired results. It is your job to know the fine detail. It is also your job to explain the decisions with language pertinent to business concerns rather than by using design vernacular. **SA**

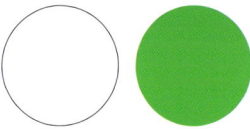

# DO count to ten when a client angers you before opening your mouth

# 1.2.3.4.5.6.7.8.9.10

Thomas Jefferson said, "When angry, count to ten before speaking. When very angry count to one hundred." As tempting as it is to lash out and attack a client when you have been riled up, it is always a bad idea. Rarely do we follow logic and give a measured response while enraged. It is not necessary to answer any question or respond to an accusation immediately. Counting to ten allows both sides to step back and, hopefully, calm down. It is much more common to look back and wonder why you were so mad than to feel that you should have been angrier. Something else to consider is whether the problem is about pride. Pride is a bad reason to engage in an angry episode. People tell themselves stories in order to survive. Let them. It costs you little. **SA**

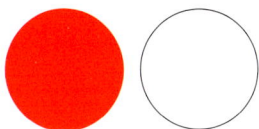

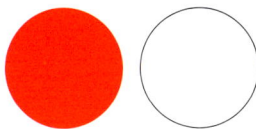

## DON'T accept your client's word as gospel

## DON'T continue to work for a difficult client

Clients only know what they already know. They are convinced that they need a small brochure and assign that as the project. This is because they have seen only a small brochure and assume that it is the best solution. Clients often give the wrong assignment. It is not the designer's job to blindly do what she is told but rather to solve the problem. That solution may be a completely unexpected medium or format. Or the problem may not be about the brochure at all but about the website and social media. Stop and assess the situation. Step back and consider the bigger issues. Never just do as commanded. **SA**

The only people allowed to shout at you should be your mother and, possibly, if not violent, your spouse. There is never a reason for a client to shout at a designer. You deserve to be treated with respect and professionalism. There are clients who are challenging because they have challenging projects. But the clients who are difficult because they are abusive should not be tolerated. At best, they will refer you to other heinous and disrespectful clients. At worst, you will be demoralized and produce bad work. **SA**

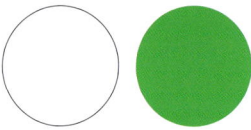

# DO stick to your side of the project's schedule regardless of your client's input

This rule is a bit of a two-way street because it requires some positive input from both sides. Creative projects are always subject to change, and as designers, we have to accept that it's going to happen sometimes. Because of this, a client should, within reason, be made to feel that they can change their mind if something strikes them as important during the execution of a project. Whatever form that takes, the challenge for the designer is to still deliver on time and on budget—if changes are reasonable. On the other hand, the client has to accept that not everything is possible and that it's acceptable for a designer to explain why a schedule or budget might not be met if a large change is requested. A reasonable client will accept this and may decide the change isn't that important. Either way, hold to your time line so that delayed projects don't end up affecting others. **TS**

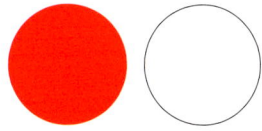

# DON'T procrastinate— ever

Procrastination is, unfortunately, one of the most common habits in the world. It always seems so much easier to put off an unpleasant task until tomorrow. The opposite is true. If you procrastinate, the task will loom larger and larger. It will seem more unpleasant and will revisit your thoughts frequently. The task will not disappear, so why ignore it? The solution is to simply buckle down and do the task.

Now is as good a time as any. It is much more pleasant and rewarding to tackle a task and complete it well in a timely manner. When you find yourself cleaning your desk for the fifth time to avoid the financial paperwork, stop. Get to work. Never put off until tomorrow what you can do today. The pressure of guilt and worry will be gone, and you can engage in more enjoyable tasks. **SA**

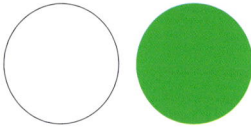

## DO talk about design as an asset

# DESIGN IS AWESOME!

We often have trouble, as designers, explaining what we do to the outside world. Did you make the formula for the soda? No. Did you do the logo? No. Did you pick the brand colors? No. Oh, so you actually print the cans? No. Come up with the shape? Mold the aluminum? Put it in the box??? No, I designed the packaging. You can see how quickly what we add to the process could get lost, though we all know it is one of the most important aspects. Design can be nebulous to the public but also to clients. Those sitting in boardrooms know that they must have it, but they rarely know what it does. It is our job to be advocates for design. Make it clear at every possible moment that design adds tangible value to what is being created and is essential. Speak in terms that the business world would understand and stand firm. Design is important. They need us. **JF**

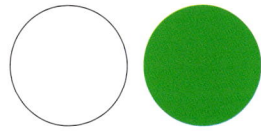

# DO keep it simple

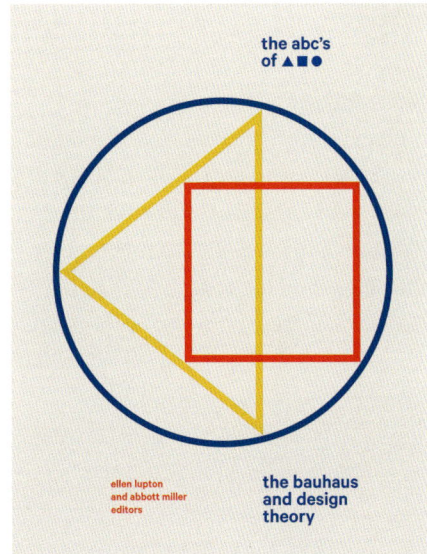

the abc's
of ▲■●

ellen lupton
and abbott miller
editors

the bauhaus
and design
theory

The options available to designers to meet a brief are infinite, and the temptation to keep adding is very strong. It is important, therefore, to remember that the primary purpose of design is to aid communication and facilitate understanding. The best designs and the most successful work are always solutions that have taken a simple, clean, and uncluttered approach. The rules in this book help guide you down that path. However, the design can only come from you.

The design process—as well as being ideas-driven—is a series of decisions taken by you to facilitate the brief. Make the right decisions and ask the right questions along the way, and your ideas will succeed. Over-complicate and clutter your designs with redundancies, and they will be confused and unappealing. In the immortal words of the German American architect Ludwig Mies van der Rohe: "Less is more." **PD**

# Author Biographies

**Sean Adams**  burningsettlerscabin.com

is chair of undergraduate and graduate graphic design at ArtCenter College of Design in Pasadena, California. In 2014, Adams was awarded the AIGA Medal, the highest honor in the profession. He has been recognized by every major competition and publication, including *Graphis*, AIGA, the British D&AD, and the ADC. Adams has been cited as one of the forty most important people shaping design internationally in *I.D. Magazine*'s I.D. Forty and is the only two-term national president in AIGA's one-hundred-year history. He is also a fellow of the Aspen Design Conference. Adams is the author of several books, most recently, *The Designer's Dictionary of Color* and *The Designer's Dictionary of Type*. He currently is on the editorial board and writes for Design Observer. He is also an on-screen author for LinkedIn Learning. Adams's clients have included the Academy of Motion Picture Arts and Sciences, Adobe, Disney, Gap, Frank Gehry Partners, Nickelodeon, and Sundance.

**Peter Dawson**  gradedesign.com

has more than twenty years of experience in the UK design arena and cofounded his practice, Grade, in 2000. Dawson has worked for a diverse and extensive range of clients over the years, including the British Museum, Thames & Hudson, Tate, and the V&A, and specializes in branding, typography and print, and publishing design. He has won a number of awards for his work, including an International Society of Typographic Designers Premier Award, several Certificates of Excellence, and a number of British Book Design and Production Awards. He is a fellow of the International Society of Typographic Designers and has acted as a visiting typography lecturer at a number of universities in the United Kingdom and overseas. In 2013, he wrote *The Field Guide to Typography*.

**John Foster**  badpeoplegoodthings.com

is the principal, superintendent, and assorted other big words at Bad People Good Things. He is a world-renowned designer, illustrator, author, and speaker on design issues. His work has been in every major industry publication, hangs in galleries across the globe, and is part of the permanent collection of the Smithsonian. He is the proud recipient of a Gold Medal from the Art Directors Club of New York as well as a Best of Show from the ADDYs. Breakthrough projects for everyone—from Coca-Cola, Hasbro, and Americans for the Arts to the Nature Conservancy, ESPN, Chronicle Books, and so many more—have established Foster as a constant force in the industry. He spends far too much time in his office, behind a giant desk for designering, drawering, and computering, with the world's goofiest foxhound at his feet.

**Tony Seddon**  tonyseddon.com

graduated from art school in 1987 and, during the following twelve years, lived and worked in London, first for a multi-disciplinary design consultancy, then as senior art editor for an illustrated book publisher. Tony now works as a freelance designer, project manager, and writer. He has authored and co-authored a number of books, including *Alphabets: Thirty Fonts, Graphic Design for Non-designers*; *Draw Your Own Fonts: 30 Alphabets to Scribble, Sketch, and Make Your Own*; *Greetings from Retro Design: Vintage Graphics Decade by Decade*; *Type Teams: Perfect Typeface Combinations*; *The Evolution of Type: A Graphic Guide to 100 Landmark Typefaces*; and *Let's Talk Type: An Essential Lexicon of Type Terms*. He lives in East Sussex, England, where his faithful lurchers are always on hand to provide feedback when he can't decide which typefaces to choose.

# Index

# Image Credits